# 31 DAYS

# 31 Days
## A New York Street Diary

## ALAN EMMINS

CORVO

First published in Great Britain in 2006 by
Corvo Books Ltd
64 Duncan Terrace
London, N1 8AG
www.corvobooks.com

A catalogue record for this book is available from
the British Library.

Jacket design by Richard Roberts.
Typeset by SJM Design.

Printed and bound in Great Britain by
The Cromwell Press, Wiltshire.

ISBN: 0-9543255-7-5

For Christine and Selma

## Acknowledgements

I would like to thank all the characters that I met on the streets and who appear in this book, as well as many who don't appear.

Also, special thanks to the Society of Authors, everybody at PTH, UHO, Midnight Run, Bowery Mission, Bowery Outreach, the Salvation Army, the Holy Apostles and All Angels (especially those who fed me), the Asian lady who bought my poem (her dollar bill held more value than simple currency), Stephen Mallon, Michael Sofronski, Laila Seewang, and Matt and Lora Dougherty (my New York contingent, for continuing friendship, spare bedrooms and sofas), my wife for being a big enough character to support this project and, finally, my daughter for not being too angry at me for the long absence.

**New York City Homeless Statistics**[*]

Over the last four years, close to 100,000 New Yorkers experienced homelessness.

Each night, over 32,000 homeless individuals sleep in the New York City shelter system, a 44 per cent increase compared to the 1990s. This includes more than 13,600 children, a 55 per cent increase compared to the 1990s. Thousands more sleep on city streets and in other public places.

There are over 1,000 soup kitchens and food pantries in New York City and 2,700 in New York State. They serve about 60 million meals each year to hungry men, women and children. Every day they turn away over 2,500 people.

Surveys show that almost 75 per cent of homeless adults sleeping on the streets of New York suffer from chronic mental illness.

Approximately 90 per cent of homeless New Yorkers are black or Latino, although only 53 per cent of New York City's total population is black or Latino.

There are more homeless New Yorkers in the new millennium than at any time since the Great Depression.

*Coalition for the Homeless, *State of the Homeless* reports 2005/6; Youth Services Opportunities Project

# Prologue

Four years ago, in New York City, I walked into a train tunnel with my friend, the photographer Michael Sofronski. We hopped up onto a small concrete wall and shimmied between two sections of fence. Once on the other side, we walked down a precariously placed plank of wood until we were back on somewhat uneven ground. We were working on an article about urban exploration – about the city explorers who explore abandoned buildings, bridges and tunnels. Three well-experienced urbanites were taking us into the tunnel to show us some artwork that had been painted deep inside.

As soon as we jumped the fence a homeless man stepped out from his makeshift house and positioned himself in front of us. Holding out his hand he said, '*Halt!* Who goes there?'

He was an elderly man. His hair was grey, as was the beard that came down to his belly. He was also slim, which reduced the garden gnome quality that the beard, rosy cheeks and green fishing hat lent him.

We explained that we were going to look at the murals on the tunnel walls. 'People live in there,' he told us. 'Don't touch anything.' Then, as we shuffled away, he called out, 'But enjoy the art. It's very good!'

He was an edgy character with a touch of menace in his voice. His twitching and fidgeting gave the impression that he could change his emotional standpoint at any time. He represented the stereotype of a homeless man: dirty, smelly, a little crazy and living in a shack made from society's discarded matter.

We walked on through a landscape polka-dotted with the tennis balls that had made their way over from the nearby tennis court. Our eyes were drawn to the odd rat, the drip, drip of water from above and the darkness that loomed ahead of us. We were alert and nervous.

But then, just before the darkness, caught in the light that poured in from the grates in the highway above, was a pirouetting figure.

Something altogether less obvious.

We moved nearer and, as we did, a young girl came into view. Her long black hair was tied with a piece of gold lamé. At her feet, you couldn't help but notice, was a dance floor.

The tunnel floor was uneven earth. It was rutted and scattered with bricks, broken buckets, odd shoes, hats, wires, shopping trolleys and tyres. The dance floor, roughly twenty feet square, was made of plywood. And there she danced – in a train tunnel, on a dance floor.

Michael and I were no longer focussed on our urban exploration story. Our minds were with this dancing girl. Who was she? Where did she come from? Why was she dancing in the tunnel?

I cut away from the group and approached her. As unassumingly as I could I said, 'Excuse me? I'm sorry to bother you.'

She stopped dancing and gave me a hard stare as the music, playing slowly due to the flat batteries in her portable stereo, whined on in the background. Her full lips were compressed, not in a pout, but in determination, as a show of strength.

'What *is* it?' she asked, with an unmistakable French accent and attitude.

'We were just going into the tunnel to look at the murals. I was wondering if I could ask you some questions on the way out.'

'No. I am leaving now. I will not be here when you come out.'

With that she picked up her little portable stereo and walked away. She had, however, answered one of my questions at least.

She was French. She was a French girl dancing in a train tunnel in New York City, with a homemade dance floor beneath her feet.

I walked back and joined Michael and the urban explorers.

Michael asked eagerly, 'What did she say? Did she say anything?'

'Yes,' I told him. 'She said she was leaving.'

Further into the tunnel we stood in front of the murals, each around three yards high. They ran connected in a long line like a cartoon strip, maybe forty yards in total, although there was no direct theme or relation between one and the next. The murals were placed in the tunnel, known thereafter as the 'Freedom Tunnel', by artists 'Freedom' Chris, Smith and Sane. In one mural an angular faced man in a beige rain mac held the wrists of an invisible somebody who was holding a gun, and said, by way of a speech bubble, 'DROP THE GUN MOLE!' While his would-be attacker said simply, 'AK!' This scene ran into a title frame that stated 'There's no way like the American way.' Another frame was styled after the branding for Coca Cola, but only showed half the logo, the 'Coca' half. But the really powerful image was of red and white horizontal stripes, over which was written the text, 'In December 1995 the forgotten men of the tunnel received city housing. They've just begun to move.'

One of the things that made these murals so special is that the only people who were able to enjoy them were the few remaining homeless living in the tunnel and the urban explorers who were brave enough to risk the unknown and the third rail to come here to see them. It was a very personal exhibition, but while Michael and I felt honoured to be taken there, our minds kept drifting elsewhere.

She was French and she had a dance floor beneath her feet.

As we left the tunnel we stopped in a sectioned-off area that looked as if it had once been a platform. It was about sixty yards long and consisted mostly of rubble and some pillars. The spaces between the pillars were piled high with debris, apart from one section, which contained five televisions, a radio and a dining table. Looking cautiously over our shoulders we went to investigate, making sure not to touch anything. On one shelf there was a salt shaker and a bottle of ketchup.

We quickly moved on. We were, after all, in somebody's home. There was no sign of the French girl as we ambled past the dance floor, not really wanting to leave. But we did see, sitting in a chair, the Guardian Gnome who had accosted us upon entry.

He was sitting with another man, who asked us, 'Did you like the murals?' Was he letting us know that they had been talking about us – or was it something else?

'Yeah, I saw you in there. You went into my house, and I was watching you.'

'We didn't touch anything!' we all sang in unison.

'I know you didn't,' he said, taking a swig from a bottle. 'Like I said, I was watching you.'

Unlike Michael and myself, the urban explorers knew what they were talking about. They stood chatting about the history of the tunnel and the artists who had painted the murals with the two homeless men.

When the opportunity arose I asked, 'Do you know the girl who was here dancing earlier?'

The Guardian Gnome's friend, who had introduced himself as JR, was grinning. 'Yeah,' he said.

'Who is she?'

'That's my girlfriend, V.'

'V?'

'Yeah, V.'

I didn't want to push him for more information about V, but the fact that she went by a single letter just fascinated me more. What did this V stand for? Veronica? Valerie? Vera? When we left, I asked the two men if it would be OK to come back and talk to them another day.

One said, 'Sure. Just don't go poking your noses into people's homes without an invitation.'

Michael and I said, 'No, no, no, we wouldn't do that,' even though, in reality, we already had.

Three days later Michael and I ventured back into the tunnel. We knew what we wanted; we were journalists and we thought we had stumbled into what could be the most intriguing, beautiful and untold story of our careers thus far.

And in the distance, bathed in the light that poured in through the grated highway above ... There she was.

She wasn't quite as cold as before: 'Ah, it is you again?'

'Yes, it is us again.'

'I do *not* want to do ... what is it, a speak with you. I know nothing of the paintings inside, so I do not know why you come back here.'

'We came to see your boyfriend.'

'He invite you here?'

'Well, yes.'

'Well, he is not here. But maybe he come back soon. It is up to you if you will wait for him.'

'OK, we'll wait if that's OK with you?'

'I do not care.'

'How long have you been dancing?' I asked.

Not wanting to talk to us, she said, 'I don't know.' Then, perhaps feeling rude, she said, 'Maybe ...' Then, possibly remembering she was French, she said, 'I don't know.'

'My wife is a dancer too.' I mentioned my wife only to try to help her relax, as if by having a wife I had already been accepted by the female fraternity and she could now feel safe. It was a stupid notion, but she did brighten at the mention of another dancer.

'She is a dancer? Here? In New York?'

Now I couldn't make V be quiet if I wanted to. She kept firing dance questions at me, questions I didn't have the knowledge to answer, though this didn't seem to worry V.

JR never arrived and, not wanting to push our luck by telling V that we would like to write a story about her, we left, saying that we would drop by again in a few days.

'Maybe I could take some pictures of you next time?' Michael asked as we said goodbye.

'Yes, this will be OK. But you must bring batteries for my radio.' She showed us her radio and opened the battery compartment so that we could see which kind of battery was needed.

The next time we visited V we were armed with batteries and a dance magazine that my wife had brought back from one of her classes. V looked happy to see us and when Michael handed her the batteries she could barely contain her excitement. She tore at the packaging.

V danced for an hour that afternoon while Michael photographed her.

We returned a few days later and met V and her boyfriend. Michael gave them some prints from his shoot. Eventually we asked V and JR if we might write a story about them, about the French ballet dancer who lives in the tunnel. They thought it was interesting, but weren't overly enthusiastic.

Then V said, 'But if you really want to write about homelessness, you need to come and live with us for a while. You can't write about it properly without trying it.'

That was the summer of 2002. A few days after that last conversation I returned to Europe via San Francisco, vowing to return to New York to do the story very soon. But the day I flew to California my wife told me she was pregnant. It wouldn't have been right to live on the streets of New York while my wife was pregnant with our first child. We returned to Europe and the story was shelved indefinitely.

It was a great regret that I never went back to write that story. V was always at the back of my mind. Whenever I read something about the homeless, some stereotypical portrayal of a thieving crack addict capable of eating a child or a rat in ten seconds flat, I would get annoyed – annoyed because I had had a chance to show that the homeless don't *all* eat babies, the homeless are not *all* doped out and trying to rob passers-by. There was another side to homelessness. I believed there was a story where those sensational headlines could be replaced with beauty, character and honesty. V was always there, pirouetting in my mind as a reminder that I could have demonstrated this. The more I read accounts of the 'mole people' scurrying about in tunnels after a rat supper, the more angry I got that I hadn't written the story about V. I found myself pacing around my living room, outraged, until it occurred to me: there was nothing stopping me from actually going and writing the story. It would be worth it just to quell my indignation.

My wife wasn't immediately taken with the idea.

'Couldn't you do something else?' she asked, and mentioned a few of the other ideas I had been toying with. But as we spoke about the homeless project I became more animated by it. I simply had to do it.

My plan was to document, as plainly as possible, the lives of the homeless people of New York City. Not just where they slept and where they ate, but who they were. I wanted to meet the personalities behind the cardboard signs and I knew I would fail if I clocked off at six and went home for dinner. I knew too that if I had money and bought stories with cigarettes, food and drink, people would basically tell me anything they *thought* I wanted to hear. I would get nothing but mythology and drama.

I set myself some rules: I would not try to explain or judge or analyse. I didn't want to delve into anyone's background.

People would tell me what they wanted to tell me and I would reproduce the information as I received it. I also decided that I would tell everybody I met that I was a journalist and that I was writing a book about homelessness. This was a simple decision; I couldn't just steal their characters. I decided that I would start this project with ten dollars in my pocket. I didn't know how long it would take to adjust, how I would raise money or gather food. This ten dollars would allow me a short transition period while I found my bearings, but once it was gone I was on my own.

I also had to allow for some practical measures. My wife agreed to my undertaking the project on the condition that I call in every five days or so to let her and my daughter know that I was alive and well, so I allowed myself a twenty-dollar phone card. I also needed some kind of safety net, in case I got hurt or arrested, so I dropped my passport and my Visa card at the office of a friend in case of emergency. That was basically it: my rules.

Once I got out there I realised pretty quickly that I would not be making all the decisions about how this book would be written. Many characters insisted on giving me their background information whether I asked for it or not. Sometimes background is all they gave me.

'Oh, you're a journalist, what do you want to know? Ask me anything.'

'Well, actually I'm not really ...'

'I been homeless for ...' and out would pour long, ranting spews of dialogue that couldn't be interrupted. Often the dialogues were random and messy, jabbing at my brain as I tried to make sense of the meaning and the rhythm. They threw me off guard and took me completely out of my comfort zone, but still they managed to be beautiful and incredible and intriguing.

My days and movements were mixed. On some I would find myself marching up and down town, across and back and forth all day long, tiring myself but needing to chase food or make it to soup kitchens on time. The areas in which I spent most of my time were Union Square, Penn Station and the Upper West Side from Westside Park to Central Park. On other days, due to sore feet, tiredness or slight depression, I would just sit in parks, watching other people live their lives and wondering what my own family was doing at that moment. But the nature of the characters I met, and their effect on my behaviour, led to a very nomadic experience. At first I used them as a safeguard, barely brave enough to leave their sides. Eventually, as I grew more accustomed to sleeping on the streets, I would branch off on my own. But I wasn't prepared for the solitude of life on the streets and very quickly I found myself missing, not just particular characters, but general and friendly contact. A meaningless chinwag was what I often sought and, without the option to call and ask, 'Hey, how's it going?', I would find myself marching in their direction, desperate as I often was just to talk, to hear my own voice.

When I embarked on this project I hoped that I might find V, and with her in mind I stepped off the bus at Port Authority in midtown New York in the midsummer of 2004. Inside my rucksack I had two pairs of clean socks, two pairs of clean boxer shorts, one clean T-shirt, a can of deodorant, a toothbrush and toothpaste, a large scrapbook and a pen and pencil.

I stood for a minute or two on the busy sidewalk of 8th Avenue with the Port Authority Bus Terminal looming over me. I looked around at all the madness: that melting pot of race, temperament and attitude. I watched large crowds scurry like ants over the crossings, daring the cars to mess with them. I soaked in all the noise, the different voices, the smells, the cars driving over metal gratings, the taxis honking. This was to be my home for the next thirty-one days: a city where the people seem larger than the gargantuan buildings that fail to pen them in.

With the sun raising a sweat on my brow I fell instantly into a blinding, shaking panic.

What on earth did I think I was doing?

# Day 1 – Welcome to the Jungle

Manhattan is saturated with news of the forthcoming Republican Convention, to be held at Madison Square Garden in August. Yesterday's *Daily News* took a look at how this will affect the homeless of midtown New York. It mentioned nothing about how the Republicans might address the problem of homelessness but, curiously, was concerned with how best to hide the homeless during the Convention. The authorities want the homeless out of sight so that Republican eyes won't have to take in the spectacle of their fellow Americans eating from garbage bins. According to the article the police have already started sweeping the midtown area and moving the homeless along. Benches have been removed too, so that the homeless have nowhere to rest or sleep.

Madison Square Garden is at the heart of Manhattan: a big block of cement from 31st Street to 33rd Street between 7th and 8th Avenue, guarded by huge glass towers. It is a landmark for homelessness in New York and it occurs to me that, if I want to document it, I'd better get down there quickly, before all the homeless have been scooped up and deposited out of sight. Already, on hour one of my project, I am diverging from my plan and, instead of heading uptown to the tunnel to find V, I turn in the opposite direction.

I arrive at Madison Square Garden later than expected. A rainstorm had me pinned under a sunshade in Bryant Park for the best part of five hours. It's midnight and due to the weather there is little activity around Madison Square Garden tonight. I sit on a newspaper on the steps in front of The Garden, just next to the elevators that shuttle commuters down into Penn Station.

If I look left and up 7th Avenue I can see the bright lights from Time Square lighting up the sky. It's an incredible display of colour and wattage. Around the entrance to Penn Station there is a neon sign with orange-dotted letters that advertise this month's sports and musical fixtures. Madonna is playing, so is Eric Clapton – not that I will be attending any such events. I watch cars, mostly yellow cabs, as they glide past on the slick, shiny road. Eventually I muster the sense to take a walk around the block. I pass a hot dog stand on the corner, where a dark-skinned man with little trade stands bored under a sunshade.

Halfway along the side street, 33rd, I notice a service road that goes under The Garden. On the far side of this I see a homeless black man with dreads, wearing a thick, padded, dusty coat and a woollen beanie hat. I am wearing a T-shirt and sweating in the humidity as I walk. The man just stands there, stock-still.

I enter the service area.

I approach the man, although I do not try to make eye contact. Instead I squat down against a wall about ten feet away from him. He hasn't moved a muscle in the time it took me to reach him, not even the flicker of an eye. Within two seconds of my sitting down near him though, he walks to the other side of the service area, where he finds a post and leans against it with his back to me.

Out of nowhere a pretty, but rather thin, black girl approaches. She is immaculately clean in tight-fitting jeans, a white vest and sunglasses, with her hair pulled back into a tight bun. Her face is thin, accentuating her cheekbones, which are high on her face. He hair is pulled back so tight that I imagine narrowed eyes behind the glasses. It must surely, after time, cause her a headache.

'Can you spare some change, sir?'

'Sorry,' I mumble.

'A cigarette?'

'I don't smoke.'

'I'll give you a blowjob for five bucks.'

Having bought a McDonald's meal during my third hour of homelessness, during the rainstorm, I only have $4.15 left from my original ten dollars. I tell myself this is OK, the quicker I get rid of the little money I have, the quicker this project can get down to brass tacks. Given the desperation of this girl I could probably get her down to $4.15. But I am not in the market for blowjobs and so I don't barter. She moves on, zigzagging across the service area hoping to find either a Samaritan or a customer. But the service area is quiet, just a handful of homeless characters with little to offer. Still she darts back and forth, just in case somebody arrives while her back is turned. Like a fly caught in a fluorescent lamp she nervously bounces from wall to wall as if she can't find the way out.

Coming down the path is a black man wearing a pair of jeans and nothing more. He has short, luminous grey curly hair with a matching goatee, out from which there pokes two inches of stubby, smouldering cigar. His bare feet make a scraping sound as he walks. His amble is suggestive of long horse rides and soiled underwear. He stops right in front of me, totters a little, turns slightly and stares straight at me with an expression that offers little joy. He stands motionless. His features are grandfatherly, the fleshy warmth long faded, leaving him looking like a Father Christmas who just got fired. His belly, though large and round, is as tight as a drum skin.

A couple of seconds pass.

Then a few more.

After a minute I'm scared to make eye contact.

He may look like Father Christmas, but this is clearly not his season.

After two minutes I'm scared to breathe in case he hears me.

What can he possibly want with me?

Should I ask him?

I am beginning to find the man in front of me menacing. I am slightly aware that I could paint him silver, stand him on a milk crate in London's Covent Garden and he would be nothing more than a dated tourist attraction, but this brings no comfort. In reality he is here, he is big, and his eyes burn with an anger and frustration I hope I will never experience.

After three minutes of being stared at, I start to sneak glimpses to the side in the hope of finding something to soothe my fears. All I find is a homeless white guy covered in grey hair and wearing John Lennon-style shades who is doing his best not to die in the far corner. He is coughing and spluttering from the very depths of his being, retching and staggering with the force of his coughs. His long white pony-tailed hair flaps about behind him as he dances with his ailment. Nobody pays any attention as he drops to his knees, rises again, falls into the wall and barks like a hound in a Sherlock Holmes novel.

Just when I think I can't be any more scared than I am, another homeless guy stumbles onto the scene. He too is white, tall and skinny and with every other step he stoops and punches the ground as hard as he can, exhaling loudly as he does. We are not talking, 'Get a load of me, I am punching the ground.' This is not a call for attention. This is a man full of rage, even more rage than the cigar-smoking statue. He doesn't appear to register physical pain, only mental pain. The service area is about a hundred yards wide and while crossing this urban pit he never once forgets to stoop and vent spleen on the ground upon which he walks. His knuckles are bleeding and every time he punches the ground he leaves a little crimson splatter – maybe so he can find his way back? I find myself staring at his grubby white T-shirt, which is plain other than the dirt embedded into it. I dread to think how he would react if he caught me looking at his face, but that is what I keep doing, snatching disbelieving glimpses that increase my trepidation.

As soon as this madman is out of sight I decide that the best option, as the man in front of me continues to bore his eyes into me, is to sit as still as I can and wish for the best. It is not a very proactive option, but it is an optimistic one.

My mouth is dry and I am on the verge of shaking. After ten minutes I am convinced that researching this book is the stupidest, most naive idea I have ever had, and only now do I realise I don't have the courage to complete it. I even start to wonder if all the media clichés *are* true, because everybody down here certainly fits the stereotype of the homeless. Maybe I have been wrong all along and there aren't any soulful characters on the street, just madmen and menaces.

I am so scared that I actually sit here working out what I will say to my wife, how I will look her in the eye and tell her I couldn't do it. My ego pricks, but there is something there, I am consumed with doubt now, I simply do not have what it takes and wonder what excuse I can offer my publisher. How can I save face? With a book about the World Tiddlywinks Championships maybe?

After twelve minutes I jump to my feet and leave the service area as fast as I can. I don't run, but I walk as if I have rough-cut diamonds loose in my underpants. I look behind to see how many of them are coming after me, but of course nobody is. Nobody has even moved. Nothing has changed. Even the cigar continues to stare intently at the space that I once occupied, as if I am still there, or as if I was never there. I walk back to the front of Penn Station and sit back down on the steps. Although I now feel safe the fear and doubt are still there, stronger than ever. I don't stand a chance of completion and consider taking the $1.75 bus back to my friend's house in New Jersey. I role-play the conversation that I will have with him, the excuses I will make. Visualising his total disappointment in me is the only thing that keeps me sitting on the steps.

I feel a little numb, shell-shocked maybe, and I have no idea what I am supposed to do next, so I sit, eyes wide open, seeing nothing.

Also on the steps leading up to Madison Square Garden sits a bulky black woman with a collection of plastic bags around her. Her black hair is trimmed short and unevenly and the dark skin on her round face shines with a neon glow. She sits toad-like in black shorts and T-shirt.

It's busier now, after a dry spell, than it was at midnight. People are starting to leave the bars and venture home.

The woman asks, '*Excuse me!* Can you spare some change?' But the man she's addressing doesn't answer. He just gets up and moves to a different set of steps.

The woman asks, 'Hey, missy! Can you spare a cigarette?' But Missy keeps on walking.

The woman asks, 'What? Am I fucking black or something? Is I one of those stinky fucking Negroes that you is too good to talk to, mo-ther-fu-cker?'

People try not to look at the shouting black woman for fear that she will hone in on them. They pass as quickly as they can.

A man heads towards the steps and makes to sit down. The black woman shouts, not at him, at everyone. The man quickly straightens and keeps going.

She says, 'You ain't got nothing I need, you good-for-nothing motherfuckers. I spit in your fucking face you come near me.'

She quietens down for a while. New people come and go. A girl sits down next to her.

The woman asks, 'Missy, can you spare some change?'

Missy says, 'Sure.' And digging around in her purse removes two single dollar bills.

'Two dollars? You gonna give me a lousy fucking two dollars? What the fuck I gonna eat with two dollars, bitch?'

The woman screws up the dollar bills and throws them back in the girl's face.

She says, 'I don't need your money, you skinny ass bitch, you fucking two-dollar cunt …'

The girl quietly gets up and walks away, leaving the crumpled money on the ground.

'That's it, bitch. You better be on your way before I fuck you the fuck up.'

People standing around turn and look at the shouting black woman, but they don't say anything. They just sneak glances here and there.

Whenever she notices she screams, 'What the fuck are you looking at, motherfucker?' Sometimes she stands: 'I fuck you up in a second flat!' Some of the people get nervous, but they don't all move on; some stand their ground, not wanting to be scared away.

She takes a couple of tentative steps forward.

Some more people move.

'That's right! That's right!'

She sits back down and takes up dialogue with herself: 'Dumb cracker bitch! Oh yeah, she be acting all sweet, I'll tell you what she is and it ain't no fucking lollypop. She's a stinking ass turban-wearing condom head *bitch*! She fucked the whole world that bitch, I can tell. But I ain't eating that pussy. I ain't *sucking* no pussy. No dick either! Fuck your own pussy, bitch, walking like you just got fucked by God. He ain't gonna fuck you any more than I'm gonna fuck you! Where the fuck you go? Where is that condom head at? I gonna fuck her up.'

The woman stands and starts looking from left to right. All she sees are the backs of other people's heads. She picks up the crumpled dollar bills and stuffs them in her bra.

I am sitting here wondering how exactly I thought I could strike up any conversations, let alone relationships, with people clearly as mad and angry as those I have encountered thus far on my first night. But these thoughts are interrupted.

'Excuse me, sir, how you doing?'

The enquiry comes from a man wearing a plain black shell suit with a beach hat on his head. He has taken pride in his neatly trimmed moustache. He glows in that enviable way that only the deeply black can, where every muscle and ridge catches and reflects light. He squats over to meet my height. Over his right arm he has a pile of newspapers. Even though I am far from it, I tell him I am doing alright and he begins his pitch without faltering. 'I'm homeless, and to raise money for food I'm out here selling my papers …'

I tell him that I am out here researching a book on homelessness and, ignoring his plight, ask him my most burning question: *where might it be safe to sleep?*

'It's er … I er … Oh, here's my boy. He'll tell you about being homeless. I gotta go make some dollars!' and with that he is gone and I am left with the youthful black man who introduces himself as JV.

'Why you wanna know about homeless?'

His dark eyes bore into me suspiciously as he tries to sum me up. I realise I am face to face yet again with anger. 'I tell you about homeless,' he spits. 'Come with me.'

He leads me round the corner to what will no doubt turn into an unsavoury experience. A mugging maybe. (Please don't take my clean socks.) Or maybe worse, maybe murder, or the sale of my kidneys to a man in the shadows?

Instead he shows me the varying scales of homelessness that exist around Madison Square Garden. The crack addicts, the mentally ill, the embittered, and the clean articulate homeless that are on the streets by choice. He assures me that they will leave me alone and, to be sure, he introduces me at the various corners of the station. As we walk he tells me what it's like to be homeless, how the homeless are treated. He is angry, and articulate enough to express it. His words are aimed and sharp. But as time passes it becomes obvious that he is enjoying the interaction, he enjoys being listened to and he takes pleasure from playing the role of teacher and protector, and as this warmer side pokes through he begins to introduce me to his friends.

'Yo, Shorty. This is my boy Alan. He gonna be around a while. You do by him how you do by me, alright?'

Shorty nods assent and we move off to the next corner,

passing the service area where I had sat scared out of my wits not so long ago.

'Don't go down there,' says JV, 'without me.'

'Do you know the people down there?' I ask.

'Do I know them? No. But damn, son. I'm the sheriff of 7th Avenue. Penn Station? I own this motherfucker.'

Just as I am beginning to relax under JV's wing, he announces that he has to go and meet some people. I feel the panic rise again, but then, as if he senses this, JV says, 'But listen, if you around tomorrow, I be here doing my thing all day. If you ever need to find me, if I'm here, I'm out front.'

The Penn Station entrance pops out of the ground just in front of The Garden: a square block with a large flat roof and plenty of overhang for shelter. There are steps either side of this protruding block which take you up half a level and place you in front of the fifty-seven imposing floors of Penn Plaza. To get to the main entrance to Madison Square Garden you walk through one of two walkways that run either side of the Penn Plaza reception, two passageways that take you beneath some of the world's most expensive office space, and on to some of the world's most expensive entertainment. At 3am, though, it is pretty quiet. There are huge pillars lining these walkways, built right up against the sides. Most of the display banners advertise coming events. I see one old banner advertising a past Elton John concert. I tuck myself behind this pillar and beneath Elton John, not a position I can say I ever expected to find myself in. I slip my rucksack under my head so that should I fall asleep I will be alerted if somebody tries to steal it. But I don't sleep. Every sound has me jumping out of my wits. I lie there awake, squinting and pretending to be asleep whenever somebody passes. There's a sour smell down here in this little cement corner, the floor is, of course, as hard as stone, but I don't care, because I can't actually believe I am doing this. All I have to do is hunker down, get some sleep, and survive tonight. Tomorrow I

will be under JV's protective wing and my project will be under-
way.

At 5am, when the sky lightens and the traffic from 7th Avenue
starts to pick up again, I stand up. I can't yet claim to have *slept*
on the streets of New York, but I feel as if I have survived on
some level. I am not, at least, tucked up in a warm bed in New
Jersey, experiencing the pangs of my failure to survive even a
single night. So I take myself off to Time Square where I reward
myself with a McDonald's coffee and a bloody great smile.

# Day 2 – The Sheriff of 7th Avenue

There's more of a breeze today. Outside Madison Square Garden the spangled banners that fly as sentinels to the station flap with gusto. Some wrap around the flagpoles the wrong way. Others flap proudly as if they know the Republican Convention is but weeks away.

JV is here, doing 'his thing'.

Another homeless fellow appears from a distance to be throwing himself willingly at the wheels of yellow cabs as they pull into the taxi rank in front of The Garden. But on closer inspection he is actually opening doors for the people getting into them. He holds out a hand for donations.

As I walk closer to The Garden I can hear it come to life.

'Buying. Selling. Who needs tickets? I'm buying and selling. You need tickets?'

'Get your tickets here!'

'What are you asking?'

'Well, how many you want?'

'Two.'

'Three hundred dollars.'

'You need tickets? You need tickets? You need tickets? You need tickets? You need tickets? Yo, miss, you need tickets? You need tickets?'

A barefooted man in a filthy white T-shirt shuffles along the sidewalk enjoying more free space than any other pedestrian. He approaches people randomly. Spare change? Cigarette?

A police officer stands and stares with a great fat cigar stub in his mouth. He shakes his head as the homeless man passes him. For a second their eyes meet, the man's expression asking, 'Who the fuck you looking at?' The man shuffles on. The officer continues to shake his head.

A handsome young boy of around twelve years, clad in Nike this and Nike that, sinks his teeth into a hot dog. He walks with his two friends. He takes a sip of soda, wipes ketchup and mustard from his mouth with the back of his hand. He and his friends are happy. They are laughing and joking as they walk along, smiling at the beautiful ladies three times their age. A tall man in a suit, talking on a cellphone, walks into the boy and his hot dog.

Into his cellphone the man is saying, 'Well, I am telling you how I want it done and you have two choices …'

The twelve-year-old boy stands in shock as he peels the remainder of his hot dog from his once clean Nike T-shirt. He turns around, looking for the villain with a suit and a cellphone. Forty per cent of the men on the sidewalk are wearing suits and talking on cellphones.

The boy stands for a second, faltering, his need to vent spleen visible, making him shake.

'Asshole!' he screams eventually, aiming both syllables at every city slicker on 7th Avenue.

But the boy's shout jolts me more than anybody else. I haven't eaten all day, training myself, as I hope I am, for a vast decrease in sustenance. All this focus on the boy's hot dog stirs my hunger to an unbearable level and I scurry to the corner and buy a hot dog for $1.75. This brings my balance down to $1.40. Tomorrow I won't even be able to afford a hot dog.

I walk back to the main steps, guarding my hot dog against the fate of the boy's, and sit down to my meagre supper.

Four girls come off the escalator from Penn Station. They are all dressed up and fighting about where to go.

'*NO!* Bullshit, we always do what you wanna do …'

'I don't care who wants to do what, the bar you want to go to is lame and you just want to go 'cause Kevin might be there … Dah!'

'Why can't we just go to that place on 1st Avenue?'

'What, *Coyote Ugly?*'

'No, not Coyote Ugly. Jeeeeezus what is your problem?'

'Guys, can we just stop fighting and have some fun?'

'Don't tell me, tell her!'

'Oh yeah, right. Like I'm the one arguing.'

JV stands talking to a tall girl with glasses and long black hair that hangs down her back.

'Hey, you too fine to be standing here on your own. What's that about? Your man not appreciating?'

'I'm just killing time,' she smiles. 'Waiting for my train.'

'Killing time?'

They are standing on the front steps of The Garden. JV is talking and gesticulating and the girl is laughing at his every move. They look as if they should be in a bar drinking cocktails. The girl smoothes her flowery cotton skirt as it lifts up in the wind, trying to cover her long white legs that end in O'Neal flip-flops. They go on talking for about forty-five minutes. Trains come and go. She falls into JV, leaning on his chest. He is whispering something in her ear while he slides his left hand down her hip and onto her bare thigh. Her arms are moving up JV's chest, her hands resting on his shoulders. Her body is arched and JV's hands sit in the small of her back. She is talking. He is talking. She looks deep into his eyes, searching for something. Then JV speaks and she bursts out laughing. She takes a step back, letting her arms slide down JV's chest until her left hand reaches out for JV's hand. She leads him away.

They walk to the corner of 31st and turn right. They stand as a yellow cab bounces past and then they cross the road and disappear into a multi-storey parking lot, being careful to elude the attendants.

The sidewalk is dense with people desperate to get to where they're going. Most head for the mouth of Penn Station as if drawn there by suction. Many stand around talking on their cellphones, making Penn Station one of New York's radiation hot spots.

But the people, despite their large numbers, are just so tiny. They live in a world where they are outsized by everything from large screen TVs that beam down from great heights to giant size training shoes that have been attached to the sides of buildings for promotional purposes. Scaled against everyday sights around them, the people of New York are like ants. At least, that is how it is if you sit with your fingers in your ears. Because when you add sound to this image, it is the people of New York that are the mad giants. With sound they become big and make this city what it is. In front of Penn Station, it is possible to just zone out and be totally immobilised by this wall of noise.

Along the edge of the sidewalk, professionals and tourists alike form a long orderly queue in the hope of getting a yellow cab sometime in the not-too-distant future. A young pretty girl doomed to a plastic smile works her way along this queue, trying to entice people into a night out at a comedy club. She tells them that it's a night tightly packed with laughter, offering the funniest comedians in all of New York and beer that is cold and cheap, 'Just like a Russian hooker, *budumdum tsss*.' People hold their hands out for the flyer. But the girl with the fake smile, fake voice and fake social interest doesn't put a flyer in their hands. She puts a pair of tickets in their hands and then asks them for forty dollars. It's a hustle, and it doesn't look as if it pays well – at least not the way she's doing it, because she is picking New Yorkers, who are without a doubt simply immune to this stuff. She needs tourists to pull this off, or at least some freshman boys who will be wooed by her looks. Not knowing this she gives herself away. She must be new in town.

JV stands to the side of the girl, who has now given up on the yellow cab queue and is instead trying to stop people as they walk by. JV is tall, around 6 foot 1 with a shaved head and big mouth; next to him she doesn't stand a chance. JV's jeans are very clean for somebody who is homeless, but his long blue T-shirt must be dirty, because he has turned it inside out to make it look clean. Over his right arm he has a pile of newspapers. The *Onion* is a free newspaper to anybody willing to walk to the corner of the block where there's a dispenser. For anybody else interested in a copy, JV can hook you up for a donation.

> Hey-hey, those some freaky glasses, where you get those?
> They like some Elton John shit.
> Listen I'm *homeless*,
> But I'm not out here asking for *money*,
> But I am trying to *earn* some money so that I can get
>     something to *eat*.
> Now I'm not gonna lie,
> These newspapers here are free.
> But I'm not trying to *sell* them to you,
> I'm asking for *donations*.
> You hear what I'm saying?
> *Donations.*
> So that I can buy some *food*.
> This is the *Onion*.
> This is some funny shit.
> You be laughing all the way *home*.
> Whadda you say, Elton John?
> Yeah, you my man, thanks bro!
> I appreciate *it*.

JV's workspace is the sidewalk in front of Penn Station and be-tween the flagpoles of Madison Square Garden. I sit watching him as he works the right-hand side with his papers until he gets a donation, then he flits to the left and works the crowd there. Sometimes he just stands in the middle, or on the steps slightly off on either side of the subway entrance where he just grins at the world as it turns. His game is a game of averages: the more people he approaches the more money he makes.

Hey, how you doing?

No? OK, you have a nice day anyway.

Hey ladies, you going to the concert?

What you waiting for? Your boyfriends?

Did I ask you if you had any change?

No, I didn't.

That's right.

That's right.

Yeah, you enjoy the concert though, I hear it's good.

Yo, dude! Don't be making love to your woman on the steps of The Garden, man!

Some of us got to work here. Go get a room.

Damn!

You be making me all hot.

Miss, can you spare one of those cigarettes?

Thanks.

You going in?

OK, get home safe now.

You want me to ride with you?

Keep you safe?

OK.

OK.

Yeah, I be here tomorrow.

Damn!

I said damn!

You too cute to be the PO-lice.

You know I just messing, officer.

JV stops in his tracks, his grin widening as he looks at a young guy leaning against one of the tall pebble-dashed flowerbeds at the front of the station. The young man has an unlit cigarette in his mouth. He has been watching JV go back and forth. Now, just as he is about to raise his hands to light his cigarette, he notices that JV has stopped and is grinning straight at him. His own expression breaks into a big smile and he spreads his arms wide to ask, 'What?'

'Don't make me come over there!' JV shouts. The guy pushes himself off the flowerbed and, laughing, walks over to where JV is waiting about fifteen feet away.

'Damn straight! What you so happy about?'

'I am happy because I am going out tonight,' says the young man in a thick East European accent.

'Yeah, where you going tonight?'

'I am going out to drink beer, many of the beer and for this I am happy.'

'Bullshit, son. You happy 'cause you're out after the pussy, am I right?'

The young man bursts into laughter and blushes. He is small standing in front of JV, and has tourist written all over him, which is no doubt what attracted JV to him in the first place. His blond hair is short and parted and looks uneven in its cut. He is wearing a royal blue polo shirt, bleached jeans and white trainers. You can tell he is not a New Yorker simply by the fact that he is way out of fashion, and has gone to great pains to be so. That, and the fact that he seems constantly in the way and ready to apologise to everyone. Still, he is a happy fellow and rather charming to boot.

'See, I know. You can't bullshit a bullshitter, son. I know you want the pussy. You make a donation for one of my papers and I gonna make sure you get the pussy. Don't laugh, son, I got the voodoo, I got your back! No, that's too much, just give me a dollar. There you go. Where you from?'

'I am from Russia.'

'Oh, the former S.U. I hear you. Now I got to concentrate … you like the black pussy?'

The Russian leans back, laughing. He takes a drag on his cigarette before speaking, 'Yes, I like the black pussy.'

'Oh, you do? Yeah, you right though, the black pussy is a

sweet thing. What you want is one of those project bitches. When you bend them over and they get up on it they be swinging their asses around left right left right, oh man, it feel good. They push back just as hard as they can *hmm hmm* a nigger be feeling that too. But listen, I got you all hooked up for tonight you hear, now give me one of those cigarettes and be gone, she waiting for you!'

The Russian hands JV a cigarette and walks away laughing.

JV approaches girls. Especially pretty ones.

He interrupts two girls who sit talking on the steps just to the left of where I sit. One wears a yellow halter-top and denim hipsters. Her long blonde hair flows freely around her shoulders. She is tanned and made up so colourfully she could be frightful through 3D glasses, but, as it is, she looks rather fetching and arty.

She looks blank as JV does his thing. Her friend, the taller of the two, is skinny in a top of Lopez-type dimensions: a piece of black cloth that barely covers her breasts. Her long silky black hair is pulled tight into a ponytail, making her already sour, nasty expression appear even more spiteful.

As JV talks you can see the contempt bubbling in her eyes. Whenever JV says something that requires a reaction she gives a little flick of her mouth, quick and sharp, such as might be the result of shock treatment. This is meant to signify that, yes, she is listening, but is growing less interested with every syllable.

But JV soldiers on.

Something changes. Something has been said that has lowered the barriers slightly. It's hard to say what this utterance could have been. But there are several aspects to the transition. The twitch has stopped. If anything it has spread itself into a frown. Not a frown of disinterest but one of questioning.

It says, 'Now I'm listening.'

Those brown eyes have softened too. For a brief second they too are questioning, but all too quickly they begin to sparkle. The frown is now a fully fledged smile. The body language now suggests something altogether different. Her spirit seems up-lifted. She has transformed from somebody who looked willing and capable of launching a mace attack on JV at any second, to somebody who will remember him as a character for a time to come.

She doesn't, though, dive into her purse and adhere to JV's request for a donation. Dollars do not flow forth. Instead she walks away with her friend, smiling, a more beautiful girl than she was five minutes ago. She looks back at JV in a manner that would befit the ending of a Justin Timberlake video.

JV calls out, 'Yeah, that's it. You keep smiling, miss.'

The NYPD mill about outside The Garden, occasionally paying attention to the crowd, but for the most part just looking for yellow cab drivers they can pick on. You can drive pretty much without regard for the law in New York, unless you are a Middle Eastern yellow cab driver. Then the slightest traffic offense seems to upset the NYPD to a disproportionate degree. One officer, a man with moustache, hat and gun, treats the failure to signal like the rape of his eight-year-old daughter. The yellow cab driver, fearing Guantanamo, nods, agrees and appears to be overjoyed with the ticket the officer gives him.

Four teenage girls, each covering their breasts with small diamonds of fabric, trip and stumble their way down town in a manner that suggests this must be their first time out in high heels.

A drunken white guy vomits at the top of the stairs.

Black people laugh.

If you were going into Madison Square Garden tonight, and you walked up the steps that lead you past the Chase Bank ATM machines in the middle and then past the big air-conditioned reception of 2 Penn Plaza towards the turnstiles at the back, you might catch a glimpse of JV. He is tucked in the far right corner counting his money.

He holds a handful of dollar bills in his right hand and one by one he counts them over to his left. His lips move silently as he counts. Nineteen dollars. He shifts the bundle back to his right hand and, just to be sure, begins to count them once more over to his left hand. Eighteen dollars. Now there's a discrepancy in his accounting. He pauses for a second and then goes through the bills slowly, not counting them but turning them all to face the right way. Any upside down George Washingtons are turned upright. Only when all the notes are regimented, only when all the bent corners are twisted straight, does JV begin his count once more. But not before taking a peek over his right shoulder, with one eyebrow cocked to check that the coast is clear. Slowly the thumb on his right hand slides the notes over, the following note always going under its predecessor in the left hand before the forefinger snatches it in. Nineteen dollars. There's no expression on JV's face that might suggest this is a good or bad take. He simply folds the bills, having accepted the total, so that George Washington turns in on himself in the middle, and he places the money in his front pocket. He walks back to the front of the station, crosses the street and walks up the block, where he buys himself an ice cream before disappearing into the subway.

Very quickly I am very lonely, missing already the comfort and ease of talking to people I know well. I want to hear the voices of friends and people who I interact with daily: the man in the corner store where I buy milk, or my neighbour who does little more than grunt in my direction as we pass on the stairs. Even the silence of a friend would be comforting now. Luckily though, this loneliness is overshadowed by the need to sleep. It is only 10pm, but I haven't had time to re-orientate myself to the US time zone and, coupled with last night's lack of sleep, I feel heavy-eyed.

On JV's recommendation I head down into the subway and, as discreetly as I can, jump a turnstile. I don't focus on where I am going, I simply follow the crowd to the sound of rumbling trains. I jump through the doors as quick as I can and slide myself into a corner seat. It is crowded. People are pushed right up against me, their bulks invading my space.

'When it's busy, Alan, it's safe!' That's what JV had told me about sleeping on the subway. But still. I don't think there's any chance of sleep. The train is at least air-conditioned.

I sit hugging my backpack, my heavy eyes trying to take everybody in without making eye contact. Occasionally my head drops. I try to sleep, and now and again do manage to drift into a parallel zone where I hear the train but more as part of another world than my own. But voices and the regular brush of legs wake and scare me. Even so, I don't leave. I have nowhere else to go and no knowledge of a better place to sleep. So I remain in this position, hugging my backpack until the crowds thin, then disappear, until 5 o'clock in the morning. Only as the train starts to fill again with the morning rush do I stir myself to leave, back to Madison Square Garden, where I know I will sit on the steps, desperately awaiting the arrival of JV.

# Day 3 – Puff, Puff and Puff

Downstairs, and towards the 8th Avenue side of Penn Station, are the men's toilets. At 5.30am, when the station is this quiet, you can make out the classical music that's playing inside the toilets as you approach. I know very little about classical music, but am a little pleased with myself for identifying this piece: it's Bach's sixth symphony for cello, recognisable to me only because my wife and I received it on CD as a wedding gift.

Once inside, the music is quite loud.

Along the left-hand wall quite near to the entrance to the toilets are three large stone wash basins. They are evenly spaced and hang below big mirrors. Further along the left wall are the urinals. Along the right wall are the stalls with their doors ajar at odd angles. At the far end you can actually turn the corner and come back on yourself in a symmetrical replica of this space.

There are three men inside the restroom. They are each naked to the waist and each standing in front of one of the large stone basins. They are all in their fifties with silver heads of hair, each absorbed by various acts of hygiene.

Although they clearly share many things in common, they do not talk. They simply go about their grooming.

One man, the one furthest away from the entrance, leans over the sink as he washes the soapsuds from under his arms. In front of him is a lathered bar of soap, a disposable razor and a can of shaving foam.

The man next to him at the middle sink is shaving. He has the tap running. Steam rises as he dips his razor into the water to rinse it clean. He stretches his face this way and that, juts his chin out and applies a long smooth stroke with his disposable razor.

The man nearest the entrance is trimming his moustache. He is in no rush. Checking himself from all angles he makes occasional and quiet snips. There's pride in his movements; the moustache has become more than simple facial hair or adornment.

All of the men, though separate from each other, appear bonded together by the music. All three appear to sway and move to the timing of the cello, as if they conduct the music with their razors and soap.

It's a corner of Penn Station in the early hours of morning. It's beautiful.

JV stands talking to a man whose grey T-shirt is stretched over his large, rotund belly, as he leans, smoking, against the wall of a kiosk. The belly hangs down, a reminder of the earth's gravity. The man seems to be nearing fifty. He has greying hair and calloused hands that appear to have worked a lifetime. His clothes are covered in plaster dust, suggesting he has just finished a shift on a building site. He holds his cigarette in his thumb and forefinger, taking drags between the quick sharp sentences, his dry face mocking JV's every word.

Oh, you're homeless *puff*
I'm so sorry *puff*
Oh, you don't like being homeless *puff*

I didn't realise *puff*
Yeah, it must be really tough *puff*
I'm sorry *puff*
I guess that's my fault *puff*
I made you homeless *puff*
I'm sorry *puff*
No really, I am sorry *puff*
You poor thing *puff*
What a tough little life you *puff*
Have *puff*
Oh, you're looking for donations *puff*
You're not *puff*
Begging *puff*
Yeah *puff*
I feel for ya *puff*
I really do *puff*
*puff*
*puff*
*puff*

JV offers his hand: 'Yeah, you know what? You have yourself a nice evening, you're a really nice guy, your mother would be proud!' Then, walking off, he turns to somebody he knows: 'Son, did you hear the fucking cracker?'

I am, unfairly, a little annoyed at JV for not sticking around. Sitting here alone I am starving, nervous, scared and thirty-five cents shy of a hot dog. I figure I need to start asking for change. If I ask only for thirty-five cents is that less of a liberty? I can't bring myself to move, to ask the question. I feel as if I am degrading myself and although I know I am not truly homeless, the people I ask for change won't know this and I feel a sense of shame about how they will see me.

I don't ask anybody. Instead I walk laps of Madison Square Garden hoping to find coins on the floor, but I don't. Time has become an odd thing, a currency that I can't spend. Hours pass and I can't motivate myself to do anything, to meet anybody. When I am not walking laps I sit on the steps, silent, worrying, achieving nothing. It is no easy feat to take myself, not to a pay-phone to call my friend to come and get me, but down into the subway, where I sit on a wooden bench, hugging my backpack and dozing apprehensively in and out of sleep.

# Day 4 – Call Me

Their lips lock together in a passionate kiss. Their tongues glistening in the bright sunlight of a Manhattan summer afternoon. Her partner's hands seek out intimate spaces, like the dimples at the small of her back, before reaching down further and grabbing a handful of butt cheek. She lets out a little giggle and pushes her breasts forward. Her partner does the same.

JV's cousin, Remy, says at the top of his voice, 'Look! It's the lesbians!'

JV says, 'Hey, ladies, how you doing today? We gonna get our freak on tonight?'

The women laugh and enjoy one more kiss before they break apart, leaving only their hands connected.

'We already told you we don't like men. We've tried that and it didn't work, we only like girls now.'

'But you know, I could help you with that.'

As Remy twists and turns in laughter I realise that Remy and JV, so smitten with the ladies, have forgotten their manners. They go through several rounds of banter before saying, 'Oh yeah, this is my boy Alan.' It's a brief introduction and lacks enthusiasm on my behalf, which is frustrating, because if these women are homeless, and the fact that they are standing at a 'United Homeless Organization' table collecting donations in a large plastic bottle suggests they are, I simply have to get their story.

Nancy and Kim are short. They both wear their hair halfway down their back. They stand, in jeans and vests, with their cleavages pumped up and pointing at the faces that walk past. Nancy and Kim met while serving prison sentences in Rikers Island women's prison, in upstate New York. They were released two weeks ago and since then have been living homeless on the streets of New York. This information comes very freely and without prompting. They wear their story like an ever-evolving badge of honour.

They don't like men, but they are aware that men like them. Nancy spots a guy who has stopped to light a cigarette. He wears a smart checked shirt tucked into his black jeans. He unclips a flip-phone from his belt and thinks about making a call while stealing glances at Nancy and Kim. He looks as if he worked out once, but now has a small paunch hanging over the waistline of his jeans. Leaning against a shop window as casually as a peeping Tom possibly can, with greying hair glistening in the sun, he takes in their every touch. His strong clean-shaven face and half-tone sunglasses hide nothing of his thoughts.

'Can you help the homeless today, sir?' Nancy asks as she fiddles with the top of the water bottle that is placed on the table in front of her. It's one of those big industrial water bottles that you would find in an office. It is empty.

'What's your name?'

'Nancy. What's yours?'

Nancy, at twenty-three, is the younger of the two women. Her hair has been bleached, but her roots and true colour, more of a dirty blonde, hang down level with her eyes. She has a round tanned face with a little outbreak of acne on her right cheek. When she smiles, everything from her eyes to her hips are involved.

Noticing that Nancy is talking to somebody new, Kim reaches over and slides her hand down the back of Nancy's jeans.

In a low voice, JV says, 'OK, we'll let you go about your business, I'll see you later.'

'OK, baby,' Kim says. 'Come back, OK?'

Remy answers, 'Yeah, we'll be back. Stay safe!'

'Yeah, we will.'

I skulk away, disappointed, with JV and Remy either side of me. But I can't let these two characters slip away, and quickly I bid JV and Remy farewell and head back to Nancy and Kim. I wait to one side. The man smoking the cigarette feels more confident now that he has the girls to himself. He steps closer.

'So what's her name?' he asks, flicking his cigarette ash to the ground and nodding at Kim. 'So, what? Are you homeless?'

'Yes, we're homeless,' Nancy says as she lets all her weight fall on one leg, allowing her hips to stand at a forty-five degree angle.

'She's my girlfriend,' Kim tells the man.

'Yeah, I can see that. So where do you sleep? Around here?'

'Sometimes. We move around a lot.'

'I'm Paul,' the man says, slipping a five-dollar bill into the water bottle. 'So do you girls, like, do anything else?'

'Like what?'

'Well, party, you know, I could get us a room and we can have some fun. When I leave you'll have the room for the night. It's got to be better than the sidewalk.'

'We'll make enough here to get a room tonight. I mean, that's why we're out here, to earn enough for a room.'

'Yeah, but if I get the room then you can keep your money, get high?'

'Yeah, maybe,' Kim says.

Nancy switches hips. 'Why don't you leave us your number and we'll call you later.'

'Sure, look, here's my card ...' and then, having second thoughts, he takes the card back. 'Actually, no. Let me write it down.'

Nancy rummages through her bag and removes a small note-book. She flicks through the pages trying to find a blank page. There aren't many left. All the pages appear littered with names and numbers.

Jeff: 917 574 XXXX
Phil: 917 254 XXXX
Brad: 646 145 XXXX
Mike: 917 347 XXXX – call me!

The notebook contains over thirty names and numbers.

Eventually a blank page comes up.

Paul: 917 688 XXXX – call before 6, or call me tomorrow.

'It was nice to meet you,' Paul says, offering his hand to be shaken. 'But you should call me. I'll take you out to dinner, get us a nice room. It'll be fun.'

'Sure,' says Kim. 'As soon as we know what time we'll be done here we'll give you a call.'

'What food do you like?'

'I want Thai,' says Kim.

'Great. I know a nice place where I'll take you. Call me when you're done.'

'OK, Paul,' says Nancy as he starts to walk away. 'Thank you!'

'*Jerk!*' says Kim as soon as Paul is out of earshot.

'Did you see the way he was looking at me?' Nancy asks.

'Right. He kept licking his lips. Yeah, that turns me on for sure, now we'll fuck you!'

'Oh, come here, baby,' says Nancy, laughing and taking Kim into another kissing embrace, causing a black man walking up the sidewalk to call out, 'Oh damn! Lesbians!'

The sidewalk on 7th Avenue is as busy as any other day. Nancy and Kim had set up their table on the corner of 27th Street at 7am this morning. They had sipped coffee and cuddled until the sidewalk had grown busier.

'We just need to try and make some money to get ahead,'

they tell a woman in a business suit who stands there with a microphone attached to her ear and pointing towards her glossy red lips.

'But where do you sleep?' she asks.

'When we make enough money we stay in a hotel on 42nd, it's forty-five bucks a night ...' Nancy is telling her.

'And when we don't make the money,' interrupts Kim, 'we sleep on a rock in Central Park.'

'Yeah, there's this rock we sleep on,' says Nancy excitedly, a smile spreading across her olive-skinned face. 'It has a great view of the park.'

Kim stresses, 'But we keep getting bitten! Show her your bites, babe.' Nancy twists round and pulls down the back of her jeans to reveal a cluster of raw bite marks. Some have bled where she has been scratching them.

'But we're trying to move into this place, we've saved the money for our first week's rent ...' Nancy begins.

'One hundred and twenty-five dollars. And we need another hundred and twenty-five for the deposit. But out here we barely make enough money for a room every other night.'

'Yeah, so we can't get ahead of ourselves. We can't get a job because we have no ID, we can't get ID because we have no address, we can't get an address 'cause we don't have a job ...'

The woman's cellphone rings and she holds up a finger to silence Nancy and Kim. She presses a button and speaks into her microphone. 'Hi Rob, I was trying to reach you all morning, basically I spoke to the buyer ...' and she starts to walk off down the street.

Kim turns to Nancy and says, 'See ya later!'

'I mean, what the fuck was that? She could afford to give us a dollar after standing there and asking us all those questions.'

'Forget about her, baby, come here.'

'She wasn't nice.'

The girls embrace and kiss.

Another black man shouts, ' Yo baby, I like that.'

Then I step in, and although I know that my intentions are

journalistic, it can't possibly look that way to Nancy and Kim. To them I must appear as one in a continuous string of letches, about to launch a pathetic bid to worm my way into the pants of two young, desperate women.

I tell them why I am on the streets. I am a journalist. I am writing a book. It is about homelessness.

Nancy and Kim look back at me with expressions that, though polite, seem to say, 'Of course you are.'

I understand. I write down my web address, the name of my UK publisher and my editor's phone number and e-mail. I tell them to think about it, and that, if need be, we can call my editor in London, who will confirm what I've said. I walk away, holding out little hope.

# Day 5 – $1 Laureate

I had two major concerns about taking on this project: sleep and food, both of which I prefer in abundance. Sleep has already been sacrificed to the cause. In the last four nights I have done little more than doze on the steps of Madison Square Garden, in subway cars and on platform benches. It's the fear that keeps me from sleeping. Having read an article on day two about two fifteen-year-old boys who beat a homeless man to death with bricks while he slept, I have had trouble relaxing. There is something so menacing about the fact that when they were caught, the boys said they did it because they were 'bored'.

Food, too, has quickly become a problem. Here on only my fifth day I am totally broke and experiencing a level of hunger that blurs my concentration. A hot dog a day is way below my usual food intake to say the least and now I can't even manage that. Even yesterday's hot dog came courtesy of JV's kindness.

But, as I watch him flit about in front of Penn Station, it is with a smile that I realise that while sleep may have been lost to the cause, the famine is about to end.

JV and his *Onion*-selling antics bring him in a fair dollar, anything from three dollars to eight dollars an hour. Of course he is seasoned, but it goes without saying that a charming fellow such as myself, complete with funny accent, should, inexperienced though I may be, be able to bring in two dollars an hour. Meaning if I put in three hours a day I will have a minimum of six dollars a day for food ... splendid!

This suits me fine. It's a far cry from abundance, I know. But it's just the right side of famished. On top of this, keeping my earnings to a minimum survival level leaves my conscience intact: not actually being homeless, I am aware that every dollar I panhandle could, in theory, go to a real homeless person, somebody that has a genuine need for it.

I feel a sense of excitement as I warm myself up to the state of beggar. The nearest I have come to begging before was behind the bike sheds aged ten, as I pleaded with a pretty blonde girl called Melanie to show me her *thing*. Having tricked me in to showing her my thing first, and having being unimpressed, she shirked on the deal. My pleas fell on deaf ears, but that was then, of course. Were she to see me now in all my grimy glory, I doubt she could refuse.

For my opening gambit (I can't sell the *Onion* as this is JV's method of choice, so I am just going all out for charming Brit beggar) I opt for, 'How are you today?' with an over-deliverance of the BBC. They love the accent, you see, the New Yorkers, I've been told. A friend in England once told me that when New York women heard his English accent, their knickers simply fell to the ground with little more than a flutter ... and here I am thinking that if their purse strings could loosen too, all the better. It's going to be too easy, to hell with my conscience; tonight I'll no doubt dine on a truffle risotto, which I'll wash down with lashings of Prosecco.

The problem is, for all this self-claimed charm and cocksureness, whenever I approach somebody I start to flinch with nervous ticks and my vocal chords simply refuse to join in. For a good two minutes I dart back and forth, never really going further than a few yards, throwing myself gladly into the path of pedestrians, who, in typical New York fashion, swat me to one side as just another pavement-dwelling nuisance.

Finally I manage to say, 'How are you today?' but I don't stop for an answer and the smartly dressed man doesn't stop to give me one. But having found the ability to speak I soldier on, darting around with my question, though never actually waiting to hear how anybody's day might be.

'How are you today? ... How are you today? ... And you, madam, how are you? ... Hello there, how are you?'

So far so good, I have speech accomplished. All I need do now is stand still and await my dollar.

The problem is they don't appear to stop. I stop and they continue. Of course I am doing it all wrong. Why shoot at moving targets when I am surrounded by sitting ducks? There's a pretty lady sitting over there on the steps, I'll try her.

'Hello, how are you today?'

'Oh, just fuck off!' she says loudly without even looking at me. I do. I fuck/scurry off to the other side of Penn Station through a flurry of giggles from all those within earshot.

I give myself five minutes to recover and try again. My feeble enquiries of 'How are you?' elicit the following replies:

'Dude, get a job!'

'I'm having a good day, thank you.'

'Move, asshole!'

'Better than you, dirt-bag.'

I become aware all too quickly that these comments actually hurt me. Of course, I don't know any of these people, I have no need to care. I certainly don't have a desire to care. Yet each and every comment stings and as they keep coming they penetrate further, they cut deeper. Do they not know I am only pretending? Within minutes of being a panhandler I have retreated into a semi-blind panic. I dart here and there, spouting my question but still never hanging around long enough to hear the reply. Eventually, I turn and am about to dart in a new direction when I bump into JV, who is at this point in tears from laughing uncontrollably.

'Alan, son, what you doing?'

'I'm trying to raise some money to get something to eat, JV.'

JV straightens up, purses his lips, and says in a mock voice, 'How are yoooooo?'

He and a group of office workers that he converses with on a daily basis fall about laughing. I turn red, feel deeply embarrassed, ashamed, pathetic, fragile, angry, small ... I grapple with a whole bunch of emotions I have never felt before. Not all at once.

'Alan, man. You gotta toughen up, son. You gotta get in their face and when they don't stop, or they cuss you out, you just move on, 'Yeah, have a nice day, sir,' and you try somebody else. You got to get over that shit if you want to eat, son. You ain't asking them, you telling them.'

That's easier said than done. I know what is in the way and it's pride. How dare they look down on me? How dare they treat me as if I am less than them? I don't even deserve to be looked at? Spoken to? Heard? Shamefully I want to drop to my knees and scream, 'I am really a writer, you know!'

Panic sets in again. I am sitting on the steps to Penn Station (my now regular panic station) with a fraught expression. I can't survive. Without a food source I simply can't survive. I don't have what it takes to carry off this project. I don't have what it takes on several levels. I am tired. I am hungry and there's nobody out here who loves me. There's nobody here to say, 'Hey, you're a splendid chap.' Simply experiencing this feeling is baffling. Can it really be so? Can my self-confidence have collapsed in such a short space of time?

I have no money left. I have dedicated most of the day, or at least as much as I could mentally give, to raising cash. All I need is a few dollars for food, but I haven't raised a single cent, which means I have nothing to eat. Never in my life have I gone a day without eating anything.

'You OK?'

It's JV, of course, standing in front of me with thirty copies of the *Onion* folded over one arm and a steaming hot dog in the other.

I look at the hot dog, thinking, 'JV if you don't get that thing out of my face you're going to lose a finger!'

Then he says, 'Take it, it's yours.'

And I know from watching him today that he has about fifty dollars in his pocket, so I get over the guilt of taking food from a homeless man very quickly and gobble down the hot dog in one and a half bites.

JV sits next to me, 'You know, Alan, what you gotta do is you gotta get a *thing*, you know? Like I got the *Onion*, that's my thing. You need to get your Alan thing, you know what I'm saying?'

'Yeah, I do.' I pause. 'I thought this would be easy.'

JV laughs, 'Nah, this ain't easy. Well, it is if you be doing it eight years, but ... you know, I was watching you. You're just too polite and ... scared. You can't be scared of these people. They are your survival and that is what you need to see when you look at somebody, you gotta see that is your survival ticket. That lady right there, she has my dinner. Plus you went to all the wrong people. After a while you start to see who's gonna give you money and who ain't. Sometimes you be surprised, but not often. Once you start seeing that, you ain't gonna go hungry.'

JV looks up and smiles, 'Yo, son. Wassup?' And off he goes.

I stay molded to the step, feeling sorry for myself. JV brings his friend over and introduces us. We start talking. JV tells him about my panhandling skills and I am able to laugh about it – a little.

His friend asks, 'So you really a writer or is that just your line?'

'I am.'

'Then that's your thing, son. I see homeless people all over this city and do you know what they do to make money? They sell poetry. You think they can write? Hell no. So if you a writer, get some cards, a pen ...'

JV butts in: 'For cards, Alan, you just walk into any café, take a handful of them postcards they have in those racks.'

'... and write some poetry, sell your poems a dollar a piece. People easier with that, man, because you doing something.'

Hmmm. I feel my spirits lift slightly as JV and his friend say goodbye and walk off into the distance. I am less sad and sorry now. I take my scrapbook from my rucksack and start writing. The next time I look up it is because JV is standing in front of me, holding out a wad of postcards. I feel moved by this gesture. It may not be love and I don't think JV would use the expression 'splendid chap', but I think he just said, 'Alan, you're alright.'

So, I have a poem, of sorts. I've never been much of a poet. Thought I was once, until I read some real poetry. But all things considered, this will do. I can't imagine anybody will be critiquing it, or indeed expecting much in the way of poetic prowess. My poem is called 'The Pigeon and the Yankee'.

> The pigeon said
> To the
> Yankee
> Alright China?
> The Yankee
> Stepped
> On the
> Pigeon's
> Head!

It's short and doesn't take up enough of the card, so I draw a picture of a pigeon in trousers and T-shirt with a Yankee dancing on his head. The Yankee is saying, 'Take *that*, and *that*, and *that*!'

It's not very profound, but it makes me smile. I take the sudden positive vibe and run with it.

'Hey, would you like to read a poem?'

'Sure,' she smiles.

It's a middle-aged woman, nicely dressed with blushed high cheeks. She smiles at first. She reads the poem. She reads it again. I wait for another smile.

'What is this? Some anti-American bullshit?'

And the Yankee said, 'Take that and that and that *and* that!'

I sit reflecting on a conversation I had had with my friend Matt Dougherty the night before I came out on the streets. We were talking about panhandling. He felt I had an unfair advantage over the homeless. I have an English accent, am rather cocky and confident, and rarely without a few words to spare.

'I know,' I told him. 'It will be like shooting fish in a barrel. I'll have to keep that in check.'

'You want a cigarette?'

I start in the direction of the cigarette packet, but pull back.

'If you want one, take one.'

But I don't want one. I don't smoke.

'I don't know why I did that …' I say. 'Sorry.'

I look at the person talking to me for the first time, a stunning Asian woman with a strong New Jersey accent. She smiles.

'Would you like to read a poem?' I ask.

'Sure.'

I hand her my card. She reads it. Reads it again.

She laughs, 'That's *stu*pid.'

I laugh, 'It's yours for a dollar.'

'You're on. I'll give it to my friend tonight. It will make her laugh.'

She hands me a dollar and laughs again. 'I'm May,' she says, offering her hand.

I shake her hand and then run across the road to a deli, where, for one dollar, I manage to secure a small square of chocolate cake.

# Day 6 – The Midnight Run

I am still *trying* to sleep on the streets of this mad city. Thus far I have had little success, spending most evenings nodding at best, generally consumed by an omnipresent fear. By 11pm I am so weary that I fall asleep on the front steps to The Garden, which is not a good place to bed down. I am so fatigued that when I wake up I don't think, 'Damn, this is a silly place to sleep.' Instead I think, 'Damn, there's a chill sweeping down 7th Avenue.' I unzip my backpack, remove my complementary British Airways blanket and, once suitably covered, go back to sleep on the steps. I am aware as I fall in and out of sleep that I feel cold; somewhere in the back of my mind I am shivering. But then before I can think to stand up I fall asleep again.

I am woken by a gentle shaking and recognise the face that stares back at me. I haven't spoken to him before, but I have seen him many times over the last few days. He is one of the regular homeless around Penn Station.

'You OK, son?' he asks gently as I look at him. 'I know. I been there too. I know what you going through. Here, eat this.'

He is holding out a hot dog.

I sit for a minute, taken aback, staring at the hot dog this homeless man is offering. I have eaten more hot dogs in the last few days than the last few years. I wonder for how long I will be able to keep them down.

For the time being, however, there are other concerns running through my head. One, I am not really homeless so I can't take this homeless man's hot dog. Two, what is this wiener sandwich going to cost me? Three, what does he care if I'm homeless? Surely he has his own well-being to think about?

I put all of these questions to one side when my body reminds me that I haven't eaten since the coffee and the ham sandwich handed out by a church on 32nd Street at 7am this morning.

'Are you sure?' I ask. 'Don't you want it?'

'No, I've eaten. Here, eat it.'

I take the hot dog and, remembering my manners, eat it in three conservative bites.

'You know, I know a shelter down town where they got a really good program that will help you kick the crack. If you want I'll take you there.'

'Crack?' I splutter. 'I'm not on crack!'

'You were shaking it up good on those steps when I woke you. People were pointing at you. You look like you craving.'

'No, really, I'm not on crack. I was just cold.'

'You sure? Because I been there and you look like you were on the down. It's nothing shameful. I just offering help is all. We all out here together, my friend. I'm clean now, been clean for a couple of years. Still smoke too many cigarettes though, but what the hell?'

We sit talking for a while. My friend's name is Sammy. He is in his mid-forties. He asks me where I am from, how long I have been in New York. But he never asks me how I ended up on the streets. His kindness is so overwhelming that I don't have the heart to tell him I'm a writer researching a book. All of a sudden what I am doing seems kind of silly. But then he offers me two dollars.

'No really, there's no need. I'm fine,' I tell him.

'Son, I can always get money. I'm sorry it's all I got on me, but take it. It's easy come, easy go to me, baby.'

'No really, I'm a journalist. I'm out here researching a book on homelessness.' This throws him a little.

'So you got money?'

'No, I am living out here – trying at least. I don't have any money.'

'So you living on the streets?'

'Yeah.'

'As a homeless person?'

'Yeah.'

'No money?'

'No.'

'Where did you sleep last night?'

'I tried to sleep on the train, on the 2.'

'On the Bronx-bound 2? Shit, son. Don't sleep there! You gonna get robbed or arrested if you sleep there. If you gotta sleep, go down into Penn Station, you know where I mean? Right down in the belly, it's warm down there too. They kick you out eventually, but you can normally grab an hour or two before they come and get you.' Sammy is hit with a brainwave. 'You know about Midnight Run?'

I had met the people behind Midnight Run, a homeless charity that delivers food and toiletries to the homeless, several years ago while working on an article. I knew them well and wanted to track them down again.

'Yeah, I do. But I don't know when they come around.'

'Now! You need to get yourself over to the corner off 33rd and 8th quick.'

With that we both jump up and head off in different directions.

On the corner of 33rd Street and 8th Avenue, gathered around the back entrance to Penn Station, is a crowd of homeless people waiting patiently for the arrival of the van. Some of the crowd are talking. Others sit against the wall, sleeping. One man stands asleep at the very edge of a steep set of stairs that are just inside the doorway. He teeters precariously this way and that, in danger of tumbling any second to a painful awakening, or possibly a non-awakening. Another homeless man coming up the stairs sees him there and gently puts an arm on his shoulder.

'You should take a seat. You look like you about to fall.'

The man says, 'Oh, OK', and slides down against the wall.

Opposite me, just inside the doors, are two young girls and a young Hispanic guy who also appear to be waiting for the van. Asleep in a pushchair is a baby, maybe two years old. The boy is wearing baggy jeans and a huge white T-shirt that comes down to his knees; on the front there's a New York Mets logo. His wife or girlfriend, whoever she may be, removes her hands from the pockets of her faded black jeans and sidles into an embrace. The second girl, standing off to the side, wears a long denim skirt with a split down the front, from which protrudes a long dark leg. On top she is wearing a peach-coloured vest that hangs loose over her thin frame. She is worryingly thin in fact, with wiry hair pinned up elaborately on her head. She leans against the wall with the most vacant expression possible. Empty, without even an inlet for hope. Her expression doesn't tell a story; if it tells you anything it's that there is no story, no adventure, no trauma, no pain, no struggle. Life is just simply this and it leads her to be standing on the corner of Penn Station waiting for the van.

The van is late, but nobody complains.

They stand.

They talk.

They sleep.

They wait.

'Is this them?' one of them asks, looking at a van that has pulled up on the corner.

'Is it?'

No.

'What about this? Is this them?'

No.

'This must be them?'

No.

Then out of nowhere the volunteers arrive carrying boxes and huge flasks.

'Hey, there they are! Where did you guys come from? Where's the van?'

'Well, we couldn't park. The van's just going round the block and hopefully we will be able to park here on 33rd,' one of the volunteers explains – a little woman with golden hair and glasses and a sweater that looks as if she knitted it herself.

'You guys want sandwiches?' one of the male volunteers asks as he sets a box full of stuffed brown paper bags on the ground.

'How about coffee?' asks another.

'We got soup too ...'

For a few minutes the crowd is tightly packed around the volunteers. Steam rises from the soup kettles and coffee flasks. I am not as familiar or bold as the others and I start to worry that by the time I get to the front there won't be any sandwiches left. But when a gap does present itself and I wedge myself in, I can see that Midnight Run are well stocked.

The woman in glasses hands me a brown paper bag with a sandwich. She asks if I want another and, after passing it to me, directs me to her right to where a man is pouring coffee from an urn. Just having these things in my hand rejuvenates me. I can feel a smile not spreading, but twitching sporadically across my face. This is all I need. Give me food and I have a chance of survival.

I tear at one of the brown bags and quite uncharmingly devour my first ever peanut butter and jelly sandwich. I am so relieved that I can't stand still. I jig around listening to the hubbub that has gathered around the volunteers of Midnight Run, who are now handing out tubes of toothpaste, soap, deodorant and disposable razors.

'Hey, miss, where were you last week? I didn't see you. Did

you have a night off?' a black homeless man in a tracksuit and baseball cap asks one of the volunteers.

'Me, I was here ... no, you're right, I wasn't. I came earlier in the week because it was my wedding anniversary.'

'Oh, it was? How long?'

'Forty years.'

'Forty years?' laughs another homeless man. 'That's crazy. What did you do, you go out for some nice food?'

'Yeah, we had a meal.'

'Was it nice?'

'It was real nice.'

'Good, good. Forty years, that's really something.'

'You want some soup?'

'What is it?'

'Vegetable and chicken.'

'What's in the sandwiches?'

'Peanut butter and jelly.'

'Yeah, I'll take a cup of that soup.'

'You don't like my peanut butter and jelly sandwiches?' another volunteer asks, smiling.

'You asking a homeless man if he likes peanut butter and jelly sandwiches? I must've eaten me a million of those things. Man, that all you got I'll eat it, but when I can smell soup, I gonna have me a cup of that soup instead.'

Sammy was right: the belly of Penn Station is warm. There is only one other person sleeping down here. He is down on the floor tucked up against the glass boundary of the seated waiting area. On the other side of this glass boundary the empty padded chairs fan out in rows. But this section is closed and not to be frequented by the down and outs.

I drop my backpack on the floor and kick it against the glass. I sit for a while, watching the world go by as if I am a commuter waiting for a late train. Directly opposite where I sit is a line of ticket offices. Most are empty. Between the ticket booths and me there is a void of about forty yards, separated only by a staircase that leads down to the station's bowels. The floor is laid with one-yard-square white tiles. A man on a buffer, his dreads swaying to the pulse of his headphones, steers his machinery up and down, giving the tiled floor its daily gleam.

To my far left I see a podium, large and white with a paneled front. Behind this stand three police officers and three soldiers. It's part of the new anti-terrorist regime that soldiers patrol the hot spots of the United States. They have seen me. They know that I am not a commuter. They know too that I am new on the scene. For the time being they let me be.

I quickly lose control of my eyelids. It is odd, realising that I am about to lie down and go to sleep while other people walk to and from trains, travel to and from loved ones, parties or work. It is 1.45am and the sensation is so strong that I know I am not about to doze. The thing that is taking me over, consensually or not, is sleep. I put my head on my backpack and drift instantly away from consciousness.

# Day 7 – Your Money or Your Wife

I am startled awake at 3am.

'OK, move it out. Come on, get up and get out, Hey you, get up and get out now! Come on. Up, up, up!'

The biggest shock of this awakening isn't the burly soldier standing over me with a gun. It is simply that when I had lain down to sleep there was just one other person sleeping nearby. Now there are around thirty other bodies, all packed in tight around me, groaning as they gather their bags and rise to their feet. I feel safer for being surrounded, for becoming a part of this temporary community that is now being scattered in all directions. I am aware that that is the best sleep I've had since coming out on the streets and I feel safer knowing now that it was communal. I slept under the protection of other homeless people. It's a protection I know I will seek every night from here on.

I stagger my way to the front of the station, the heels of my trainers scuffing the buffered floor. I have just had the longest sleep since coming on the streets, yet I am still exhausted and

in need of rest. I cross the road to an all-night deli where JV
(after going to the seated area upstairs under the pretense of
drinking his coffee) sometimes sleeps, although not tonight. I
think about going down into the subway stations. When thrown
out of the deli he often sleeps down in the station, crooked up
on a bench. But I won't be able to jump a turnstile now, when
it is so quiet. Ultimately, I have to get away from Penn Station
anyway and this is as good a time as any. I need to visit another
part of the city, meet some new homeless people that live in different surroundings and experience a different New York. I
have already spent too much time hanging around Penn
Station, so I decide to walk all the way down to Union Square.
I have whiled away many an afternoon in Union Square and so
I know it to be a place popular with the homeless. I plan to join
them on the benches and sleep away the rest of the night. It is
this idea of sleep that keeps me trundling along.

Cars drive sporadically down 7th Avenue. There are guys
shouting out of limousine sunroofs as they whiz past. I come
across the first pedestrians down on 27th Street. A middle-aged
man and woman approach on my side of the avenue, arguing
at the tops of their voices.

'Fuck you! Get away from me!'

'I was right fucking there!'

'I can't believe you just let that happen.'

'Let it fucking happen? Let it fucking happen? He had a gun!
You listen to me, bitch …'

'Oh, you wanna act tough now, motherfucker? You the man
now, you piece of shit …'

I pass them by, trying not to make eye contact.

'Now you the fucking Don, tough guy? Where the fuck were
you while we were being robbed? Where was the tough guy
when that son of a bitch was robbing us? You're nothing but a
pussy bitch …'

'Yeah, go easy now! I'm not gonna take your shit!'

'Oh! What are you going to do, cocksucker? I tell you what
you're going to do. You're going to stand there like the quivering

prick you are – say nothing! Do nothing! You worthless fuck pig. I see ...'

There's a loud crashing noise. It is the woman's head bouncing off the shutter of a budget perfume store. As she bounces back her boyfriend kicks her in the stomach. She goes down and her boyfriend follows and crouches beside her while he punches her repeatedly: one-two, one-two, left-right, left-right in the head. Her screams and the horrifying thud of fist on skull fill the night air. It is over in about four or five seconds. I have barely comprehended what is happening before the boyfriend or husband, whatever he is, stands and marches off up the avenue. His woman lies there bleeding, up against the shop front.

I take a few tentative steps towards her. Even from fifteen feet I can see the woman's bloody face. She rolls around a couple of times, tattered and beaten. She groans as she struggles to her feet. She doesn't see me, let alone hear what I am saying. She turns after her partner and staggers away. I follow a few steps, not quite sure what to do.

'Is that fucking it? Just what I expect from a faggot cocksucker like you! You can't even beat a woman, you malignant pussy!'

Now I know exactly what to do: *nothing*! I am not getting involved in this. They are clearly *both* mad. It strikes me that were I to step to this woman's aid, she would be the one to turn on me. I move on, but this word, this *malignant* – it throws me a little. It is just about the last word I ever would have expected to hear in this situation. What a vocabulary. With words like *fuck, motherfucker, pussy, prick, bitch, cocksucker and malignant,* this woman can take care of herself. For my part I have a new realisation. I am once again walking down the avenue, down, down, down, the way they had come just a minute earlier, and apparently there's a chap down there robbing people – *with a gun*!

Balls to the foul-mouthed woman being beaten up the street. I am in fear of being robbed down the street. I am not scared of what I might lose, but because I have nothing *to* lose. A half-used notebook, a British Airways paper-thin blanket, a toothbrush, toothpaste and two pairs of dirty socks and underpants. My fear is of telling a would-be robber that I have nothing; my fear is that he will think I am holding out.

*Listen here, you quivering malignant pussy, I have nothing, I tell you! NOTHING!*

By the time I reach 20th Street I am over my fear of robbery and, falling asleep in mid-stride, am in more danger of being run down by an errant yellow cab as I sleepwalk into the middle of the road.

When I do finally arrive at Union Square I stand blinking wildly. All the benches are empty, there's nobody asleep on the grass, even the wall around the Washington Memorial is devoid of the regular bodies. Where have all the homeless gone? What happened to the Union Square I know?

When entering this project, people warned me vigorously about the menace that is the homeless man. But on so many occasions in so few days, they have watched my back. I don't feel safe at night without them. There must be a reason why Union Square, usually with a high quota of the homeless, is currently empty. So I keep walking, through the Square, across 14th Street, down University Place, dozing until I walk into a *Village Voice* dispenser. I turn right on 10th Street and there he is, my protector, asleep under a blanket on the other side of the street. Ten yards up from him there's another breathing bundle of bodyguard.

I line myself up so that I am directly opposite the first man, lay my bag down, lay my body down, and, for all it's worth, draw my BA blanket around me. I fall deep and fast.

'Dude! Like what the fuck?'

This particularly exasperating question wakes me up. As if sleeping on a concrete sidewalk, with my body numb and the road just feet away, isn't bizarre enough, I now find myself staring back blankly at the inquisitor.

He says, 'You're not a real bum!'

He is right. I am not, nor have I ever been, as he put it, 'a real bum'. But just how would he know? I am certainly dirty enough at this point. I have a bush on my face, my jeans are caked in grime and one need only point a snout towards my feet for there to be little doubt that they haven't seen clean air in days. Let's also not forget, *I am asleep on the sidewalk*! I have never before laid eyes on this fool, nor his girlfriend, who is now also bent over me questioningly. There is no way that they know me, or my reasons for sleeping on the sidewalk.

'Dude, you're not a real bum, get up.'

'What do you expect me to say to that?' I ask him, now leaning up on one elbow.

'Dude, you were just with us at the party!' he goes on emphatically.

'How can you even do that?' the girlfriend asks.

'Right! Not ten minutes ago you were at the party dancing with us and now you're on the sidewalk asleep! I mean, like, what the fuck, dude? How can you relax like that?'

I say, 'You have me mistaken for somebody else.'

'Why are you being such an asshole?' the girlfriend wants to know. 'You just spent most of the night with us and now you want to act like you don't even know us?'

'Listen, really. You have me mistaken for somebody else. I haven't been to any party.'

'Dude, stop fucking about. Come on. Let's go!'

'I don't know what else to tell you. We haven't met before. I haven't been to a party. I have been up at Penn Station until, I don't know, an hour ago.'

'You fucking asshole! How can you do that to us?' the girl demands almost tearfully.

'Yeah, screw you, man! We're outta here!' And with that they start to walk. Then the boyfriend turns his head and over his shoulder adds, 'But I know that's not where you live!'

It's a line of pure comedy genius, but I am not a good audience tonight. I rest my head back down on my bag and try to not feel so vulnerable.

It's 5am when I walk back into Union Square. I don't know if it is or was a trick of the light, or if I missed some kind of spectral gateway, but now the place is littered with the sleeping homeless, both on benches and on the wall around Washington, and, regardless of the reason, I am delighted, and make for a bench of my very own.

Obviously enough I suppose, the public benches of New York City were not designed with a good night's sleep in mind. They are pleasant enough to look at: wooden slats in a gilt iron frame. And the good thing about the benches of New York City is that you are rarely very far from one. But the bad thing about the benches are the circular armrests. It is not the armrests at either end of the bench I take offense to. It's the one in the middle of the bench. Really, what is it doing there? At best it is anti-social, but right now, to a fear-ridden exhausted Englishman, the middle armrest is a pain in the arse ... or more accurately, a pain in the legs.

If I were longer-limbed I might be able to curl my legs around this obtrusive armrest, taking my knees out and off the bench and bringing my feet back on the other side. But I am not longer than I am and so the metal ring digs into the back of my calves.

I scoot down a bit.

Lying on my back I am hoping that I can bend my legs over the armrest. But no, now it digs into the backs of my knees. It's not torture. You'd be hard-pressed to get my life's secrets out of me by laying me down on a New York bench, but still the discomfort is too much to sleep through.

I try my side again, but have to lie so far out on the edge of the bed that gravity becomes an issue. Did I say *bed*?

I stand up and look around. Union Square is no stranger to the bench or the bench-dwelling sound-asleep homeless man. So how are they doing it?

Aha! The answer is obvious. You slide your legs through the armrest. Of course you do.

Have they lost their minds?

It's an odd thought to be having, but as I look at the home-less man just twenty feet away, with his chest rising and sinking in slumber and his legs fed through the middle armrest, I am aware that I could walk up to him now and stamp on his head. Which raises the question: have I lost my mind? No, it's a question of vulnerability. That's what is bothering me: seeing him there, held fast by the middle armrest. Even if he woke up as I approached, there would be little he could do to defend him-self.

I try to get a grip. There are over ten other homeless men asleep on the benches around me and that's just on my side of Union Square. They are perfectly safe. They are not being set upon and bludgeoned. I wonder for a second what I had ex-pected. I chuckle silently to myself and slip myself into the bench, feeding my legs through, puffing up my backpack and pulling my cap down over my eyes.

But now I can't see!

OK, push the hat back. Deep breath. Close my eyes.

But now I can't see!

I have never known fear like this. Once again the idea of fail-ure looms over me. I breathe, close my eyes again, think of my daughter, imagine her asleep next to me. The sun is breaking through the blind and though I still want to sleep, I can't be-cause my daughter keeps tapping me on the nose with the heel of her foot. She giggles and repeats, giggles and repeats. She wants to play. I know it would be easier to get up and play. But I am exhausted, inexplicably so. Completely and utterly pooped.

I leap from the bench. I leap into the bench. I don't leap any-where. I just feel a sharp pain in my legs, just above the knee where I am held fast by the armrest. More importantly my worst fear has been realised. I am under attack. Attacked while sleep-ing. A sneak attack.

I hear him coming, from behind me, through the bushes.

This is what wakes me, a snapping twig. But as I had imagined when looking at the other homeless asleep and pinned down, I can't get up in time to defend myself. I fling my arms around, trying to stave off my attacker at the same time as pulling myself out of the bench. And though this epileptic defence/escape appears to be a sad option, I surprise myself by going about it with aplomb. I flap and I flip, continually banging my legs into the armrest, continually banging my head on another armrest while smashing myself in the face with both hands.

It's hard to say how many seconds pass. Like when you catch yourself nodding, you feel as if you have been asleep for minutes, but discover the minute hand on the clock hasn't actually moved.

I am alone, almost, just me and a squirrel prancing like a fool in the bush behind, and of course a dozen homeless people sleeping soundly around me. The squirrel looks amused; if he had a friend with him he would say, 'Wehey, we've got a live one. Get *him*!'

I am the fool. I think I have lost my mind. The idea of failure looms over me.

I can do this.

I try again. I'm asleep.

No, I'm not.

I'm under attack.

A sneak attack.

The worst kind.

A pigeon this time, just mincing past, letting me know that he knows I am the virgin of the park bench-dwellers.

I let him know that I know he knows by allowing terror to flash across my face for a few seconds.

I can do this.

I try again.

I look at the ground around me, the concrete path that runs around Union Square. There's something wiggling, crawling so slowly I almost miss it. It is opaque, until the rising sun catches it, then it is there, clear as day. There are more of them, hundreds of them, they are everywhere, crawling, wiggling; is it some kind of tiny worm, a centipede?

I look closer for legs. I don't see any, but still they're closing in fast.

I panic.

When planning this book I hadn't thought about minute urban flesh-eating worms with a penchant for Englishmen.

Who had?

I leap from the bench. I leap into the bench. I think I am losing my mind.

# Day 8 – Everything from THIS to THAT

In the daylight hours, as the sun rises above the buildings and finally allows its warmth to spill down, Union Square becomes a hive of activity. The paths inside Union Square run like a figure eight on a two-dollar digital watch, its circles filled with grass. At the south end of the park, high up on a plinth, George Washington rides a horse. At the north end Abraham Lincoln stands proudly with his cape draped down his back, looking out over the homeless bodies that snatch sleep in the park. Right now there are seventeen people asleep in Union Square Park. Most are on benches, but three lie on the low wall that curves around Washington and his horse.

At the end of the square, in the bottom right corner, half a dozen steps lead you down to a subway entrance and a fountain. But with no money and nowhere to go I ignore the subway entrance. Instead I flop down on the long steps and with nothing in mind I just sit and watch.

I notice, behind the fountain, a shopping trolley. It is the two flags that catch my attention at first: a small American flag and an Olympic flag, attached to the trolley by sticks, flap lightly in the breeze. But then I notice that the trolley is loaded with two large trash bags. I can tell by the way they bulge that they are filled with cans and bottles.

'Perfect,' I think to myself. This is my first day in Union Square and already I have a plan. I will sit and wait for the owner of the trolley to come back. He will be my next subject.

After a minute or two I become aware of an argument. Just three feet to my right, on the slope that runs along next to the steps, a young olive-skinned boy aged around six sits on a new shiny pushbike. His helmet is securely strapped on, his gloves are fastened around his wrists with velcro and his feet rest on the pedals, yet his mind is not ready. He squirms on the bike as his father assures him that it is OK: 'You can do this.' Yet the boy is not convinced and as the father gives him a gentle push-off he twists his handlebars and comes to a crashing halt just two feet from where he started. He stands up quickly, embarrassed, as he yanks his trousers up and kicks the saddle of his bike with his right foot. The father is trying not to laugh as he retrieves the bike and brings it once again to the top of the slope.

The square is starting to get busy with people going to work, tourists looking at maps and dog-owners rushing to and from the dog run. Park workers are emptying bins and scooping litter from the floor; youths sentenced to community service are helping them. The sun is out and already hot, my body is sticky with moisture. I ask a passer-by for the time.

'No! Oh, *sorry*, 8.15.'

Once again the boy is mounted. His hands grip the handlebars tightly. His right foot sits ready to push on the pedal as his father talks into his right ear. But still the boy is not ready. There's just something about the downward slope, the lack of stabilisers and the stream of pedestrians that pass by the bottom of the slope that doesn't sit right with him.

'No, I can't, I can't!' he cries and is already getting off the bike before his dad can do the push-off. The bike falls with a clank to the ground. People pass by.

Gently the father and the boy stand talking. The father tells the boy that he *can* do it, that the forward motion will make for easier balance. The boy tells the father that he is scared. They go back and forth for a couple of minutes until the boy is struck with an idea that will help him succeed.

He says, 'You show me first, then I'll try.'

The father jumps at this idea and quickly hands his newspaper to his son for safekeeping. The father is about 5 foot11, wearing blue jeans, sandals, a white linen shirt and a black baseball cap. On his back is strapped a small Nike backpack. His olive face is clean-shaven and handsome. He is not at all shy of riding the child's bicycle around Union Square. Careful not to knee himself in the face he sets off down the slope with a grin.

The boy screams, 'Yeah, go, Papa! Go, Papa. Yeah!' and bounces up and down clapping his hands. His father does a lap of the fountain at the bottom of the slope and then pedals back to his son. They both giggle, the son kisses the father and then pushes him out of the way. There are no fears now; he may be a little stiff as the blood leaves his tightly gripped hands, but now *he* gives the countdown.

The handlebars wobble immediately. The bike tries to move but can't ride against the wheel that sits at a 90-degree angle. Then the boy straightens the bars and slowly the bike starts to pick up speed.

'Arrrrrrrrrrrrrrrrrrr!'

He is off. You can hear him screaming as he heads towards the pedestrians. At the bottom of the slope he tweaks the handlebars to avoid a woman with her face buried in the low-fat decaf latte and an old fart who feigns cardiac arrest at the sight of the one-mile-per-hour boy. He rides around the fountain, just as his father did and then stands up on the pedals as he powers his way back up the slope, screaming and laughing. There is no gentle stop to this triumph: the boy dives from the bike into his father's arms in mid pedal. The father holds his son in the air and spins him round.

'You did it! You did it! I told you, you could do it!'

'I did it! I did it!'

Behind the father and son who kiss and hug in abandon, an MTV poster boy swings a large black rubber cock around his head. The rubber cock is so big that any thoughts of practical usage must be pushed to one side. The poster boy proceeds to beat his friend around the head with it.

'Dude, what is that?' asks an unrelated poster boy who just happens to be passing by.

'Dude! It's a huge rubber cock, dude! Here, take a look!' and from one poster boy to another, the rubber cock arcs through the air.

The boy on his bicycle quickly goes from strength to strength. He no longer rides down the slope to my right; he now rides down the steps to my left. His father sits by the railing to the subway entrance, one eye reading the *New York Post*, the other cocked at his now kamikaze son who twists in and out of pedestrians, circles the fountain and crashes gently into the shopping trolley that I have been keeping my eye on.

'Use your brakes!' the father calls out. The boy untangles himself and rides on.

A boy and a girl stand on the corner. Both carry a clipboard and a sign saying 'Help beat Bush!' It's an invitation they offer to everybody passing by.

'Would you like to help beat Bush? Sir, help beat Bush? Madam, would you like to help beat Bush in the upcoming election? Sir? Beat Bush?'

Some people stop and sign the petition unquestioningly, without even stopping to read what they're signing. This would be a really good ploy on the part of the Republicans. Picture Bush in the Oval office: 'They hate me? How can we use that? I know, let's tell them it's a petition against me, but really ...' Others explain that while they would like Bush to be beaten in many ways – one woman even confesses to praying for the defeat – they are not willing to put their names on a public petition.

When I turn back to look for the two flags that mark the

location of the trolley, they have gone. I am irritated with myself for getting distracted. I just know there's a story attached to those flags. But then my attention is drawn to something else. Leaning on the wall to my right a boy stands eating a chicken salad. It's a strange breakfast, but he appears to be enjoying it. He is a young boy, maybe seventeen, short blond hair and rosy cheeks. His beige jeans are neatly pressed, as is his blue checked shirt. He shovels the food into his mouth as if he is running late, as if he just has to eat something before he goes and does something important for his future, perhaps a college interview.

But then a pigeon attacks him.

The pigeon goes straight for the plastic container holding the chicken salad, flapping its wings in a bid to snatch at the succulent meat. It's quite daring for a pigeon, normally so cowardly and nervous. The boy waves his arm at the pigeon, trying to shoo it away.

He says, 'Wha fff gee ukkk whe!'

The pigeon is relentless if not successful. His only victory is that he has spoiled the salad for the boy, especially as half of it now lies on the floor.

Angry now, the boy changes tack and stabs the pigeon with a plastic fork – not a deadly blow, but hard enough to make the pigeon squawk and make haste.

The boy looks at the ground, shaking his head.

He looks at me with an expression that says, 'Can you believe that? I got my ass kicked by a pigeon.'

He looks back at the ground, at the green leaves and red onion, at the whole juicy chicken leg with its crispy skin that lies on the ground.

Then somebody else swoops in and stakes a claim.

But it's not a pigeon.

It's a black woman.

She doesn't look as if she's homeless. She is clean and presentable, if dressed a bit bizarrely in a mismatched outfit of flowery skirt, vest and earrings.

The black woman is also hungry.

Clearly.

She wipes the dirt off the chicken leg and takes a big bite as she walks away.

The boy does not stab the black woman with his fork. He simply stands there dumbfounded. It is clear he has never seen such desperation. It is clear he has never seen an American scoop down and pluck food from the floor. It is clear he didn't know such hunger existed in New York. He thought it was all a scam, but there was no scam, the woman hadn't asked for anything. She was simply hungry.

The boy looks at me with an expression that says, 'Can you believe that? I got my ass kicked by my sheltered upbringing.'

I smile back, 'Didn't we all?'

He puts the rest of his salad down on top of the wall he is leaning against. He stands there shaking his head. He looks completely flabbergasted and has lost his appetite.

He will not forget the day he got his ass kicked by a pigeon.

This is as good a time as any to tell you that the steps on which I sit killing time, watching the world go by and hoping that the trolley might return, are shallow. I would say, without a ruler, that they are around six inches deep, *max.*

'Oh, what the fuck! You motherfucking cock. I nearly broke my fucking neck. What the fuck is this shit! The city's trying to kill me, the cocksucker!' shouts a middle-aged thin white man, who appears to have thrown himself willingly from the step upon which I sit. 'Did you see that?' he asks me. 'I nearly broke my motherfucking neck? You got a cigarette?'

He kicks the step with his white sneakers. Sitting down next to me he unbuttons his blue blazer to reveal a white and navy polo shirt with a red number 84 on the right breast. I don't have a cigarette but this doesn't seem to bother him. He doesn't stop talking for the next hour. His name is Tony.

### Tony's Rap

Man, *last night*
I had this black bitch
Crack head
She was sucking my cock, man
You know what I'm saying
She had her lips pressed all tight around it
Bitch was good too
She was sucking for hours
She went from the crack
To my cock
From my cock
To the crack
Dumb bitch
I weren't doing no crack though
I ain't gonna lie to ya
I'm in the rehab now
I'm straight
I done my time with drugs
But I never did crack though
Coke was my thing
But not any more
I go to meetings everyday, man
To keep me straight
I ain't gonna lie to you
I was a little bit high last night
Not on the crack though
Just you know
A couple of snifters
As they say
That's why she had to suck my cock
For so long
You hear me
I was so loaded
I couldn't bust a nut

So she had to keep sucking it
Wadda ya gonna do, huh?
But it ain't like the old days
I miss the old days
I used to live in
Well, I mean work in
One of the old porn cinemas
Up on 42nd Street
Well, I used to live there too
I made a deal with the manager
He paid me OK
And I was allowed to sleep there
In the cinema when I wasn't
You know
Working
That's all changed now though
Porn cinemas all closed down
But I can't go back there anyway
Some fellas up there
They wanna see me
I ain't been back since they stabbed me
I owed some dude fifteen bucks
For some coke
And he knew I was fucking about too
I was being an idiot
I told his boy to go fuck himself
And two days later
I didn't even know I was being stabbed either
I was so high
Found a gun in there once
In the cinema
It was when the city was offering
Three hundred and fifty bucks
For hand-ins
You remember that?
Anyway I goes into the precinct

And I says – you still giving money
For hand-ins?
And the cop says – why?
You know somebody who wants to hand in a gun?
And I says yeah
*Me*!
And I says to him now listen
Don't freak out
I'm bringing it in
And I ain't gonna take it out myself
But I got a 9 mm in my backpack
So he takes my backpack
And he opens it up
And he calls out
Hey, Pete
Come over here
Look at what this kid just
Brought in!
His friend couldn't believe it either
'Cause sitting there in my bag
Was a silver 9 mm
They gave me a receipt
I was like *yo* – this better not bounce!
They said nah, it won't bounce
And they sent me upstairs
I handed the receipt over
And this dude gave me
Three hundred and fifty bucks
I split that straight up, man
A hundred on coke
A hundred for a room
A hundred for hookers
And fifty for clothes
And I went straight up into the Carter
You know the Carter?
That place is fucked

But I was up there for a few days
Getting high
Fucking hookers
I'd get them up there
Fuck the shit outta them
And be like
Here's twenty bucks
Take a hike
But I ain't got money for
Hookers no more, man
But maybe after the weekend
There's this rave on at this club
All the fucking yuppies
I'm going over there
I got the money for my ticket
And I got a jar of pills, man
For the headaches
All I gotta do is file the logo
Off the pills and then
I sell them as E
Yuppies don't know the difference anyway
They never did
That's how I got by
Back in the day
Selling fake dope
But I'm not gonna lie to you
I got a dope deck in my pocket
You know what a deck is
Right?
But it's not for me
It's for this Wall Street cat
He comes by in his car to collect
But I'll be honest with ya
I don't get high any more
I've been clean for like two years
Like six months I've been clean now

Hey, did you see the way that kid
Left his wallet on his bag
Over there?
If you weren't here
I'd have snatched that already
Or maybe it don't matter if you're here
Stay there
I'll be back
Whistle if you see him coming.

# Day 9 – Joey O'Shea and the Boy Savage

At the south end of Union Square, around the George Washington memorial, there is always a crowd of hard-core characters. A mix of over-pierced punks, skaters and vagabonds. It is always the same crowd. Loud, not only in voice, but in fashion and attitude too. They have made this section of the park their own. The low wall that circles the Washington statue is made uninviting by their raucous presence. I have wanted to break into this crowd for some days, but it is only now, when I see two of the regulars sitting on the grass off to the side of the main group that I feel I can approach and introduce myself.

It could be the opening scene for a gay condom commercial. Savage (christened Thomas Savage) is sitting next to Joey on the grass in a park. He is pointing out different flowers and Joey is naming them in Latin, his Belfast accent long since drowned out by his upbringing in midtown's Hell's Kitchen.

'That one there … to the left?'

'Yeah, the yellow one.'

'That's the butterfly bush, *Buddleia davidii*; the one behind it is a cornflower, *Centaurea cyanus*.'

Joey, I can't help but notice, wears brown Armani trousers and a blue Abercrombie crew neck T-shirt with rolled up sleeves. His hair is long, dark and pulled back into a ponytail. His forearms are tattooed. He wears, as homeless men so often *don't*, sandals by Reef. Joey tells me he has a degree in pathology from NYU and a master's from Columbia.

'This over here, the little spiky thing, like a spiky ball, that's a globe thistle.'

Joey's chin is scarred, both on the left-hand side and underneath the jawbone. His teeth are misaligned and chipped as if he's been beaten with a crowbar. Yet these features don't suit his otherwise soft and handsome face. Someone somewhere repossessed his million-dollar smile.

Thomas Savage is twenty-three years old with short blond spiky hair. Savage's features can only be described as beautiful, feminine. He has the kind of face that will get you bullied and name-called at the age of fourteen, but a lucrative billboard campaign when you are in your early twenties. Savage is also clean of cloth and skin. His girlfriend is seventeen and lives with her parents in a penthouse apartment on Fifth Avenue. He hasn't seen her for five days. The day her parents discovered that Savage was homeless they whisked her away to a private retreat in Kentucky.

Savage says to Joey, 'You got any more of those chocolate puddings?' His South Carolina accent is slow and drawn out. It carries well. It's also slightly croaky. Savage talks like a frog that's just smoked a pound of good quality skunk. It's a complete contrast to Joey, who speaks fast and low: 'Igot twomore, youwantone?'

'I wouldn't say no-o-o.' Savage erupts into bar-fight-type laughter, all nose and apprehension. 'Where did you get them anyway?'

'At that mission I go to, they had boxes of them; people were just filling their bags up. I'll take you there tonight if you wanna go. Keep it quiet though.'

Joey and Savage sit in the afternoon shade of an elm tree eating chocolate pudding.

Nodding his head Joey says, 'Look at Robert, he's fucked.'

About twenty yards away a homeless man is lying crooked on the ground, virtually dead. He lies half in the sun and half in the shade, an empty vodka bottle by his head. Underneath his black leather waistcoat his skin is bare, and golden, like his goatee beard and receding curly hair. Dangling from his neck is a small pocket radio. Robert looks as if he has just fallen from a Harley.

'Poor Robert,' says Savage, with a mouthful of chocolate pudding. 'I don't know what his story is, but I'm guessing it's pretty bad.'

'Yeah. Robert's fucked up.'

'He does say some nasty shit, though.'

'Yeah, but I don't know he means it. I think maybe he's shit-scared. I know he's a Vietnam vet.'

'Oh, he is?'

'Yeah. I'm not saying that has anything to do with it. Nobody will ever know what Robert's story is; he's still running away from it.'

Joey removes a piece of dry, stale bread from his backpack. After breaking it up in his hands he walks over to Robert and he crumbles it over Robert's body and face. Joey walks back to Savage, 'Everybody needs a release of some kind, right?'

'Oh dude, that's fucked up, look, here they co-o-ome.'

Savage and Joey laugh – Savage loud and nasal, Joey quiet and shuddering – as pigeons flock and start pecking at Robert's body and face.


Tonight, as on most nights, I feel anxious about where I am going to sleep. It is 9.30, and, for the last hour, whenever I have sat on a bench I have started to fall asleep. Once again I am starting to doze while I walk. Where do the homeless go when they want an early night? Until around midnight Penn Station is like a madhouse. Central Park is quiet in the middle if you're dumb enough to go in there. Sidewalks are packed and the smaller parks are still patrolled by the police, which rules out the benches. I could sleep on the grass in Union Square, but as

I walk past there is a guy taking a piss on it. It isn't a pleasant sight and although he does his thing on one small patch of grass, the act still quashes any urge to sleep there. In the other grass square of Union Square Park, a beautiful oriental girl is fucking her boyfriend. With her skirt covering the both of them, she is riding him slowly and rhythmically. I fall asleep sitting there, but am woken up by a group of guys clapping from the bench next to me.

I walk up Broadway, disconnected. Here I am, tired, weary, and desperate to find somewhere I can lay my head and be safe. There they are, millions of them, at least that's what it feels like, marching towards me, shouldering me here, nudging me there, and complaining when I don't move out of the way quickly enough. But, through the sea of bodies, through the gaps in the tanned flesh and Hilfiger sweatshirts, I see a warming sight. I don't know what makes me look to the right as I cross 20th Street, but I do, and on that corner, slightly behind me, is a man sitting on a raised ledge in front of a shop window. The shop is the Bombay Company, a retailer selling reproduction antique furniture that you assemble yourself. In the window are four chairs, a dining table, a rug and a lamp. Above the window is a racing-green awning. This front window is the only one that is set back from the outer wall, leaving a small platform about a foot off the ground, three feet in depth and around twelve feet long. The ledge has been covered completely in card. At one end sits a black man with a big bushy beard and a bald head. He looks like Mr T without the mohawk. He is reading the *New York Post*, sitting with his feet off the ledge and crossed. He doesn't pay any attention to the people marching up and down Broadway even though, essentially, they are in his living room.

'Hey, how's it going?' I venture.

'It's going good,' he says, barely raising his eyes from his newspaper.

'Is it safe to sleep around here?' I ask.

'*I* think it is. I been sleeping right here on this ledge for the last, what, nine years I'd say.' His voice is gravelly, so he even sounds like Mr T.

'Nine years you've been here? That's crazy!'

'It's not that crazy. Nobody ever bothers me so I stay, simple as that. Oh, and I only sleep here in the summer, mind. When it starts getting cold I go back to work and get me a room. I don't like the cold, no sir. But then as soon as it starts getting warm again in the spring, I'm back out here.'

He tells me he used to work as a cycle courier: 'You know, delivering the pay checks to these big firms, but I quit that. I was getting knocked off my bike too many times. Last time it happened I just took the bike straight back and said, 'I'm done, pay me up, I'm outta here.' The road's too crazy these days. It's a shame too, real nice guy running the place. He just gave me my job back every year. But you know, I'm getting too old, I can't be getting run over every day like I used to. I don't know what I'll do this year, but I'll find something.'

I can't help commenting that some people would think him crazy, quitting his job every year to come and live on the streets.

'Yeah, I know, but I think hundred-dollar shoes are crazy. And what do I need to work for? I don't want all the stuff people want, the car, the house, the stereo and the ... the crazy shoes. I live in one of the most wonderful cities in all the world. All I want is to be able to roam this city, watch the people in this city, eat some food and read my Bibles. I don't bother nobody and nobody don't bother me. It's just that ... that cold really gets to me. I don't like the cold, that really screws with my lifestyle ... Nine years, yeah, it must be nine years I be sleeping on this ledge. Where you been sleeping at?'

'I've been sleeping in Penn Station.'

'Oh, that's not good, that gets messy up there. Don't they throw you out? I heard they be throwing people out on account of the convention?'

'Yeah, you can get away with a couple of hours and then they throw you out. But the convention isn't until mid-August, it's a couple of months away.'

'Yeah, but they be starting early. Get the job done before the deadline come into play.'

'What's your name?' I ask, offering my hand, which he takes without looking and gives a firm shake.

'Jerome,' he says, with a quick nod to the space on his right. 'You can squat down there tonight if you like.'

Instant relief. I will sleep under the protection of a man who has been out here for nine years. I don't tell Jerome about my story. I am too tired, and in fact too scared that he will send me packing. Screw the book. I just want to sleep. I just want to feel safe. The book can wait until another day. I huddle down in the corner and fall instantly and securely into my first deep stone-clad slumber.

# Day 10 – Cover Me, I'm Going In

Jerome wakes at 6.03am, swings his feet over the side of the ledge, and sits up. Next to him, in the corner of the ledge, is a brown bag that wasn't there when he fell asleep. He picks it up, unscrunches the top and leans forward questioningly, then holds it out so I can see. Inside the bag, in a plastic box with a clear lid, are six pieces of sushi. He scrunches the bag back up, walks over to the trashcan and throws it away.

'You're not going to eat that?' I splutter, wishing he had at least offered it to me.

Jerome smiles. 'You don't eat sushi on the street. You don't know how old that stuff is. Chances are it has been there since midnight, so it could be bad. I don't want to be the one to find out.'

He takes his white laceless trainers and slips them on his feet. He begins to tidy up. Newspapers are folded and slipped into the holdall. A brown bag containing empty fruit-drink bottles and power-bar wrappers is taken over to a trashcan. The cardboard on the ledge he folds in half and then in half again. Jerome takes the card to the other side of Broadway and wedges it between two mailboxes.

With our bags over our shoulders, Jerome and I walk down Broadway, cross 16th Street and enter Union Square. We stop at the drinking fountain on the right and rinse our faces and necks with water that we catch in our hands. The park is quiet. People are asleep all around; only animals move under the grey sky as Jerome and I, on our way once again, head for the subway. He rummages for a couple of seconds through his bumbag until he finds a Metro card. He looks over to me and asks if I have a Metro card. I don't.

'Here,' he says, holding one out to me. 'I was given an extra one yesterday, you can use that.'

We swipe our cards through the turnstile and head towards the 6 train. The station is quiet, just a handful of early morning commuters scattered along the platform.

Jerome and I have an entire row of seats to ourselves. A girl sits opposite and slightly to the right. Her stripy polo shirt is stretched over her taut pregnant belly. She looks very sweet, with friendly eyes, a mass of light brown curls and a nervous thin-lipped smile. She's about eighteen years old. Sitting next to her is a grey-looking man in a grey suit and pastel blue tie over an old white shirt. He is reading the *New York Times*.

Leaning towards him the girl says, 'Sir?' The man turns and looks at her. 'Would you mind moving over?'

He looks around at the empty train. If she wants more space, he appears to think to himself, why doesn't *she* move? Yet, without a word to the girl, he slides two seats over.

The girl holds a small white paper bag. She scrunches the top tightly. She places it on the seat that the man vacated. She looks down at it. Picks it up again. Re-scrunches it. Puts it back on the seat. Twists it. Turns it. Picks it up again. She strokes out some of the creases in the side of the bag, checks the scrunch and puts the bag back on the seat. She appears to be satisfied. She puts her hands flat on her thighs and looks down at her T-shirt, brushes it with her hands and then puts them back on her thighs. The train lurches into a bend and the paper bag begins to slide. She grabs for it, picks it up, scrunches it, smoothes it, puts it back. The train lurches out of a bend, she grabs for the bag and picks it up again.

Next to me Jerome is asleep. The girl looks at him and then gently pats her white paper bag, now sitting safe and secure on the seat next to her.

The doors open at 116th Street and Jerome steps off the train. I follow him as he makes his way up and out of the station, crosses the road and walks along to number 170. He pulls at the locked door and sighs.

Street vendors move about, setting up tables and unpacking their merchandise. Cartoon bubble guns, sunglasses, leather belts, batteries and all kinds of knick-knacks are laid out in neat rows.

Two smartly dressed black men of differing heights approach. The taller wears a grey suit; on his head he wears a kufi. The other, shorter and rounder, wears a navy-blue suit and gold-rimmed glasses.

'Hey, fellas,' says Jerome.

'Hey, you all set?' asks the taller one, called Leroy, towering like a retired NBA star.

'Well, they didn't get the tickets, so I don't know exactly what we're doing.'

'They didn't get the tickets? That's crazy! Why didn't they get the tickets? We have nothing without the tickets. Damn!'

'I don't know. You'll have to ask her when she gets here.'

A lady arrives. She says hello to the waiting men and slides a key in the door.

'We didn't get tickets?' asks Leroy as they all climb the staircase.

'No,' she says, looking back over her shoulder.

Leroy calls up, 'Well, why not? We need those tickets.'

'Just wait and listen. They offered Lynn a ticket. They said she can go, but she told them straight, we are all one and they have to deal with all of us or nobody.'

'And what?'

'And ... they chose nobody.'

'So how are we gonna disrupt the mayor's meeting if we can't get into the conference?'

'We have a plan.'

Jerome chuckles: 'Tee hee hee.'

When we finally get to the office of Picture the Homeless – a Bronx-based charity which prides itself on being both for the homeless and run by the homeless – the petty-cash tin is opened and breakfast sandwiches are sent for. Homeless members of PTH arrive one by one, grabbing sandwiches as they do. Jerome introduces me as a friend. When divvying up the tasks one of the office staff asks me if I have any skills that could be useful. I tell them I am a journalist and to let me know if I can be of any help.

A homeless lady asks, 'Have you written for anybody we know?'

I tell them, as we are in New York, 'the *New York Post*, the *Daily News* ...'

Very quickly somebody cuts in, 'So how did you end up on the streets?'

I stutter to a grinding halt. It dawns on me that I haven't told Jerome why I am on the street. All I wanted was sleep when I met him. I had intended to tell him, so that he could make his own decision about whether he wanted to be a part of it. But at 6am when he awoke me from a sleep that could have lasted another five hours, it just hadn't occurred to me.

Jerome can't find out like this, it would seem like I have intentionally cheated and lied to him. Somebody else comes in and starts ranting about the arrangements, freeing me of any obligation to answer the question. But still I know I have to clear things up. I will tell Jerome first, later today when we are alone, and then I will tell the people of Picture the Homeless. For the time being, though, there is a mission to embark on.

Twelve people carrying picket boards, banners and leaflets sit and stand on the 6 train as it makes its way down to midtown. They are of mixed race, mixed age and mixed gender. Some look excited as the train shoots along swinging passengers this way and that. Others look simply indifferent. At Grand Central Station we all get off, gathering together on the platform to make sure nobody is left behind. Once everybody is accounted for we make our way up to ground level. The excitement builds. The mission for the day is to be *heard*, to be *accounted* for. This morning Mayor Bloomberg is unveiling his new 'Ten Year Plan' for reducing homelessness in the city of New York. He is doing this unveiling in the Hyatt Hotel above Grand Central Station. He has invited many of his peers to join him for breakfast at the Hyatt. It's a big deal curing homelessness, and it must not be done without the accompaniment of a warm breakfast and freshly squeezed juice.

Picture the Homeless are not so much angry about the contents of the plan. They haven't yet seen it. Apart from the team that put the plan together, nobody has. They are angry because they weren't consulted about the contents. They are angry that yet another mayor has come along waving a flag and hollering homeless cures without even speaking to the homeless or the key organisations that already work with the problem. It's a point they have plastered on their banners and flyers.

In a last minute bid to quieten Picture the Homeless, the mayor's office offered them one seat at the table. It was offered to Lynn, the main coordinator, who isn't homeless. She rejected the offer, reminding the mayor's office that PTH is a charity for the homeless, run by the homeless. If anybody should be sitting at the table, it should be one of the homeless. If there is any input the mayor needs on dealing with the homeless problem, surely that input on some level should come from the homeless themselves, Lynn argued. But the offer was not amended. It was Lynn or nobody.

Consequently, PTH is here in loud force. They are not only vocal, they are armed with fluorescent orange, green and yellow flyers. On the front of the flyers is a large black and white photograph of a wrought-iron garden table with two chairs. Nobody sits at the table, hence the caption above the image: 'Once again we weren't invited.'

The Hyatt is a four-star hotel. Upstairs the mayor and his merry men are having their breakfast conference. Downstairs the not-so-merry men and women of Picture the Homeless hold a no-frills conference.

'OK,' begins Lynn. 'Listen up. What we need here is press coverage. Leroy, Jean and Hugh, you guys have your routine memorised, so get yourself in front of the cameras as often as you can. Do interviews wherever possible.'

The hotel is incorporated into the Grand Central terminal building. The team spread out around the hotel, handing out flyers to anybody that will take them.

Sam J. Miller, a fresh-faced white boy in a pinstriped suit and dirty-collared shirt, is the Organiser of the Housing Committee of Picture the Homeless. 'OK, I'm going into the Hyatt to flyer. Who's with me?' he asks. Then to me he says, 'Alan, why don't you come and help me?'

He is a handsome-looking fellow, Sam, with his short waxed hair and neatly trimmed beard, if a little excitable – he is not homeless himself, but he is passionate about the cause.

'Sir, good morning, important news on the mayor's homeless plan … Sir? Miss? Madam? Important news …'

Sam is greeted by a long run of apologetic smiles. Only one woman takes the flyer, looks at it as she walks away and then screws it up into a ball while shaking her head. There's another man shaking his head. On his jacket he wears two badges: one that reads in capital letters 'HYATT', and another that reads 'SECURITY'.

'You can't be in here with this. This is private property and you have to leave.'

'Why?' asks Sam belligerently 'I'm not bothering anybody!'

'I just told you why. This is private property and you can leave or the police will arrest you for trespassing.' Sam doesn't need to look around for the police, he already knows that half of

NYPD's finest are stationed all around the hotel. But what is a cause without at least one arrest?

He says, 'But I'm just flyering. I don't understand the problem.'

'I'm not explaining it again,' the security guard says. Then in a deep booming voice he adds, 'Leave! Now!'

'Do you even know what I'm flyering about? This is a serious issue!'

'It don't make no difference what your flyers say. This is private property and you are trespassing.'

'Do you not care about the homeless?'

'Right now all I care about is getting you off the property.'

The security guard looks indifferent. It isn't so much that he doesn't care, but he has a low-level secure job that, if he just keeps his head down, he will keep. He doesn't seem so proud of his suit or badges, but he does seem to prefer them to the shabby outfits of the Picture the Homeless crew milling around the hotel entrance.

'Well, maybe you should read a flyer and …'

'Get out now!' the security guard shouts.

Sam joins the other group members outside.

'I just got totally busted, they threw me out,' Sam says to Linda, the organisation co-director and Sam's boss.

'Out of where?' she asks.

'Out of the Hyatt.'

'Well, what were you doing in there? Now it's closed to all of us and we've only been here five minutes. What happens when I need to go in there? They'll be watching us.'

'It doesn't matter, they can't stop you going in there, it …'

'Yes, they can stop us. It's private property.'

'No, but I wasn't in the hotel. I was just off to the side by the entrance and they threw me out.'

'OK, OK, well just start giving out flyers.'

'Right! I'll flyer the entrance to the hotel from the Grand Central walkway, inside the station. They can't throw me out of there because it's private property. Who's coming with me?'

If Sam had a sword he would cry, 'Chaaaaarge!'

Around the corner to the main entrance, on 42nd Street, a policeman stands tucked slightly into a nook. He enjoys his work, which today amounts to smiling and greeting any female that looks like she might have once graced the covers of *Maxim.*

'Good morning, mam, how are you today?'

'Morning, mam.'

'You look lovely today.'

'Morning.'

'Nice blouse.'

'How are you?'

'Good morning there!'

He smiles away at the women, who for the most part find him cheeky and charming and smile back, happy at least that they are getting something for their tax dollars.

About fifteen yards up from the community flattery officer stands Jerome. He leans out slightly on his right leg, holding out bright orange flyers in a way that people can read the title on the back of them:

> WHY AREN'T WE AT THE TABLE?
> You can't solve homelessness without involving homeless people.

Rather than forcefully handing out flyers to anybody and everybody, Jerome stands holding the flyers in a way that allows people to read the title as they pass, allowing them to make up their own mind as to whether this is an issue that concerns them. He doesn't give out as many flyers as the others, but the flyers taken from Jerome are read there and then, or are folded up and slipped into bags. He stands unfalteringly, always with his weight pushed forward on his front leg and an impassive expression.

'What is this?' a beige-suited woman asks, sliding her glasses down her nose.

'It's about Mayor Bloomberg's ten-year plan to end homelessness.'

'What about it?'

'Basically, every time we get a new mayor he comes up with a plan to reduce homelessness to some itty-bitty number. Guess what? These plans never work! The only thing you know about these plans for sure is that every time they come up with one, they do a little dance for the media. They have to have a breakfast or a lunch, invite all their friends over so they can pat each other on the back. Well, we're just a bit tired of them sitting up there in their breakfast meetings, eating their nice food and drinking their hot coffee, when what they should be doing is standing down here, speaking to us, *the homeless*, about the problem. That's why they always fail. They don't even know why we're out here. If they did they might be able to put together a plan that actually works, because they'd be armed with the correct information.'

'OK, well, thank you.'

'You're welcome,' Jerome smiles.

The woman takes a flyer, folds it and slips it into her handbag as she walks away.

When all of Jerome's flyers are gone he walks around to the front of Grand Central where the other members are handing out flyers. There are some news crews there: WB11, MSNBC, Channel 7. Cameras are rolling. A newspaper photographer takes pictures of the people holding the banner and singing songs. Jerome stops for a few seconds and watches the people who are all too keen to be interviewed. He listens to the words of an eight-man chant: 'Money on shelters is ill-spent. Give us the money to pay our rent!'

Leroy moves from one camera to another, his lines rehearsed and previously discussed with the other group members. Jean does likewise, beaming for the camera. Jerome stands, blank-faced, for a few more seconds, then gathers another handful of flyers and walks back around the corner where he stands alone, away from the fanfare, holding up his flyers. Even round the corner, the chanting can be heard faintly.

'Money on shelters is ill-spent. Give us the money to pay our
rent!'

The words of the chant have been poorly chosen, perhaps on
the spur of the moment. If you were to take Leroy to one side
and ask him what he wants – is it a free ride? Does he simply
want the government to pay his rent for him? – you'd better be
ready for a long, well-thought-out intelligent, 'No!' You would
get the same from Jean and Hugh. What they do want, as in the
case of Leroy, whose uninsured house burnt down to the
ground, is financial help – not when they are homeless, but at
the point just before people become homeless, when the
money could be used to prevent homelessness instead of sus-
taining it. The lyrics don't convey this message, but still the
PTH members are caught up in the song. They are riding the
wave of the chant but have no idea where this wave set out
from. If they would just take a second to listen to their words
they would know why the passers-by huff and puff in disgust.
They would know why the woman, rushing to or from this or
that, who may well have two kids, three jobs and a problem
making ends meet, doesn't appreciate their ballad for free
rent. But they don't take that second. It's not simply that they
are caught up in the cause, the struggle, they are caught up in
each other, in a euphoric camaraderie. They bounce on their
feet as they sing, waving their banner in the air, falling head
first into the stereotype of the homeless freeloader who can't
be bothered to work to pay for housing. The men bouncing up
and down with the banner do not want this, but they are lost in
an emotion – a joy – that, while rather touching, causes them
to misrepresent themselves.

On the subway back to the PTH office the talk is animated.
Those that didn't really know each other this morning know
each other now. Photographs are taken to record the laughter.
The successes of the morning are discussed.

'Did you see Maryanne Schretzman? She's the deputy com-
missioner to Linda Gibbs and she came down begging us,

positively begging us, to work with her,' Linda tells the group over the rattle of the train.

'I saw that.'

'Who did the WB11 interview?'

'That was me,' says Leroy.

'They did a thing with me too.'

'They did? That's great,' says Lynn. 'Now who spoke to Channel 7?'

'I did.'

'How did it go?'

'I think it went great. We'll see when we get back to the office. We should make the 12 o'clock news.'

Sam, in a very mocking voice, says to me, 'Hey, Alan, we met one of your friends.' He hands me the business card of a *New York Post* photographer. Sam's voice and mannerisms are laced with disbelief. He makes it clear that he doesn't believe I'm a journalist or have ever written for the *Post*. Not feeling in a position to clear this up right now, I take the card and look at it. It's been at least a year since I did any work for the *Post*, having moved away from New York some four or five years ago. Yet when I look at the card, much to my own surprise, I do recognise the name. Luiz C. Ribeiro. He is the photographer that was assigned to my very first *New York Post* story, an article about illegal after-hours bars in the city.

'Do you know him?' Sam asks.

'Yes, we only worked together once, but …'

'Oh *really*?' Sam asks.

I turn away and look over to Jerome, who stands off to one side, listening quietly.

# Day 11 – Targeting Your Audience

When I arrive at Penn Station, where I go for the company of JV, he greets me with: 'Yo, Alan, son. The lesbians are looking for you!'

'What? Really?' My excitement confirms JV's already established ideas about any relationship I might have with Nancy and Kim.

'Yeah, Alan's got the moves! You gonna get freaky with the lesbians, huh?'

'No, JV, I am not going to get freaky with the lesbians. Now where are they?'

'Ha! See. You can't wait to get there. You don't have to lie to me, Alan.'

'JV,' I say, but his attitude is making me laugh. 'I am just going to follow them. Where – are – they?'

'Yeah, right!'

'JV?'

'They're right there,' he says, pointing. 'You see? They at the United Homeless table making out.'

As I march off JV shouts, 'You better come back and tell me all about it, Alan. I'm your friend, remember.'

Nancy and Kim appear pleased to see me. They greet me with smiles.

Laughing, Nancy says, 'We know you're cool, we had you checked out.'

'What do you mean, "we had you checked out?"' I ask.

'We have a friend who works at a drop-in shelter,' Kim tells me. 'He used to be homeless. We went to see him and we told him about you. We were laughing 'cause we thought you were full of shit. We gave him the piece of paper you gave us and he looked you up on the internet. He showed us your bio on your publisher's website and then he called your editor ...'

'No, he didn't call them,' Nancy cuts in. 'He said he would if we wanted him to.'

'Oh, OK. Anyway we know you're who you say you are. We saw the picture on your website of you with your daughter ...'

'She's so cute.'

'Do you miss her?'

Nancy and Kim go on to ask me a bunch of questions, yet it is hard for me to find a gap where I might slot an answer.

'Anyway, Alan, we will finish here with the table at one, then we can go and hang out,' Nancy says.

Kim says, 'Oh, first I got to go and get my medicine.'

'Cool,' I manage to squeeze in. 'Should I meet you after?'

'Or you could just come with us,' Kim offers, with a shrug.

'Come with us, Alan,' Nancy says.

We ride the subway to 102nd Street. People are starting to arrive at the methadone clinic for their daily dose, their medicine. The clinic sits halfway along a block, half a block from Central Park. Its double doors are made of stainless steel frames with a vertical glass panel. Around the frames is a horrid faded and depressing blue façade.

Nancy and Kim sit on the wall of a trough out of which one lone tree sprouts.

They wait.

But it's only Kim who is feeling sick. It's only Kim that's on methadone treatment. Through those glass doors is everything she needs.

'You'll be alright soon, baby,' Nancy assures her, and then, looking up, she says, 'She'll be alright once she gets her medicine.'

It's 3pm now; doors open for the afternoon shift at three thirty.

A man walks up from the left. His clothes, like his long hair, are bedraggled and dirty. He has the telltale half-empty sports bag over his shoulder. He has Disney-shaped eyes that are black and droop down most of his face. He looks at Kim.

'Oh shit, they keeping you waiting?'

Kim looks up. 'They don't serve until three thirty.'

'Oh shit, really? What is it now?'

'Three.'

'Fuck. I didn't know that, this is my first time here. I just got in from West Virginia last night. What are you on here?'

'One-eighty.'

'Oh fuck! One-eighty, a little thing like you on one-eighty, that's crazy. What do you think they'll start me on?'

'I don't know, not one-eighty.'

'I was on one-forty in West Virginia. You think they'll give me that?'

'Not just in off the street. They might start you on eighty.'

'Oh man, I can't be doing no eighty. If all I get is eighty I'm gonna need to score some dope.'

'They ain't gonna just give you one-forty 'cause you tell them that's what you got back home. But it's real easy to get bumped up here.'

'What? Five a day?'

'No, all last week I was being bumped up ten milligrams a day.'

'Are you fucking kidding me? Ten a day?'

'I just kept telling her that I was still sick. I started on one-forty, a week later I was on two-ten …'

'Two-ten?'

'Yeah, but that was fucked up so I took myself back down to one-eighty.'

A very pretty girl with piercing eyes and a sweet teenage smile leans against a wall, listening. Her long curly hair is pulled back in a ponytail and held in place by a blue scrunchy. After a short pause she interrupts, 'Who do you see to get bumped up?'

'Your nurse. You still sick?'

'Yeah, but I'm only on thirty and I don't need a lot more. But thirty's not getting me through.'

As the time crawls nearer to three thirty more people arrive. Another man, in his late twenties, arrives hand in hand with his five-year-old son.

At three thirty, people are allowed in. They take up chairs in the waiting room until their name is called. It's typical of an institution waiting room: brightly coloured uncomfortable chairs and walls lined with sensitive advice posters and helplines.

*Do you know somebody on drugs?*

*Do you know somebody suffering from addiction?*

*Do you know somebody that shares needles?*

These attempts at softly, softly are frankly bizarre.

*Do you know somebody that needs help?*

Bar my fortunate self, all of these *do you know somebody* questions could be answered by everybody else in the room with, 'Yeah. *Me!*'

After their drink some come back and sit in the waiting room; others walk straight out of the door. In the background the guy from West Virginia is arguing: 'But the girl out there gets one-eighty and she's half my size …'

'Oh, thanks,' whispers Kim. 'You're really fucking smart.'

The man and his son are sitting in the waiting room. The little boy is already throwing himself into gangster poses, desperate to imitate his father. He's already got the baggy jeans and the basketball vest over his white T-shirt. He has the Nike trainers and the Yankee cap. All he needs now is another four feet of height.

The father speaks. He says, 'Hey, Kimmy, how you doing?'

'I'm doing OK.'

Nancy talks to the boy, 'Hey, sweetie,' then to the father. 'He looks so cute in those pants.'

The father says to Kim, 'Do you need anything?'

Kim says, '*No!*' in a slightly terse voice.

'I got everything, what do you need?'

'I don't need anything.'

'Look here …' The father pulls out a cigarette packet and after a sneaky look around takes his son's hand and tips the contents out into it. The tiny dime bags of heroin look big in the little hands. The father signals to the son to go over and show Kim what's on offer. The boy stands with attitude, lips pouted in what is supposed to be a menacing grimace. He has watched his father do it a thousand times before. He knows how to act. He takes a step, but as he does Kim stands, red-faced and angry. She looks as if she is about to explode, but can't, because she can't afford to be thrown out of the clinic, not before getting her drink. Her name is called in the nick of time and she leaves the room.

The father smiles at his son encouragingly. First you recognise a market, then you target your customer and if you can get them all in the same room bugging out from product withdrawal you can just keep targeting them and targeting them and targeting them. 'Look, son, here comes another one.'

I look at the little boy with his doomed future and think of lotteries.

Kim doesn't calm down until we are in Central Park, where we sit watching rollerbladers go by while the girls tell me stories about the daily dose of men who try to get them into cheap hotel beds.

I leave Kim and Nancy in the park and start a long hike back downtown. I walk along Broadway, follow it down to Time Square, and then slip down 7th Avenue to see if JV is around. It's 9pm and Madonna fans are swarming past. Ticket touts argue with potential customers about why they still want $150 for a ticket when Madonna is due on stage any second. Even the touts' runners argue for a better price in a bid to earn themselves some commission.

JV dumps his papers on the wall and walks up into the corner. He is counting his money, going through the well-practiced ritual. Forty-six dollars. He smiles, turns and with a raised boyish brow makes his way back to the sidewalk, ignoring his stash of papers that he has on the wall. He bums a cigarette and stands smoking it. He overhears a conversation between two teenage girls dressed up as Madonna.

'I guess you have to call out,' one girl says, laughing.

Her friend joins in the laughter, 'You call out.'

And laughing some more, in her leather catsuit with tinfoil cone breasts, she says in a deep mimicking voice, 'Tickets? Tickets? Tickets? Get ya tickets! Buying, selling. Need a ticket? Need a ticket? Need a ticket?' The two girls fall about laughing.

JV stands a few feet away nodding his head, 'Oh, you girls having a good time, huh?' he says. 'What you up to?'

The girl, dressed as Madonna dressed as Marilyn Monroe talking as a boxing presenter says, 'Need a ticket?'

JV says, 'Yeah.'

'Are you serious?' she snaps back, now talking in her own voice.

'How much you want for it?'

'Eighty bucks.'

'Get the fuck … I'll give you twenty bucks.'

'Yeah right, it's a $90 ticket. The price is on it.'

'Yeah. But Madonna's on stage now and you missing it. I'll tell you what, being as you all dressed up and shit, I'll give you thirty.'

'Sixty?'

'Forty!'

'Fifty?'

'Forty!'

Turning to her friend with the tin breasts Madorilyn asks, 'What do you think?'

'What the fuck? We're missing the show standing here.'

JV hands over forty dollars in singles. The girls laugh.

'Yeah, you keep smiling,' says JV. 'I see you in there.'

Five minutes later, on the other side of the Penn Station entrance, a guy in spandex shorts and a string vest buys a Madonna ticket. JV takes the hundred dollars, slips it in his pocket and walks away, trying not to smile. In total Madonna will play six nights at Madison Square Garden. She is good for business, even JV's business.

I want to ask, 'What has Madonna done for me lately?' but know only too well that Mad owes me nothing.

JV pauses in front of me for a minute, then says, 'Hey, Alan, what you doing now?'

'Nothing.'

'You want to take a ride uptown, see my hood?'

'JV, I'm going to get busted soon if I keep jumping turnstiles.' The problem with this turnstile jumping is that I am not yet as discreet as I need to be.

'Don't worry, Alan, I got your back, just go in front of me, I got a Metro card.'

On the subway JV takes up two seats and goes to sleep. Somehow he manages to wake up before his stop. He steps off the train, the only person getting off at this station at this time. At the top of the stairs, as he steps out onto the pavement, he takes a deep breath, his nostrils flaring. This is his town, his hood. This is the Bronx.

The road is a dual carriageway separated by a central reservation. The opposite side of the street is dark. It is residential apart from the one fast food joint with lights that are too bright. On JV's side of the street there's a deli, its doorway crowded with youths talking and hanging out. There's also a fried chicken store and a pizza take-out.

This is still New York: the mad uncertainty continues to lurk round every corner – in fact more so. But here the people seem even bigger on account of the buildings being so much smaller. Most of the buildings are just five or six floors high. They are dark and dirty. The road is busy with cars speeding in all directions, but the sidewalk is desolate compared to the sidewalks of midtown. It's an odd feeling, to walk down into the ground in midtown, get on a shiny cage of metal for twenty minutes, and then come back up onto the earth's surface to a completely different scene. This is what midtown would be like if you took away all the tourists – the Bronx is like an apocalyptic midtown.

JV walks along in no apparent rush.

He passes people on the left.

'Wassup, son!'

He passes people on the right.

'Wassup, nigger!'

Now and again he'll stop and bang shoulders.

'Yo, nig, where Lisa at?'

'I don't know, man.'

'You see her tonight?'

'Man, I see her earlier but that was like six or summin …'

'Yo, son, you see her, tell her JV here and he waiting, alright?'

He walks on.

Around a corner walks a tall muscular black man wearing a doo-rag wrapped around his head, a white T-shirt and some bright yellow Nike tracksuit bottoms. He is flanked on either shoulder by at least two other black kids. They walk along and into the deli. Two kids stay outside, the rest go in. When the big man finally comes out he spots JV.

'Hey, nigger. Lisa know you're here?'

'I looking for the bitch right now. I called her, she said she meet me here.'

To one of his sidekicks the big man says, 'Yo. Go tell Lisa JV waiting on her ass!'

A sidekick skips off.

'You alright?' JV asks.

'Same ol'. What about you? You keeping good?'

'Yeah, you know, I keeping it.'

While he's waiting JV crosses the street and turns a corner. He approaches a young guy in a black tracksuit and a cap.

'Yo, gimme a twenty.'

The guy throws a small plastic bag of coke on the sidewalk about three feet away.

JV pays and scoops up his bag before crossing back to the other side.

Lisa, now standing on the corner, says, 'Nigger, I be standing here and everybody like, "Yo JV looking for you …"'

'Yeah I here, I just stepped off the block a second.'

Lisa wears tight jeans, a black shirt and a gold 'L' that hangs around her neck. Her her is pinned up elaborately on top of her head and she looks like she's made an effort compared to those around her.

'You good, baby?'

'I'm good, you know me.' Looking back over his shoulder JV says, 'This is my boy, Alan.'

Lisa and I nod and smile at one another before she turns back to JV.

'OK, give me a hug, the shit's in my back pocket.'

JV takes Lisa in his arms and caresses her back. He slides his hands down and inserts both hands into the back pockets of her jeans.

JV says, 'Yo, nigger, I think I found it!'

Laughing, Lisa says, 'Just take the shit and go. You bringing the money back tonight?'

'Yeah, I be right back, alright?'

'See ya, baby.'

JV slides the deck of heroin that he just took from Lisa into his front pocket and heads back to the subway. Now I understand why he's not jumping turnstiles – you don't risk getting caught skipping a two-dollar fare when you have ten grams of uncut heroin in your pocket. He walks down the platform, and when he's sure nobody is looking, he stands by a payphone on the platform, opens his coke bag, tips half of its contents onto the back of his hand and snorts it in one go.

For a second he looks around, then he licks the back of his

hand, fiddles with his nostrils and waits for the subway train that will take us back into Manhattan.

I ask him, 'Why did you buy off the street if you're dealing?'

'Why?' he says. ''Cause it's split. My people own one half of the street and only deal H. The other side of the street belongs to some other cats, and they got the coke.'

At midnight, just off 8th Avenue, JV stops and sits on a flowerbed with his cousin Remy. Remy starts unwrapping the leaves of a buck-fifty cigar, a blunt. Carefully he pulls at the skin so as not to tear it. When he is done he fills the skin with grass and re-rolls it.

'This motherfucker's late,' JV says as Remy lights the blunt.

'Motherfucker's always late.'

'Yo – not always!'

'Was late last week.'

'Yeah, he was too.'

'Week before that too he was late.'

'Yeah, but fuck it, easy money.'

'Oh shit, look at this Asian girl coming here!' says Remy.

'Oh damn, lady, look at you!' JV says as the girl passes them by. 'You wanna smoke some weed with two handsome black men and ...' JV looks at me and laughs, 'an Englishman?'

'Fuck you, nigger!' she shouts back.

Remy nearly falls off the flowerbed. He is laughing and choking from misinhalation.

'Did that bitch just say "nigger"? Yo baby, you ain't hood!'

'Fuck you!' she calls back.

'No, fuck you!' shouts JV.

'Yeah, nigger!' calls Remy and both he and JV fall to the ground laughing.

That's when a shiny Mercedes pulls up.

JV says, 'Oh, talking of niggers, here's my white boy.'

The Mercedes is a brand-new SL350, black with all the trimmings. U2 are playing softly as the window winds down. A thirty- something white guy in a suit sits in the driver's seat. JV hands over the deck of heroin. The driver hands him money. They bid each other farewell and the car rolls crisply away.

No love lost.

And very little time wasted.

# Day 12 – The Lord's Smile Can Be Seen in Curious Places

Jerome is a classic New Yorker. He loves the city and enjoys nothing more than sitting in one of its parks with a copy of the *New York Post*, or better still one of his Bibles. He likes watching his fellow New Yorkers go about their day, or just sitting in the sun taking in the sounds and smells. He can talk too, and with that voice of his you don't tire of listening. Often, if he has made no plans, Jerome will get up in the morning, head off to a church for an early sermon and then trot to the nearest park for a place to sit and watch.

When we go our separate way in the morning Jerome shares with me his plans for the day. He tells me of a mission that gives out food in the evening.

'If you want to meet up before, I can take you there,' he says. 'You know where to find me.'

Yes I do, in the park.

Jerome sits on a bench in Gramercy Park reading his King James Bible. *And on the seventh day God ended his work, which he had made …*

Sunlight breaks through the trees and casts patterns on the

path in front of the bench. There are lots of people on benches. Some read, some write, some talk and some sleep. The girl sitting next to Jerome talks on her cellphone. Her long tanned legs cross in front of her; her sandals are off and to the side '... No I can't, I have a lecture at two and then at six I have to start my new job ... No, I make better money behind the bar, so ... Yeah, but he's such an asshole to work for, I just thought it was time to move on ...' Her free hand twists at the string tied around her neck. '*I did not fuck him*, who told you that?' She wears a lemon-coloured vest. 'He's not even attractive, why would I fuck him?' Her straight blow-dried brown hair lies in feathers down to her freckled shoulders.

Jerome's reading becomes fragmented.

*And God blessed the ... seventh day ... and sanctified ... it ...*

'... Yeah, OK, call me tomorrow ...' she breaks into stifled laughter. 'I did not fuck him! ... No, no, OK, yeah, I did do that, but that's not fucking him. It does *not* amount to the same thing ... 'Cause ... It just ... Call me, OK? Bye.' She closes her phone.

Jerome says, not to anybody in particular, but to anybody who wants to listen, 'If nobody objects, I think I'm gonna lie down over here on the grass.'

Nobody objects.

Jerome slides yesterday's *New York Post* onto the bench to re-serve his seat and he crosses the path to a patch of sunlit grass. Using his bag as a pillow he lies down on his back with his King James held high.

*... in the day that the Lord God made the earth and the heavens ...*

After ten minutes Jerome can feel his underneath moisten from the heat. He rolls onto his right side, re-puffs his bag and continues reading.

*And every plant of the field before it was in the earth ...*

Without meaning to, without wanting to, without conscious application on his part, Jerome's eyes peer over the top of his Bible to the girl on the bench, with her parted legs and short skirt.

*And the Lord God took the man, and put him in the Garden of Eden …*

The Lord smiles at Jerome from a curious place. Jerome smiles back into the dark crevice even though he tries not to. He looks back at the Bible.

*Thou shall not eat it …*

He looks back over the Bible.

The girl senses that Jerome is looking at her. She is aware that she has no underwear on and she knows that with her right foot up on the bench the way it is, Jerome can see right up her skirt.

Jerome looks up at the girl's face.

She smiles down at him.

Slowly she takes her right foot down, places it a fair distance from her left foot and parts her knees.

Jerome giggles.

A man on a neighbouring bench shuffles his newspaper.

An arthritic woman painfully peels an apple with a penknife.

The girl's legs snap shut. Bang!

Now she giggles.

Jerome, shaking his head but still smiling, turns back to the Bible.

*Now the serpent was more subtle than any beast of the field, which the Lord God had made …*

The girl slowly opens her legs.

Jerome smiles.

The girl smiles.

Jerome let's his head roll from side to side.

The girl takes her left foot and puts it up on the bench.

A tanned guy in a suit and sunglasses walks past the bench, talking into a little stick microphone that is attached to his ear.

The girl puts her leg down and looks away as he walks by.

Then she takes both her feet and rests them on the edge of the bench.

Jerome closes the Bible with a snap and leans up on his elbow while the girl runs both hands through her hair.

She turns her head to the guy sitting on the neighbouring bench. He is a thin, weasely-looking man with a big nose and silver-framed spectacles. He is clean-shaven and his eyes have turned beady.

The girl stares intently at her neighbour, letting her hands rest on her knees.

Jerome's eyes flick back and forth and across, from between her legs, to her face, to that of the weasel, and around and around and around. Finally, the man, having sensed the attention, looks at the girl. She quickly turns away. He goes back to his paper. She goes back to him. He turns. She turns. Jerome turns.

The girl now stares at the arthritic apple peeler and pulls faces, sticks her tongue out, all the time while flashing herself at Jerome.

The old woman turns with a speed her hands don't possess, and the girl brings her tongue back in just in time. 'Do you need some help with that?' she asks, nodding at the apple. The arthritic woman passes the girl the apple and the penknife that she is using, telling her to be careful, the knife's sharp. She thanks her.

Resting her arms on her knees the girl peels the apple, letting the first slice of peel drop on the floor in front of her.

'Oh, I'll get that in a minute,' she says, smiling at Jerome who sits wide-eyed and happy.

Thin strips of apple peel lie on the floor. The girl cuts a slice and passes it to the old woman and then returns to the peeling, to Jerome. They giggle to each other. The man with the newspaper folds it and gets up. He walks away briskly. The girl slides forward a little, bringing herself to sit on the edge of the bench.

The girl laughs. 'Wow, I'm getting cramp in my legs.'

She puts her legs down on the ground. Closed.

She opens them.

'Sir, do you have the time?' she asks Jerome, beaming broadly.

Looking at his watch Jerome tells the girl, 'It's 1.23.'

'Oops,' she says. 'I have to go.'

She passes the peeled apple to the arthritic woman next to her.

'Thank you so much,' the old woman says, taking the apple.

'You're welcome,' the girl says. She turns to Jerome.

He says, 'I guess I should say thank you too?'

'No,' the girl says. 'Thank *you!*'

With that she stands, jiggles her feet into her sandals and walks away.

Jerome goes back to his Bible.

*But of the fruit of the tree which is in the midst of the garden, God hath said, Ye shall not eat of it, neither shall ye touch it, lest ye die.*

# Day 13 – The Hook and the Hamburger

Joseph Lucas is a character straight out of a made-for-television movie about cross-bred goldfish that grow teeth and eat human beings – whole ones, or maybe just the arms.

One of the first things he does is offer me his hook to shake. 'I'm Joseph, where are you from?'

Joseph is drunk. He is enjoying a small McDonald's coke that he tops up with vodka. Even though we are in the new shiny multi-screened McDonald's on 42nd Street, I don't see the McD's memorabilia; instead I see Joseph Lucas. It would be easy to imagine Joseph Lucas on a trawler, with nets and flapping fish, and drunken fisherman telling stories about how they lost their arms.

It was a whopper.

A *whopper*, I tell you.

Gold, with teeth.

However, Joseph Lucas lost his arm as a result of 7,000 volts of electricity surging through him. He should have died. He should have died from the fall as well as from the electricity. The accident happened when he came home one day to find that his electricity had been cut off. Drunk and in a stupor, he climbed the pylon just outside his house and decided to main-line it. He woke up in hospital one and a half months later with only one arm.

Joseph points his hook at my dollar-menu cheeseburger. 'Is that food nice?'

Yes, the two mouthfuls of cheeseburger are nice; when you're this hungry, a deep-fried shoe would taste good.

'Adam ...'

'No, not Adam, *Alan.*'

'Adam ...'

'No, Alan, with an l.'

'Listen, Adam, I'm not gonna lie to you,' he says, leaning to-wards me, resting his hook on my shoulder as if we are dear friends. 'I need some money for food.' There's a pregnant pause as Joseph removes a vodka bottle from his bag and pours it into his coke. Maybe it is the drink blurring his vision, but, as he hits me up for money, I realise that to Joseph I must look like a tourist. 'Also,' he says with a mischievous smile, 'I'm not done drinking yet!'

Joseph Lucas has been homeless since 1992.

'Do you think I like it? Ask me.'

He doesn't. Not one bit.

'I hate it. Since '92, right after I divorced my second wife. We were only married a month ... Ah! I hated her guts, I mean re-ally *hated* her guts!'

Which begs the question: 'Why did you marry her?'

'Well, at first ... what's your name?'

'Alan.'

'Adam, I'm Joseph Lucas.'

Joseph Lucas is a little thin white man with shoulder-length wiry hair. He is the type of character usually associated with scaring away birds. His hook, poised to snap at any moment in any direction to highlight any point, scares more children than birds. Yet he is harmless and lost. On his left hand he has a tat-too, and mixed within the faded image are the names of his three children.

'From my first wife. She was another bitch!'

On the other hand are tattooed three figure sevens and the name 'Bruce Lee'. On his lower arm there's also a tattoo of … 'I don't know what that is …' and a dagger. Joseph's forearm is covered in scar tissue from the accident. So is his jaw and most of his upper body. He lifts up his T-shirt to show me.

'You want to hear a story? My mother-in-law, from the first wife, she was a filthy stinking whore.' Joseph takes an aggressive suck on his straw and then slams the cup down on the table. 'She wanted me dead. She used to tell my wife she'd be better off if I was dead. She wished for me to die. She said I was a lazy fucking asshole drunk, that all I did was drink whiskey and listen to Johnny Cash.' Joseph takes another sip of his drink. 'That part's pretty much true,' he says, grinning. 'Anyway, the mother-in-law, she died when she was only forty-two. That's what happens, you see, if you wish other people dead. God kills you instead.'

Joseph Lucas came to New York to serve a three-year prison sentence for breaking and entering.

'I never stole anything,' he reflects. 'I just needed to warm up and use the phone.' In his drunken state Joseph left the details of his phone calls written down on a pad by the phone. '*That was really stupid.*'

Joseph's face is flushed red with alcohol. He tells me he has been in detox sixty-eight times. He was released from his latest stint just yesterday.

'If you're going to go in, Adam, ask to go to St Vincent's. There you get to wear your own clothes and there's a TV at the end of your bed. Not up on the wall in the corner, at the *end of your bed.* I'll be back there at the end of the week. You can just come in with me if you like.'

'But didn't you say you just got out yesterday? Will they let you back within a week?'

'Ah, see, what I got out of yesterday was a different clinic, see …' Joseph goes on while tapping his nose with his hook (his good hand holding the vodka). 'I know what I'm doing.'

Joseph slumps back in his chair and sucks on his drink some more, looking over his nose contemplatively. The screens on the wall to the right show the history of McDonald's. They play interviews with its founder, Raymond Albert Kroc, and show black and white stills of the first ever restaurant. Oriental girls sit and coo at the screens while eating burgers twice the size of their heads. Latinos queue for the toilet. Mothers chastise children for being children.

Joseph has a tear running down his left cheek. 'But I don't want to keep doing it.' He bites his bottom lip for a second. 'I just don't know how to stop.'

People pass by. The effort of not looking at the now-crying homeless man with a hook is visible on their faces.

'I've tried to not be homeless. They got me a room once but I missed the friends that I drink with. I missed them a lot. I didn't know how to be in that room, alone. It was so quiet. I fucked it up. I hate my life. I hate being homeless. I hate being an alcoholic. It's so hard, but somehow I can't stop. The only way they'll help me, if I'm not dead by year out, will be to lock me up and throw away the key. I don't want to die like this. I want to see my kids again. But I don't want them to see me like this.'

People walk past Joseph Lucas as if he isn't there. If this were a normal day, and I was sitting here shoving a quick junk fix down my throat, I too would have ignored him. The sight of Joseph is just too depressing to contemplate. But for right or wrong I am here, and so I sit with Joseph while he cries.

After a short while he says, 'Come with me.'

I follow him out onto 42nd Street where he squints up into the bright sunshine and heads up towards Time Square.

He says, 'I need to make some money, so just hang back but keep following.'

He stops at various groups of people, mostly young guys who stand talking and smoking.

'Listen, I'm not gonna lie to you,' he tells them. 'I need some money for food … Also, I'm not done drinking yet!'

Joseph repeats the line to every group that he stops at. Most shrug him away. Others turn their backs. Now and again somebody gives him a cigarette. Once in a while, a dollar. He moves on, working the crowds like an old pro.

Saddened by the sight, I let the gap between us grow, until he slips away.

Whenever I have passed through Union Square in the last few days I have looked out for the two flags flapping in the breeze that would indicate that the mysterious trolley man might be nearby, and I was beginning to give up hope of ever seeing the trolley again. That was until now.

I can see the flags. But they are all I can see. The trolley and the man with the trolley (if there is one) are blocked out by the huge crowds of people who line the street to watch the Gay Pride Parade. I'm standing on the corner of West 10th Street, where it cuts diagonally onto 6th Avenue. Crossing the street is proving to be difficult. The crowds are dense and on the other side of them are barriers. The police are controlling the crossings and only letting people through when there's a break in the parade.

I don't have a problem with that. I'll just stand and wait, as long as I can see the flags I know where the trolley is.

But the flags start to move.

They get smaller.

I try to push my way to the front of the crowd – at least then I could see where the trolley goes, or be the first to cross when a gap presents itself. There are so many people that I really have to push.

I have been homeless for two weeks now. It shows in my appearance. I can't smell myself, but I must smell, a bit at least.

When I push past people they think nothing of it as I come from behind.

Then they get a look at me.

They say, 'Ooooh!'

They say, 'What's that smell?'

One says, 'Get lost, you stinking bum!'

And that's when I freeze.

I am not a street-arguing type of person. Street arguments normally turn me a deep shade of red and have me looking for some kind of shelter. The words *who're you fucking looking at* have never left my lips.

But for whatever reason I wasn't about to let somebody call me a 'stinking bum', even if I did stink. Something stirred in me. If I were a real homeless person, I'd be able to unleash a torrent of abuse that would reduce this asshole to a quivering shadow of his former self. I've seen them do it. It's a simple equation: if you're homeless you are expected to be crazy, if you're crazy you're capable of anything, if you're capable of anything and coming down on the average Joe, the average Joe stains his Calvin's.

But I'm not really homeless.

I'm just Alan. But I don't want to be Alan right now. So give me something to hide behind. I want to be crazy. I want to make this little George Michael clone pay for his one silly little comment. Even though it really doesn't amount to anything.

Why? I don't know. Maybe because my back aches, or because my feet are sore, or possibly because I am hungry … maybe.

I recently read *The London Pigeon Wars* by Patrick Neate. In this book there is a character called Murray. He is a very spontaneous character, capable of anything. His dialogue never ceases to amuse me. He's a character that every male wishes he had a little of.

He says things like, 'Sorry I was late, china. Got held up, know what I mean? But I didn't interrupt you, did I? You interrupted yourself.' And, 'So much for the superhero. You're a fool, china, a fucking fool.'

I can't do this as Alan, but apparently I'm willing to have a go at it as Murray, because I find myself turning and saying loudly in my best barrow-boy prose, 'Oy, spandex!' As far as comments go, this one garners a lot of attention today as I could be addressing every other male on the sidewalk. 'You got something you wanna share with me, or what?'

He knows who he is. He says, 'No, I have nothing I want to share with you at all.' Which causes a friend of his to snigger.

'What was that, sweet cheeks? I didn't hear ya! It's no good flapping your gums while talking through your nose! Speak up if you got something to say!'

'Oh, go away.'

'I'm not going anywhere, shortcake. I'm all into you now. Look at ya, standing there like a wilted lily. What? Speak up!'

'I didn't say anything.'

'That's right, china, and best you don't.'

'Just leave him alone,' says an older man with a handlebar moustache and lots of leather.

I say, 'Tell ya mum to stay out of it, this is between you and me.'

'What is your problem, homophobe?' I'm asked.

'I ain't homophobic. I'll mince with the best of ya I will, but what I won't have is some cunt with a loose mouth and tight underpants giving it Berty big bollocks behind my back! You 'ear me, china?'

I realise that I am overacting and being incredibly immature and thank my lucky stars that nobody I know is here to witness this little outburst. I think I've got my point across, though, for a minute, but soon find myself surrounded by the spandex and leather brigade, who look like they're about to smash my face in.

If I *were* a homophobe, this here could be the most potentially degrading beating of my life.

I am saved the spectacle of being straight-bashed by a Mr NYPD. At least it looks that way for a second, but Mr NYPD really is a homophobe. He's the new breed of homophobe that's trying not to be. His expression says, 'Don't worry, queers, I'll deal with this.' And as he lays into me they seem happy to accept this misguided help.

Turning to me he says, 'Get outta here!'

I say, 'I need to cross …'

He shouts, 'Get out of here now!'

I give a glance back over my shoulder to where once I could see the flags of the trolley. They are nowhere to be seen.

They have moved on. It would appear best I do the same.

# Day 14 – Some People Obey a Darker Lord

A teenager wearing a New York Knicks vest and a baseball cap that sits skew-whiff on his head walks along the sidewalk on Broadway. His right shoulder hangs down as if it weighs a few pounds more than his left. He walks as if he has sprained his left ankle, but this is just for effect. He spits out his chewing gum in irritation. Irritation at what, I don't know. The bubblegum, green and shiny, hits the sidewalk and comes to an immediate, bounceless halt. It enjoys a few seconds of rest before being picked up by a Boateng loafer that jumps into the road and takes a cab ride.

The sidewalks up and down New York City are marked with little black circles. Chewing gum, spat out and collected by unsuspecting footwear until eventually it is ground into sidewalks and unsuspecting carpets. The dead chewing gums are everywhere, little black spots that are eight to twelve inches apart.

Another prominent pavement dweller is the cigarette butt.

*There's one!*

They aren't as frequent as the chewing gum, but they are there, maybe every yard, every other yard in a drought. Some are no more than little brown butts, sucked of life and discarded like unwanted memories. Red lipstick marks the spot. Others are half-smoked and still send off smoke signals. Others are extinguished and trodden flat. But some show an inch of white unsmoked tubing.

*There's one!*

Now and again you find a whole one.

*There's one!*

On 30 March 2003, Mayor Bloomberg's Smoke-Free Air Act came into effect, making it illegal to smoke in public places. If you wanted to smoke in a restaurant in New York City you used to have to go and sit at the bar. Now you have to go outside. Now even the bar is off-limits. Now, even if all you have is a bar, it is off-limits to smokers.

The mayor said, 'Today's bill signing is an historic event for New York City.'

Outside bars all over New York City, clusters of people stand sucking the life out of dead things, desperate to get back inside the bar before Rodriguez takes a swing at a home run.

They look relieved!

They light up. Take a long deep drag, rising on tippy-toes as they take the dark cloud deep into their lungs. Relief and tears in their eyes, they exhale, inhale, exhale, inhale and come down off their tiptoes. If the game is hot, if Rodriguez's bat does connect with the ball, they might drop their cigarette on the floor there and then, half-smoked and still alight.

*There's one!*

Then again, at seven bucks a pack, they might just do away with the exhale …

Inhale!

Inhale!

Inhale!

… and explode back into the bar, blowing an entire cigarette out of their nostrils, thinking, '*Bloomberg needs to get up earlier if he wants to get one over on old Stevie!*'

In New York, before the Smoke-Free Air Act was passed, the average smoker smoked a cigarette in three minutes. Since the

Smoke-Free Air Act was imposed, this time has come down to two minutes.

The average New Yorker doesn't waste tobacco, he smokes it down as quickly as he can, his hit coming quicker and faster. His resistance adjusts accordingly. But his friends, the ones who want to get back in the bar quickly because A: they are missing the tail end of a really good story; B: it is starting to rain; C: the guy on the bench opposite is staring at their breasts – they drop half-smoked cigarettes on the floor. Now, when they are out socialising, they have to smoke two cigarettes to get the fix that one cigarette used to give them.

The Smoke-Free Air Act must surely have been the brainchild of the tobacco industry.

The sidewalk in front of bars and restaurants is a good place to find a half-smoked cigarette butt, should you be looking for one.

*There's one!*

Some homeless people just scoop those butts right off the ground and light them up without stopping. Joey likes to collect as many as he can and put them in his empty Drum tobacco pouch. Later he will sit in the park making roll-ups. But for now he keeps walking, walking and looking for and at butts.

*Oh, she's gorgeous!*

*There's one!*

I walk with Joey as he searches. He sees a cigarette on the floor, full and fat and unsmoked. There's a woman standing next to it, smart in her purple blouse and grey business skirt. Her long curly black hair shines in the sun. She is waiting for somebody. The cigarette lies just a foot away from her high-heeled shoes. I expect Joey to stride over, smile, squat and retrieve the cigarette. But instead he stands off to one side. He leans against one of the big red *Village Voice* dispensers. A couple of minutes pass. The woman answers her cellphone and takes the 'I'm running late' quite well. She keeps waiting.

Joey waits. He says, 'I just don't want to go, you know, barging over there, I wanna give her some space. No need to scare her over a cigarette.'

This is rather a strange notion. The thought of a homeless New Yorker being concerned about picking up a cigarette by somebody's feet doesn't fit with my idea of New York. But maybe he is right to err on the side of caution; you never know how a New Yorker might react. The woman might simply offer Joey a fresh cigarette from her own packet, or equally she might plant a pointed toe in his groin before unloading a can of mace in his eyes.

The woman is still showing little sign of moving. Joey waits. He grows impatient as he looks from the cigarette to the woman. He turns and looks around. He seems nervous, as if he is worried about who might see him. It would not be surprising for another homeless person to come along, see the cigarette and without as much as a pause for consideration scoop it up and light it in one smooth movement.

Joey, tapping the newspaper dispenser with his fingers, says, 'Come on, lady.'

Another minute passes.

'Oh Jesus Christ, look at this.' *This* floats towards us wearing a low-cut white cotton dress that stops halfway down her tanned thighs. There are pleats and frills and a pair of red sandals. Joey asks, 'That's an Oscar de la Renta dress, right?'

The girl smiles and bounces past, 'Yes.'

He says, 'It's one of my wife's favourite designers – *was,* I mean, *was* my wife, not *is* her favourite designer.'

The girl keeps walking.

Joey looks back to the woman guarding his cigarette. She's gone and in the two seconds it takes him to get over there, cat-like, so is the cigarette.

If the numbers say that there's 60,000 homeless and we take a conservative half of that number and we say that 30,000 homeless people a day bum a conservative three cigarettes a day, that's 90,000 cigarettes. That's 4,500 packets. That's $31,500 ... a day!

If you are homeless and have more cigarettes than you can smoke at one time, you have no right holding on to them.

'I saw you had another cigarette in there. What's that about?' demands Nathan of Joey, hurt and hunched.

We have returned from butt collecting. Joey sits talking to Savage in Union Square, while he rips the butts apart and taps the tobacco into his Drum tobacco pouch.

'I have this one I'm smoking now,' Joey tells Nathan, 'that one in the packet, and that's it, that's my last smoke.'

'Dude, I don't have any smokes, shit. What's that about, fucking holding out on me? I give you smokes all the time.'

'Like when?'

'Like – all the time.'

'Like when? Name a time.'

'Oh, like, yeah, I'm gonna name a time – like it was Tuesday and 4.15, yeah right.'

'Why don't you just go and bum a cigarette from somebody that has some?'

''Cause.'

''Cause what, asshole?'

''Cause I can't be bothered.'

'Can't want a cigarette that much then, can you?'

'Just gimme the goddamned cigarette!'

Somebody else enters the conversation. To Joey he says, 'Hey man, what's up, spare a cigarette?' He smiles. 'Thanks, man.'

Nathan says, 'You fucking asshole! That's it, you don't get shit from me from now on!' and he walks away.

Savage has given up smoking.

'I just got sick of people looking at me like I'm a piece a shit. I can bum cigarettes real good, I just hate doing it. People look at you like it wasn't a cigarette you asked for, it was a fucking lung – *snort giggle snort giggle.* Yo, dude, can I get a lung?'

Nathan, having not gone further than ten paces, comes back.

'Joey, Joey, Joey, hey Joey, can I at least bum a roll? I'll roll it my-self?'

'Why don't you go and collect some cigarette butts and roll your own?'

'Just give me some tobacco, Christ. It's not like you bought it.'

'Do you have any idea how humiliating it is collecting butts off the sidewalk?'

'Yes!'

'No, you don't, 'cause you've never done it. It's degrading. It's humiliating. Do you really think I go through that so you don't have to?'

'What is everybody's problem? We're all out here together, man.'

'Is that what it's like when you go collect your pizzas?'

'That's my fucking hustle, man …'

'Right and that's fine. But don't come here with that 'we're all out here together, man' bullshit, when two days ago you come over with four free pizzas and you wouldn't even give a slice away to anybody.'

'I was hungry.'

'You weigh what, a hundred and fifty? You needed to sit there and eat four pizzas in front of everybody?'

'Can I get a cigarette or what?'

'Yeah, you can, when I'm done sorting the tobacco.'

Robert doesn't smoke butts from the ground very often. He cuts an imposing figure – one that can't stand straight from drink and that might fall on top of you any second. There is no mistaking, for Robert's victims that is, the easiest way to get rid of Robert – just give him what he wants. So when he stops in front of you, with his weight on his left leg while his right leg is still trying to walk on and he growls, *Spare a cigarette!*, most people give him what he wants. He uses the same technique to acquire money.

'Spare a dollar!'

He is not asking, he is telling.

'You! Yeah, that's right, spare a dollar, give me one of those cigarettes too!'

I head up to Penn Station to see if JV is around. He isn't, but I do bump into the little sprightly black girl in shades and tight-fitting jeans from the first night. She says, 'Come on, I know you got cigarettes, man. I'll blow you for cigarette?'

I can safely say I will never understand smoking.

# Day 15 – Meth Talking

Kim and Nancy come out of the Hello Kitty shop on 42nd Street, where I stand looking after their luggage. They scoop up their bags and walk briskly towards 9th Avenue, past the Loews cinema, turning right at the corner.

'What did you get?' Nancy asks.

'A notebook.'

'Can I see it?'

Kim pulls up her sweatshirt and removes a pink notebook from her waistband. She passes it to Nancy.

'Oh, cute,' Nancy says as she removes the plastic wrapping.

The notebook is pink; on the front is a black cat in a pink and yellow bobble hat. 'It's cute, isn't it?' Kim asks.

'Yeah it is … look at the cat!' Kim says as she holds the notebook out for my approval.

They both giggle.

Then Nancy asks Kim, 'Did you need a notebook?'

Kim goes to answer but stops herself. She thinks for a while, the question crawling all over her face: Did I need a notebook?

'Sure … well, no. I don't need a notebook, what would I need a notebook for?' She's asking me, but I don't really know what to say so I shrug my shoulders.

Kim says, 'That's really dumb, why did I steal a notebook? I ain't got no use for a notebook.'

We keep walking. It's a while before anyone speaks.

Nancy says, 'Maybe you can use it for addresses and phone numbers or something.'

'Right, exactly, I'll use it as an address book. I needed an address book anyway.'

Nancy passes the notebook back to Kim, who stops and puts it in her bag.

We walk on in silence.

Nancy, Kim and I sit in McDonald's sharing a Chicken McNugget Meal. Nancy and Kim share the large coke that came with the meal. I have managed to scrape together enough extra coins for a coffee. Kim can't stop talking.

'... my ex was a bitch, a total bitch ...' Kim is telling me.

Nancy says, 'Ugh!'

Kim says, 'No, Alan, you have no idea!'

'Tell him what she did to you when you were pregnant!'

'Oh God! He doesn't wanna hear that, he's got a chicken nugget in his mouth!'

'He don't care, tell him!'

I swallow the nugget quickly.

'OK, so I was pregnant ...'

'I thought you didn't like men?' I can't help but ask.

'Well, I don't any more – sexually that is – but I used to be married ...'

'OK.'

'But that's a whole other story, we'll get to that ... Nancy, what was I talking about?'

'Your bitch of an ex-girlfriend!'

'Oh yeah. So I got pregnant and my ex-girlfriend always beat me. I was always covered in bruises and had black eyes. She broke my ribs and what else ...'

'Just tell him what she did!'

'I'm getting to it, babe. Give me some coke.'

After a long suck on the straw Kim says to Nancy, 'I love you so much, babe!'

'I love you too, baby!'

The girls start kissing and caressing each other.

The man sitting at the table next to us chokes on a french fry.

The two women sitting on the other side of the room get up and leave, ushering their bewildered children hastily down the stairs.

When Nancy and Kim finally stop kissing, Nancy turns to me. 'Alan, isn't she just, like, really hot?'

'Oh, I hate it when she says that.'

'Baby, but you are! Isn't she, Alan? Tell her she's hot.'

'You are a very attractive girl. You should be happy that your girl thinks you're attractive.'

'I didn't say attractive, I said *hot*.'

'Yes, but I'm of a generation where the word 'hot' is generally used in reference to temperature.'

'I do like it,' Kim interrupts. 'It's just that I don't see myself that way. I mean, Alan, listen, I would never be wearing clothes like this …' Kim turns to the mirror on the wall and grabs her breasts, gives them a quick adjustment and straightens her tight fitting vest. 'I like to wear baggy clothes.'

'Oh God!' Nancy butts in. 'If I let her dress herself in the morning she would look like a boy.'

I laugh.

'No, she's right, Alan. I would. I wear all baggy shit.'

'But baby,' Nancy says, turning to Kim, 'you don't need those baggy clothes, you are so hot the way I dress you.'

Leaning in and just getting the words out before a flurry of tongue kisses, Kim says, 'Oh thank you, baby!'

After the kisses, Kim asks me, 'So what was I talking about anyway?'

'You were telling me about your ex-girlfriend. She was a bitch, she used to beat you and you were pregnant.'

'Oh shit, Kim! He's paying attention.'

'Oh right,' says Kim, almost shouting. 'I was pregnant and she stuck a knife up my vagina and gave me an abortion.'

This is a rather shocking piece of information to receive. Not just for me, but also for the other, now on their feet and mounting the stairs, patrons of McDonald's. Very quickly we have the entire floor to ourselves, though neither Nancy nor Kim notice this. I sit stunned, shrouded in silence, and feeling oddly guilty and completely at a loss for some kind of rational response. As soon as I get over the cringing wave that courses through my body I have to ask her, as gently as I can, how she allowed that to happen – didn't she fight back?

'I couldn't fight back. *I was fucking doped!*'

'Do you know what she did, Alan?' Nancy adds.

'Tell him, babe.'

'No. I can't, I'm getting too angry. You tell him.'

'She injected me with dope! I was asleep on the sofa and she injected me with dope and I went into a nod, all doped out, and she stuck a knife up my cunt and cut my baby out. I'm sorry, but that's what she did. Twice, actually. She did the same thing a year later, but that time she didn't use a knife she used a …'

'Can I just … I have so many questions and I don't think …'

'No, Alan, just ask. You're a friend, come on. It's all in the past anyway, I don't care.'

'How were you even with this person after she did this to you? I mean, how were you there for this to happen a second time?'

Kim's voice resonates through the McDonald's 'I was scared. Every time I tried to leave she beat me shitless!'

She strikes me as the kind of girl that would do everything she could to kick my ass if I tried to hurt her. She has a fire and energy about her that suggests she would probably succeed and I can't imagine anybody beating her. She strikes me as a bit crazy and unpredictable, not the kind of character easily bullied let alone …

'Oh, I'd fight now. I'd put your head through the fucking

window, probably. But I'm not the person, thank God, that I was back then. You know, I've done two stretches in prison since then.'

I'm trying not to judge her, but it's hard. How could she be so irresponsible, getting pregnant again, knowing all this?

'No, you're right. It was fucked up. But I was fucked up. I couldn't think straight. And if … the truth is, at the time I was selling my ass, I was a hooker, and that's how I got pregnant both times.'

Nancy sits filing her nails and fidgeting with her purse. Kim's talk is not the hushed, 'This is for your ears only' kind of talk. It is the loud, 'If you don't like it, get out of McDonald's' kind of talk and it isn't about wanting to tell the others in the restaurant, because they are long gone, it isn't about shocking people. It is just the way Kim talks, loud and clear and with apparent horror. It is not just the details I find horrifying, but also the fact that she relates these details as if they are just part of life, any life, a normal life. They are things you simply have to accept and try to move on from, or escape from – whichever takes your fancy.

'I've sold my ass like … God, you have no idea how many men I have been with.'

'What were you in prison for?' I ask.

'The first time was drugs. I was carrying dope with my husband and we got caught. They found it in our car. We came up with this plan that if we both blamed each other and insisted that the drugs belonged to the other person, we'd both get off, 'cause they wouldn't be able to prove which one of us the drugs belonged to. But actually what happened was he got off and I went to jail.'

There's a pause.

'And the second time?' I ask as I sip my cold coffee.

'Oh, the second time? That was armed robbery.'

I choke on my coffee incredulously. 'Armed robbery?'

'Yeah, we held up a convenience store and crashed the car when we were trying to get away.'

Nancy says, 'It's a fucked-up life, isn't it, Alan?' but I don't know if she means life generally or Kim's particularly.

'Yeah, but Alan, I don't mean to be rude, you come from a wealthy background, right? I mean your family had money and you went to college and everything ...'

'Well, it's not comparable either way, but we're a working-class family, I didn't get to go to college ...'

'But I mean you had a normal, loving upbringing, right?'

'Well, I never *used* to think so ... but now ...'

'Typical teenager,' Nancy laughs.

'Right,' smiles Kim. 'Can you imagine him as a teenager?'

While Nancy and Kim joke around, I am getting worked up and forgetting my own rules. The idea of sitting back as the patient observer has gone out of the window.

'You can't possibly think I was spared a life like that because I might have gone to college? Or have lived in a nice house with a shiny car? What happened to you is fucked in any context, Kim. It's not your economic heritage. It's not a part of a normal life and you must know that, otherwise how do you ever have a chance of happiness?'

Kim pauses for a second, taking my words on board before she continues. 'When I was thirteen years old I was raped by one of my dad's friends. When I told my dad he beat me for lying. He made me apologise to his friend for what I said. The friend kept raping me because he knew he could get away with it. After several beatings I stopped telling my dad.'

Nancy says, 'Alan, I can't believe she's telling you so much, it took a long time for her to tell me this stuff and I haven't even heard all of it.'

'It's the meth, baby. I can't stop.'

'Right,' nods Nancy. 'That's what I was about to say, it's the meth.'

I sit numbed for what feels like a long time, before managing with much effort to say, 'Then we should hang out another day.' I feel guilty, like an intruder. 'I don't want you to tell me things that you're going to wish you hadn't.'

'No, don't go! I want to tell you and, you know, put it in your book or don't, I don't care. Maybe this story will help somebody one day.'

Nancy says, 'Stay, Alan, really.'

'But, Alan, fuck it. That's all done with now. I have my baby here,' Kim says as she slips her arm around Nancy and pulls her in tight. 'You know I get angry sometimes 'cause like, I'd really love to have kids some day, I mean not now, but in a few years when we've got our shit straight. I'd be such a good mom, Alan, I really would, I have so much love in me …'

'She does, Alan.'

'But because of what that *bitch* did to me, I can't ever have kids. My insides are just a mess. I mean that second time the doctors were just about able to save *me*. And it's just … I'd be such a good mom, Alan. I know I'd have to get straight-straight. I mean my arms now, look at them, covered in track marks …'

'She was injecting coke!'

'Yeah, I can't sniff coke, when I do it I have to inject … *don't ask*. Nancy, is there any soda left?'

# Day 16 – A Belly Full of ... God Knows What!

There's a steady flow of human traffic entering the Bowery Mission as Jerome and I arrive. Some head sternly to the front, others sit on packed benches at the back. Some wear headphones. Others fall asleep with the ease of snakes, coiled on the end of benches and resting their heads on the backrests.

Somebody starts playing the piano. Under the hushed hymn of the homeless who turn up to sing, although not for their supper, the voice of the piano is soft. It's nearing 8am and the people here want breakfast.

Some people get up and leave.

More arrive.

And just when I start to feel as if I am in a bus station rather than a church, a man appears. He is in a suit – a clean suit. His clean face is trimmed and neat. He is sculpted, dust-free, buffed for the morning service, then wheeled out – though not in a chair.

Standing securely on his own, still youthful, legs he says, 'Good morning, everybody ...'

It's hard to say whether it is the word *good, morning* or *every-*

*body* that carries the most weight, but two-thirds of the people sitting in the pews slouch further down.

The suit says, 'Thank you, Lord, for the air in our lungs …'

A man in the third row starts a fit of coughing. It is not for comedy, and for this reason nobody laughs – except Jerome: 'Tee hee hee.'

The suit says, 'Thank you, Lord, for the little details in life … the little details that, more often than not, we take for granted …'

The noise from the headphones on the man sitting in front of Jerome gets louder.

The suit says, 'I pray, Lord, that you will encourage them to listen up …'

And, 'I pray, Lord, that you will show yourself …'

And, 'I pray that you will prove yourself to each person who is here today, God …'

And, 'Bring miracles, Father …'

Outside a large lorry can be heard speeding through the empty early-morning streets.

The suit says, 'Amen!'

And now we are going to sing. But first the suit says, 'Are you ready?' He looks around at the many faces 'Right …'

The suit sings, 'I must tell Jesus …' his voice rings around the chapel, loud, confident and alone.

He continues to sing, '… all of my trials, I cannot bear these burdens alone. In my distress he kindly will help me. He ever loves and cares for his own …'

Then one by one the homeless start to join in.

They sing:

> I must tell Jeeesus! I must tell Jeeesus!
> I cannot bear these burdens alone
> I must tell Jeeesus! I must tell Jeeesus!
> Jesus can help me, Jesus alone!

Then more people join in, infecting others, who follow them:

> I must tell Jesus all of my troubles
> He is a kind, compassionate friend
> If I but ask him, he will deliver
> Make of my troubles quickly an end!

As soon as they stop 'telling Jesus', they start being 'lifted by love'.

They sing:

> I was sinking deep in sin, far from the peaceful shore
> Very deeply stained within, sinking to rise no more
> But the master of the sea, heard my despairing cry
> From the waters lifted me, now safe am I
> Love lifted me! Love lifted me!
> When nothing else could help
> Love lifted meeee!

The suit asks, 'Any requests?'

'Number 37!' a deep baritone calls out.

'37! At our church up in the Bronx, we sing a lot of current songs. You know, fast songs, with fast beats and all that stuff. This song, and I love this song … 'cause there's something about these hymns, because they're all written out of, out of turmoil, out of pride, out of circumstance, out of painful situations … and, you know, sometimes you need to just forget the rhythm and, you know, just read through these and you can discover how these words came out of broken people. People that were hurting or were weak or something … But what amazes me is how no matter what we go through, if we support our alliance to the Lord, God will give us a new song. *Amen!* God will give us a song that will identify him, that will glorify him and, er, encourage us and encourage one another. *Amen!* People ask why others come forth with songs, with hymns and spirits of songs and so forth, and why, and it's because it comes out of hearts that are grateful and plentiful for what God has done for us in our lives. *Amen!* And then, I don't know about you, but when I look around and I see things happening all I can say is,

'Oh Lord, my God Almighty, I am at a loss of wonder to consider all the worlds that thy hands have made. I see the stars, I hear the rolling thunder.' And by the power of God the universe is explained.

'Powerful words, you know. You think about the power of the galaxy, the rotation of the earth, the moon and stars and the holy planets ... they are precisely tuned to be one ... whatever, or whatever scientific word. You might know someone who knows the word, but, you know, God who created heaven and earth has everything to just perfect timing ... All the rotation and time and the seasons and the ... All of it. All these things. And think how great God is, amen!'

Without much of a warning the preacher breaks into song 37:

Lord my God! When I in awesome wonder
Consider all the works thy hand hath made,
I see the stars, I hear the mighty thunder,
Thy power throughout the universe displayed;

Then sings my soul, my Saviour God, to thee,
How great thou art, how great thou art!
Then sings my soul, my Saviour God, to thee,
How great thou art, how great thou art!

He says, 'Lord, in such a city, such a city with almost 10 million people, this city of people who are surrounded by each other day in and day out. *Lord*, sin unfortunately has disguised the beauty of your creation. But Lord, mankind, human beings or those that are in this chapel this morning are the top of your list, for each and every person that's here is not here by accident or by mistake ... please, God, open their hearts to the seed that you have for them today ... With a double-edged sword, God, we could cut through our lives, through the sin and carnality and flesh.'

The preacher takes a moment to introduce his family. The chapel bursts into loud and energetic applause. He insists that his daughters stand and face the congregation. His wife too, complete with newborn baby in her arms, takes her bow.

'Now, a couple of days ago I was saying how we take the miracles of God for granted. We assume, we take for granted ... just being able to sit here ... with lights on ... food waiting ... clothes in the basement ... showers running ... you know those are miracles, *amen*. The really are! And it's important for you people here, you guys in the program, the guys off the street to see, every time you come here, it's *God, God* handing you things. It's *God* giving you things, a*men*. And when you come here you need to be thankful to God for giving you this place. You know, I see it myself, you live in a state where God is constantly blessing you and you don't even realise it ...'

Eventually God himself intervenes and two hundred men file from the chapel to the neighbouring dining room for porridge and tea or coffee.

Most of the homeless eat as if they have somewhere to be. In a sense they do have somewhere to be: back at the front of the queue for a second serving. There will not be enough food for everyone to have a second serving and so those that would like more food eat fast.

Jerome asks, 'What are you up to now, fella?'

'I don't know,' I tell him.

'Well, there's some pretty good food coming down at Tompkins Square Park if you want to come along?'

This is one hell of an invitation. I remember reading an article about Daniel Rakowitz, who, to cut a long story short, hacked his girlfriend up in a bathtub, threw various pieces into a cooking pot and served her, stewed, to the homeless of Tompkins Square. Needless to say, I bid Jerome farewell and ponder my next move as I walk slowly back to Union Square.

I have wanted to talk to Robert for some time. He is always staggering around Union Square, abusing and being abused by those around him, yet the right time to approach him has never really cropped up. Then, out of the blue, he comes and sits next to me on a low wall in the square, where I sit with yesterday's *New York Post,* waiting to see if Joey comes by. It's a conversation of sorts, though I don't get to take part in it. I just nod to let him know I am still listening.

**Robert's Rap**

*Featuring three teenage missionaries from Alabama.*

OK
This country is so fucking badass
And Anglo-Saxon
The fucking Saxons ran New York
Those Irish fucking pigs couldn't even fight a wife
That's how fucking badass
The fucking English are
Screaming fucking badass warriors
*Warriors!*
I'm telling you, partner
Straight up
We, we, we, we …
Killed off the Vikings
Killed a whole bunch of them
They came into our monasteries
We had battles
But the fucking done deal was
We killed their fucking king
That put an end to it
We moved north
That put an end to it
The fucking English
Killed their fucking king
Swutt
Cut him off
They were done
That was the end of the Vikings
That was the end of them

Fucking English whacked the Vikings
Dude
Whacked 'em
The King of England – *for fun*
Conquered France and Normandy
*For fun*!
Went over there
Did his shit
Captured the King
Sat down with the King of France
And said, *Yo*
Check it out!
*You're OK*
*I'm OK*
Ha, ha, ha, ha …
That's no bullshit
The fucking King of France
Was scared to death, dude
That's no bullshit
Straight up
Fucking King of France
Scared to death
Of the fucking King of England
But he didn't kill him
He just sat him down
Said, *Yo*
Check it out!
*You're OK*
*I'm OK*
Badass Anglo-Saxon
I love history
My ancestors built the fucking pyramids
It wasn't the fucking *Shag Heads*
It was us Americans
It was the beginning of civilisation
They were the white people

If you're white
You're straight
Write it down
Write this shit down
Fucking pyramids
The god damned fucking
Who?
The Zodiacs?
Nah!
It wasn't them
White people ruled the fucking earth
They stepped in towns and they came to fight
Goddamned fucking geniuses
They were mathematicians
Fucking geniuses
They mapped out the fucking universe
I'm talking six to seven thousand years ago
Those were white motherfuckers, dude
I'm telling ya
Straight up
A nigger
Ain't worth shit
Look at the fucking couch monkey
That's all a fucking nigger is
A fucking couch monkey
Black fucking
You know why they're black, right?
'Cause they fucking stupid
*Stupid!*
The nigger brain ain't no bigger
Than a fucking …
A fucking …
A fucking …
Cashew nut
A nigger
Ain't worth shit

That ain't true
A nigger is worth something
Thirty-five cent
That's the cost of a bullet
Thirty-five cent a pop
Pop
Pop
Pop
Pop
Pop
Pop
That's like …
Two bucks right there
Which is nothing
When you think about it
It's just two bucks!
There are three fucking million
KKK members
In this fucking country
The clan ain't Anglo-Saxon
CLAN?
CLAN?
Now that's a wobbler
That's a wobbler
What it is, is I wanna see your paperwork
Wanna claim white boy
I wanna see your paperwork
It's, it's, it's
It's not ssssswit sssssswut
ssssswit sssssswut
ssssswit sssssswut
I wanna see your Anglo-fucking-Saxon shit
Fucking greatest kings
Of fucking England
Were Anglo-Saxon
You know who that is

Up there?
Riding his fucking horse?
George Washington
He won the Civil fucking War
No …
That was Abraham Lincoln
250,000 dead
In a field
Fucking knights
We're fucking knights, dude
Give us our armour
Our fucking sword
Wipe out
Sssssssswut
20,000 knights
Dead in a field
You imagine that
We're on a campaign now
Conquer the Middle East
That's religious shit there
Now we got a real big problem
We got a real big problem
They're just blowing shit up
Suicide bombers
And it's not so much the Iraqis
We all fucking wired, dude
You saddle up
You get your shit on
You battle
And you fucking die
And that's it

*Afternoon, sir, how are you?*

I'm good.

*What's your name?*

Robert.

*I'm Daniel*

Let me tell you something
We're sitting here
Talking about religious fucking battles
Jesus
Christians
Knights
They go to fucking battle
Have some fun
That 9/11 shit
That weren't religious
Goddamned Arabics
They don't give a damn about
You, you, you, you, me, you …
Or anybody
Put them in a field with a bunch a knights
Done deal
Straight up
Done deal
Those fucking bastards
Those bastards
Laid out in the fucking field
Bleeding

*Robert, do you have Jesus in your soul?*

Yeah, he's another one
Jesus
He knows about bleeding

*He did that for you, Robert*

Right, for all of us
Jesus
He's dead now though

*You know, Robert, if you just ask the Lord for forgiveness*
*He will forgive you*
*Robert, all you have to do to start receiving the Lord's guidance*
*is open up to him*

A nigger ain't worth shit

*Robert …*

What's your name, sweetheart?

*Julia, but Robert, listen to me … you're drunk right?*
*No, no, no, no, no, wait, Robert, I'm just asking because Jesus*
*can help you with that*

Vodka

*It's never too late*

VODKA!

*No matter how much you've sinned*
*He will always love you*

*She's right, Robert, all you have to do is love him back*

Jesus said
In the Bible
That he would rather that a man fucked a whore
Than let his cum spill on the ground

*Oh, Robert, he never said that …*

It's in the Bible
Jesus said that
Check it out
Write this down
Jesus said
Rather than let your sperm land on dry ground
You should take your cock
Stick it in a whore
And fill her up
Jesus said that

*No, Robert, you have it wrong*
*Jesus said, 'Don't waste your sperm'*
*What he meant by that was ...*

Go take a whore
Stick it in her
And fill her up
Then get the fuck outta Dodge
Ha Ha Ha

*Robert, please, it's not too late, open up to the Lord, Robert,*
*and he will show you*
*The light*

Jesus was a badass Anglo-Saxon

*Robert, Julia is trying to help you, do you want to go to hell,*
*Robert?*
*Yes, Robert, if you carry on the way you are and you don't em-*
*brace the Lord fast*
*You will burn, Robert*

Julia come here, you sweet little thing give me a kiss ...

*No Robert ... Stop! Take your ... Robert, no ... No! Take your*
*hands off ... He-elp!*

I follow Joey through the gap in the wrought-iron fence. There's a huge statue to the left, ringed by another waist-high iron fence. A stern-looking chap sits on a bench facing us as we enter. He and Joey greet each other as they do on most evenings.

The statue is of an even sterner-looking fellow. He sits in an armchair, all done out in a three-piece suit and an elaborate beard. He holds a walking cane in his left hand, but, going by his expression, you might easily believe that it's not for conventional purposes. He leans back in the chair, sits with his legs slightly apart, looking straight ahead. He carries the air of an important man. He looks like an achiever. He is Peter Cooper, 'Engineer, manufacturer, and philanthropist.' In 1828 he started the ironworks where he built the USA's first steam locomotive. Joey walks past Peter and crosses Cooper Square, which is actually a triangle, and dumps his small yellow backpack on one of the benches in the middle of a row.

'I keep my stuff here,' he says as he slips past the bench and pulls out a black binbag that's been stuffed deep inside a bush. The bag is full of clothes. He rummages inside for a minute, until he finds what he is looking for and changes his T-shirt.

Joey returns from behind the bush with two large pieces of cardboard, one of which he hands to me. He wastes little time removing his trainers and preparing for bed. He ties his trainers by the laces to the armrest that will be nearest to his head, then he places his backpack up against the armrest. Getting on to the bench, he threads his legs through the circular armrest in the middle. He covers himself with his blanket, using his feet to spread the blanket all the way down, then he drags the cardboard up off the floor and covers himself. He lies there inside his shell, feet poking out of one end and his head poking out of the other. Having studied all this I now follow suit.

I sneak glances over at Joey, who lies with his eyes closed. That's not to say he is asleep. He just closes himself off to the world. He listens to the cars that pass just a yard away on the other side of the bush. But he doesn't react to the honking taxi, or the thunder of a lorry, or the screaming of a fire engine as it barrels down 3rd Avenue. He just lies there, dead still, not even a flicker of an eyelid.

He manages this for almost twenty minutes.

*Bing!*

His eyes are open.

Leaning against a tree on the other side of the triangle is a bright-orange hard-shelled suitcase. Joey wonders how he missed it when he came in.

I watch as he slowly starts to uncoil himself from the bench.

He gets to his feet and leisurely slides his trainers on. He doesn't tie the laces but stands and walks to the left, to the furthest point of the triangle, where he slips in between some bushes and urinates.

He turns and slowly walks towards the hard-shelled orange suitcase, but he doesn't stop.

He walks right past, pretending not to notice the out-of-place object.

He walks up past the statue, past the stern-looking gentleman, now fast asleep on his bench. He looks around. Who else is there? Anyone?

No.

But who would leave an expensive bright-orange suitcase leaning up against a tree? Joey doesn't know.

He walks another slow lap of the park to make sure we are alone and then collects the orange suitcase and carries it over to his bench.

The orange suitcase is on Joey's lap. Gently he fiddles with the latches and lifts the lid.

Drugs?

No. Ladies' clothing.

The case is full of ladies' clothing, all new, unworn and still with the sales tickets attached. Joey holds up a white linen blouse.

Gap: $39.99

Next he holds up a pair of green combat pants.

Levi's: $59.99

'Look at this,' he says, holding up a T-shirt for me to look at. 'Somebody's been on a thieving spree.'

Randomly Joey picks out garments and holds them up for inspection. He feels the fabric and checks the prices. He wonders about the size. Once he has seen everything in the suitcase he starts to slowly fold and slip the clothing neatly back into position. He closes the lid and carries the suitcase back over to the tree.

Without another word to me he is back inside his cardboard shell.

His feet poke out from one end.

His head pokes out from the other.

Behind him a taxi honks loudly, but he doesn't hear it.

What he does hear are footsteps, light and slow. Joey cracks open an eye and watches, as do I, an elderly, dirty-looking white woman walking past. She is halfway between Joey and the orange suitcase. She stares at the suitcase and instantly flicks her glowing eyes back to Joey. She walks fast, not towards Joey but *at* him.

Ten feet.

Six feet.

Two feet.

Joey sits up. 'You need to get the fuck away from me!'

I lie rigid on my bench, wondering how this will play out. She looks crazed and I start to wonder about the length of her fingernails. But the woman quickly backs off. She marches over to the suitcase, pulls up the handle and stomps away, dragging it behind her.

Joey remains up on one elbow, watching her leave.

Another man arrives in the triangle. He is drunk, carrying a bottle of vodka and a small transistor radio that is quietly playing jazz music. He sits on a bench, places his radio down beside him and drinks from his bottle until finally his heavy head is resting on his chest.

Joey too calls it a day and, once again cocooned in his box, falls effortlessly asleep.

An hour later six youths enter the park. They are loud, but, surprisingly, neither Joey nor the sleeping jazz fan stir. The youths take up the bench two down from the radio. There are five boys and a girl, all with a hint of goth. They sit drinking beer and smoking joints, talking and giggling.

One of them gets up and walks over to the bench with the sleeping jazz fan. He picks up the radio and turns it off. For a second he looks as if he is going to put the radio back; then he takes it over to his own bench and slips it into his backpack.

None of his friends pass comment.

An hour later everyone is asleep – except for myself and Peter Cooper, who sits watching, ready to bring down his cane should anybody be foolish enough to urinate on his plinth.

# Day 17 – Single, Pregnant and Stranded

Mary sits outside a deli in midtown. She sparkles in the mid-day sun, her wavy golden hair lining her grubby face.

Mary is nineteen, and her big burgundy backpack lies next to her. In her hands she holds an open book, a horror story: *House Of Bones* by Dale Bailey. Her knees are pulled up to her chest, her face pushed down. She doesn't want to interact. If you want to contact her you should do it via the plastic cup that sits at her feet. Read the sign if you have to, but she doesn't really care.

> I am pregnant
> My husband has left me stranded in New York.
> Homeless
> So many crazy welfare appointments
> That are supposed to help me
> But they won't give assistance for a min. 45 days
> I can't even get a bed in a shelter …
> The point is I'm desperately
> In need of your kindness
> And compassion
> Please help.
> Thank you.
> God bless.

The sign goes largely unread, until an aging man with tight curly grey hair and dark dazzling eyes stops and gives it a read through, his lips moving as he takes in the words.

He has held cardboard signs. He has told stories: untrue stories and true stories.

He looks into Mary's eyes.

'You need to get out of the sun, little lady,' he tells her.

She says, 'Yeah, I know. I'll be here for a little while longer though.' Her voice is husky. 'It's a good spot.'

'Oh, I hear you.'

There is a flash of recognition between the two – but not because they have met before.

The old man shuffles into the shop.

He peers into one in a row of large refrigerators that holds drinks of every imaginable colour. He studies his own reflection for a while, then sharpens his eyes and pushes his vision through the glass.

He says loudly to the deli, 'Yo! How much are these here? These Snapple things?'

'Dollar fifty!' the Indian deli-owner calls back.

'Dollar fifty? What?' The rhetorical tone is noted and the deli remains silent. He removes two lemon Snapples from the fridge. At the counter he hands over a dollar bill, then, sorting through change, he finds five quarters, four dimes, six nickels and five pennies.

He leaves the deli.

'Here you go, sister ...' He hands one of the Snapples to Mary.

Mary looks up briefly from her book. 'Thanks, man, that's really cool, have a good day!'

'Get out of the sun,' the man tells her.

Looking back down into her book, Mary says, 'Yeah, I will, I promise.' And she lets out a little giggle.

At 2pm Mary *is* ready to get out of the sun. She drinks half the Snapple and zips the bottle up in her bag. Her plastic cup is half full. She tips it out and places it back in the centre of the table, quickly throwing a dollar's worth of quarters back in to weigh it down. She sorts the quarters out of the pile first and stacks them in neat little piles next to her on the sidewalk.

Someone slips a dollar in her cup.

'Thank you!'

The dollar bill is quickly whisked out of sight.

Twenty quarters stand in a stack. George Washington's face appears on all of them, offering forth once again the wisdom of his words: 'In God We Trust!'

But it would appear that Mary has given her trust to somebody else.

Most quarters have Liberty's Eagle on George's flip side, with wings held high and draped, head twisted defiantly to the right. But now and again the eagle has been replaced with a state symbol. A quarter from Kentucky has the image of a horse standing at a fence, with a house on a hill in the background, and the motto 'My Old Kentucky Home.' A quarter from South Carolina has the image of a palmetto tree and a Carolina wren. This is 'The Palmetto State.' A New York quarter, with its Liberty Statue, is inscribed 'Gateway To Freedom.' The New Hampshire coin says 'Live Free Or Die.'

Mary says, 'That should say "Live Free *And* Die."'

Soon there are four stacks, each amounting to five dollars.

25 x 80 = In God We Trust

The dimes, of which Mary counts twenty-seven, also say, 'In God We Trust.'

27 x 10 = In God We Trust

The nickels, too.

16 x 5 = In God We Trust

Mary scoops up the four stacks of quarters and slips them into the front pocket of her jeans. The rest of the coins she drops back into the cup. The cup goes in the bag. The bag goes on the back. The back marches down the street at a 37-degree angle.

Mary disappears into the crowd.

I am sitting with Joey and Savage in Union Square. Our shoes are off and we sit with our bare feet twitching in the breeze. Sometimes we talk, sometimes we don't. Sometimes Savage plays his harmonica. We are waiting for the Salvation Army Mission to open at 7pm. After the sermon they give out food bags.

Right now it is 4.27.

This is what we do: sit, wait, talk, don't talk.

Savage broods over his girlfriend, who is still in Kentucky. Joey calls out the names of flowers and birds.

'That one there is a finch, *Carpodacus mexicanus.*'

'Oh, look at tha-at, that one's trying to fuck the other one! That's right where you fucked that punk chick last night.'

Grinning, Joey asks, 'You saw that?'

'What do you mean, "You saw that?" Everybody saw it, you were fucking her right there on the gra-ass. We were there. Like, ten feet away.'

'Yeah, but I pulled the blanket up over us.'

'We could still see your ass moving, dude! You think 'cause you took your sweet time we didn't know you were fucking her?'

Joey laughs. 'That was the idea, yeah.'

'Guess what?'

'When does your girlfriend get back?' Joey asks.

Savage looks at his feet, 'Tuesday. I can't wait, I really miss her.'

'Do you think she'll be able to keep seeing you?'

'Oh, I know she will. No matter what they say. It fucks me off though. I mean, my family isn't as rich as hers, but I come from a real wealthy family. My dad's a lawyer, you know. But they just take the homeless thing like I'm some kind of fiend. Like I'm gonna rob them or start injecting heroin up her ass or something.'

Joey sits giggling. 'That's what people think about homeless people, dude. Ain't nothing you can do about it.'

'She already had a coke habit when I met her. She's seventeen years old. I'm the one trying to get her off the shit. Her parents are too dumb to know what she does. Too dumb to know that they're buying her coke for her.'

Joey suddenly turns to me and says, 'Here comes Crow and Country and them. They can't come to the mission with us, dude, so don't mention it. I feel bad saying it, but they'll go in there all drunk and cracked out and fuck the place for everybody else.'

I have met Crow, who, oddly, has cropped and *bleached* hair. He is another Union Square regular, often shirtless, showing off his tattoos and body-piercing.

'Were you there last night?' Savage asks Joey. 'When Crow fucked that guy up? No, that was before you came …'

'What happened?'

'These college kids got into it with him about God knows what, I didn't hear that. These three guys were threatening him, but one guy with all the mouth just wouldn't let it go. Crow goes to his bag and pulls out this can of lighter fuel. He cut the top off with a *knife* and dumped the whole can on this guy's head. He sparked his lighter and held it inches from the guy's face …'

'But he didn't catch, right? I mean Crow's still around, so …'

'Right, it didn't go up but this kid just whacked his pants, dude. He was screaming, "Please! Please! I'm sorry! I'm gonna go up. Please, please! Don't do it! Don't do it."'

'Crow's fucking crazy too. He would do it.'

'Everybody thought that was it. The guy's friends just froze …'

'You seen Crow's tattoos, right? The Aryan Brotherhood tattoos?'

'Yeah. He is fucking crazy. He said to the guy "One fucking word and you're finished." The guy was just begging.'

'What happened then?'

'Crow let them go. Kid was just standing there shaking, but finally his friends got him the fuck away. Crow and the others were just laughing about it like it was a fucking joke.'

'I'm done. I gotta get away from this shit. It's everywhere, thieves and fucking junkies. I mean, look at this girl over here. She's young and cute and she's a fucked-up junkie.'

Joey nods to where Mary stands alone on the grass. She is spaced. Her body collapses and she doubles over, her head plummeting to the ground. She looks as if she'll headbutt the floor, but at the last second her back arches and she straightens up.

'She was there the other day, doing this shit,' says Savage. 'And that other girl? The young fifteen-year-old girl that hangs around and just fucks anyone?'

'The one whose dad works for the UN? She's staying in that hotel on Park?'

'Yeah, her. She was watching this girl and she called me over to watch. She was like, "Check this out! This girl's doing some really cool Tai Chi." I was like, "That's not Tai Chi." She said, "What is it then, is it like, Japanese?" I said, "No, that ain't Japanese." Joey joins in the laughter, 'That's the nod!'

We all sit laughing.

Joey says, 'Oh, man. That's fucked up! She was on the nod and she thought it was Tai Chi?'

'She'd been watching her, like, fifteen minutes, just, like – wow!'

# Day 18 – Nancy-Kim Go Flash, Flash

'Listen, baby, you can't come in with me …'

'But it's stupid that you're gonna do it, I should do it.'

'No way! I'm not letting you do it and that's it.'

'But if you get caught …'

'I know what's gonna happen if I get caught, OK? Don't remind me before I go in there.'

'You're gonna do another year, Kim, Jeez. If I get caught all I'll get is a warning.'

'Nancy, I just said don't remind me. Stay here.'

Kim marches into the convenience store. The door swings closed behind her.

I watch as Kim walks briskly along the aisles. She doesn't look around for security cameras or mirrors, she already knows where they are. But she does look for staff members and security guards who might be following her. When she is sure she is not being followed she makes her way to the photo lab at the back of the store and stands browsing the disposable cameras.

She picks up two Fuji cameras and walks towards the check-out at the front of the store, stopping on the way to check out a new range of eye-shadow.

She slips one of the cameras into her hooded zip-up sweat and tucks it into her armpit. From the rack she removes a small bottle of 'Liquid Eyes' from the Maybelline stand. She reads the side of the bottle, *long wear, no crease shadow*. The colour is 'Eternal Espresso'.

She applies, she twists, she turns, she smiles.

She slips the other camera into the other armpit and walks back to the disposable camera display where she collects two more Fuji cameras.

She walks back to the make-up aisle again. This time she takes a look at lipsticks.

The Maybelline Wet Shine Diamonds range takes her fancy. She flits between 'Plum Solitaire' and 'Rhinestone Pink', but finally settles on 'Gems 'n Roses'. Before she removes the lipstick from the rack she slips another camera into her sleeve.

First the top lip. Then the bottom lip. By which time the fourth camera is also nicely tucked away.

Kim unzips her sweatshirt to show that she has nothing to hide and confidently marches out of the store. I follow her, but we don't acknowledge each other.

Outside Nancy says, 'For fuck's sake, Kim! I've been worried out of … Nice lipstick! Did you keep it?'

'Of course I did, baby. You didn't think I'd come out without anything for you, did you?'

'No, I knew.'

'Come here. Give me a kiss!'

Smooch!

A black man shouts, 'Oh damn, did you see that?'

Nancy and Kim make haste away from the storefront.

Once around the corner, Nancy asks, 'How many did you get?'

'Four. Come here, baby, I wanna put some of this eye-shadow on you.'

'Four?' gasps Nancy as she tilts her head back into the light. 'You took four in one go?'

Applying some 'Eternal Espresso' to Nancy's left eye, Kim says, 'Yeah, but there was nobody near me and I just wanna be done with this, you know?'

'I know… How do I look?'

'Hot.'

'How hot?'

'Like I-could-fuck-you-right-here hot!'

Smooch!

A black man shouts, 'Lesbians!'

'Kim, do my lips.'

'Here, pucker up, buttercup.'

It's 4 o'clock in the afternoon; the 6th Avenue sidewalk is busy with people heading home or to bars. Some of them hold coffees that cost more than the digital cameras Kim has just stolen.

'How much money did you say you had?' Kim asks Nancy.

'Thirteen bucks and some change.'

'OK, so we got four cameras, that's another twenty, so that's thirty-three. We need four more cameras and then we can go pick our shit up and get hooked up for the evening.'

Nancy grins at me and, rolling her eyes to the sky with a nod of the head, says, 'Isn't she crazy, Alan?'

And I'm thinking, 'Yeah, just a little bit.'

Nancy and I sit outside the Rockefeller Center sharing a coffee. We are tired and dirty, but Nancy cares less about that than whether Kim can measure up as a petty thief. Right on cue Kim arrives in the NBC doorway. But it's instantly obvious that there's a problem: Kim is trying to run, but is being held back by a three-hundred-pound woman who appears to have accosted her on her way out.

'Kim!' Nancy cries as she stands dropping the coffee to the ground.

'Nancy, run!' Kim shouts back.

But Nancy is reluctant to run. She freezes, on the verge of a decision that could be potentially dangerous. She scowls at the woman. If Kim is arrested, she is going back to prison. She steps towards them.

A crowd is starting to gather.

'Nancy, no! Don't! Just run!'

Nancy does run. But not away.

'No!' Kim struggles with the woman and, seeing Nancy come nearer, makes a decision of her own.

She turns and punches the woman in the face.

*Pow!*

The woman gasps. So do those passing by. But the woman no longer has a hold on Kim. Instead she is holding her swelling eye. Kim wastes little time in making a run for it. Nobody tries to stop her and by the time she reaches the corner Nancy has caught up with her. They run straight out into the road, side-stepping a speeding yellow cab that nearly runs them down before they run off towards 5th Avenue.

The woman sits on the floor, trying not to cry. She says it doesn't hurt much, it's the shock more than anything.

By the time I get back to Union Square, it is pulsing with activity. At the top end, men dressed in ancient battle garb beat the crap out of each other with wooden swords. People stand and watch in amazement. Young girls wonder how men can be such idiots. Why would they dress up like this and beat the crap out of each other? Young guys wonder if the young girls will think them idiots if they have a go.

At the bottom end of the square, protesters beat each other up with words, forgetting that they all arrived together, that they are all fighting the same cause, and instead argue among themselves about who has had too much time on the megaphone, or whose turn it is next to shout into the megaphone, or who has cared about the cause the longest, or who loves the megaphone the most.

'Hey, you've been talking for thirty minutes. Now let some-body else have their say!'

'I'll be done in a minute.'

'You'll be done now!'

'Sonny, I'll be done when I'm done.'

'Don't call me Sonny. Give me the megaphone!'

'I was shouting into megaphones long before you even knew about the struggle.'

The crowd start to giggle and chant: 'Don't give it up! Don't give it up! Don't give it up!'

'That's right, people!' The man, long-haired and bearded, has apparently modelled himself on Jesus. 'Don't ever give up! We have to unite! We have to stand …'

Couples sit side by side, holding hands, sharing sodas, nibbling sushi and wishing the protesters would go somewhere else. Skateboarders perform kick-flip ollies off the steps. They sail through the air in what is, when you really look at it, an amazing feat: they fly over the top of people who sit talking, with their hair flapping in the breeze and their skateboards spinning beneath them. It's a move that is very likely to end in pain for all those within spitting distance. Yet they defy not only gravity but also the danger that somebody might easily be going home with a skateboard wedged in his head.

There's a guy setting up for an evening's busking. He comes complete with amp and microphone. He looks around nervously as he tunes his guitar. Just over the way is a huge Virgin Megastore. He dreams of being in there. But Union Square on a bustling summer evening, with its fiends and lovers and lawyers and layabouts, isn't a bad place to start out from. As soon as he has his amp just so, he strums a cord and a few people turn his way. He puts the guitar down and opens a sand-wich.

Then there's the Boy Savage.

Thomas Savage is balancing on the flat of one hand and spinning himself around.

Meet the Jackhammer!

He is not part of a crew of break-dancers. He is not at this moment even with a friend. He is alone, dancing on the concrete as the sun sets behind tall buildings.

Jackhammer.

Between moves he stands up for a few seconds of rest. He dusts off his denim waistcoat, loosens his fingers and twists his head about to relax his neck. He looks around to see if anybody he knows has arrived on the scene.

There's nobody around apart from the three hundred strangers who are all engaged in other activities.

Savage is glowing, slightly red and perspiring lightly. He looks almost fictional, an urban comic book nomad, as he arches backwards until his hands touch the floor behind him.

Crab?

He stays there for a few seconds, appearing to stretch himself. Then he flicks his legs up until he is in a handstand. Locked in position he seems to view his surroundings as if seeing them the right way up for the very first time. Then he lands on his feet and brushes his clothing back into place while circling the spot he had just balanced on, before diving into another rotating handstand.

Madness?


As dusk settles, I sit with Joey on the other side of Union Square. I am interested to know why somebody as smart and able as Joey finds himself homeless. I realise that if I want the answer I am going to have to break one of my rules and ask a direct question.

'It's … I … Two …'

'Listen, Joey, if it's too personal just tell me to shut up, you don't have to tell me.'

'No, I want to tell you. It's just … I want to. There aren't that many people out here that you can talk to, you know, but … I've been out here about two years. I told you I was married, right? Yeah, well … We had a little daughter, Jessie. She was just the sweetest kid, you know. Everybody loved her and I took her just about everywhere with me. She was beautiful, just like her mamma. So, I took her with me down to the store one day and I was carrying her up on my arm like this and some dude came and tried to rob me. He had a gun and I told him to go fuck himself and he came right up on me and I just kept telling him to fuck himself and basically he shot me through the side here.' Joey points to the scar on the side of his face. 'And the bullet went through my mouth, out the bottom and into Jessie's head. She died.'

And all of a sudden the world is truly an evil place.

'Shit, Joey!'

'Hey, how could you know, it's not your fault. You know, I'm glad you asked, man, sometimes you just need to say it out loud. Otherwise you get confused and start to wonder if it's real.'

'Did they catch the guy?'

'Yeah, some black dude, he's in jail right now. But you know from there … Fuck … My wife always blamed me, you know … I mean, she never said it directly, but I knew she did, like it was my fault. Everything just fell apart. One day I couldn't take it any more. I quit the department at the museum, stuffed a few things in my rucksack and just walked out. You know, I wasn't doing anybody any good where I was. I just needed to get out, so I did.'

'Have you spoken to your wife? Your family? I mean, do they know you're safe?'

'Yeah, they know. I speak to my mum when I can. She still lives in Belfast. She kind of knows what's going on but we don't talk about it. My wife came looking for me once. She knows I'm out here but she also knows I want nothing to do with that life.'

Joey and I sit in silence for a long time. We don't go to the mission for our food bag – Joey can't take the preaching tonight – so we sit, hungry and silent, until it is time to go to Cooper Triangle to sleep.

# Day 19 – A Table for One in the Trashcan Diner

Is this a half-eaten Cajun chicken wrap from Starbucks I see before me? Still in its wrapper?

It would appear so, and let me tell you, having failed miserably at panhandling and poetry and having not eaten since yesterday morning, the half-eaten Cajun chicken sandwich from Starbucks really raises my spirits. It looks fresh and unsoiled by the surrounding trash. It looks tasty and though I can't smell it for traffic fumes, I know once I raise it to my lips it will smell tasty.

All I need to do now is pick it up.

Like a punctilious pedestrian I look first to my right.

I look left.

All seems fine.

I look right again. I can't see anybody I know.

Not that I care of course.

I look left again.

Just to be sure I take another but this time unswerving look to the right.

The coast looks clear.

And left again …

And … now I am looking ahead of me. There's a man standing on the other side of the trashcan – a homeless man. He
doesn't look at me or acknowledge me in any way. What he
does do is lean into the trashcan, flick a *New York Post* to one
side, spot the Cajun chicken wrap from Starbucks, pick it up
and march off with it.

New York is a large and noisy city, but right now I don't hear
any of this noise, what I hear is a puppet voice in my head, and
what that puppet says is, 'That's the way to do it!'

What I say is, 'Son of a bitch!' I was here first, this is my trashcan and to prove it I give it a good hard kick. Fuck! That was
my Cajun chicken wrap from Starbucks still in its wrapper.
Naturally, I am now ten times hungrier than I was while stood
salivating over my find, and that was hungry. Does the bastard
know nothing of manners? Did he not know that at some point
in the not too distant future I was planning to pick that wrap up
and eat it?

Like a coward emerging from behind a bush long after the assailant has left his victim for dead, I say, 'Where is the bastard?'
But I know I am not going after him, because I am too scared
to confront somebody who can walk up to a trashcan on 5th
Avenue and remove food so unashamedly. So I kick the trashcan again and a girl passing by flinches and gives me a dirty
look and I know why. It's because there's a dirty man within
touching distance who keeps kicking the trashcan and ranting
to himself.

An hour later my pride is still stinging. It is not simply because
I am hungry and sifting through trashcans for something to eat
– although that is mainly it – but also because having battled
with the degradation of this situation and having come to terms
with it as best I can, I am losing the battle. I have learnt nothing from my earlier experience. You don't have to sort through
many trashcans in the early New York afternoon to find something edible, even something decent, to eat. But still, starving
though I may be, I continue to scan left and right because I

don't want people to see me take food from a trashcan. So I stand here, soiled and dishevelled, leaving little doubt as to where I slept last night, and lean over the trashcan with an enquiring look as if trying to suggest that really, I dropped my wallet in the trashcan and while burrowing down into the trash for my wallet my Rolex fell off.

If I had just picked up the chicken wrap straight away this would all be over. I would have eaten it and it would have kept me out of the trashcans until tomorrow. The Midnight Run van is expected tonight; I could even stock up with sandwiches and be good for the next day. But I didn't pick the wrap up and so I am consumed with a hunger that I have never previously experienced. I also fail to take the pizza slice I find in a trashcan on 8th Avenue, up by Columbus Circle. I look at it for a long time, one lone slice in a large box. A cheesy triangle covered with peppers and onion and chicken and spinach. But then I see two policemen walking towards me. They are about thirty yards away, but still, I don't want them to see me take the pizza from the trashcan.

The NYPD, brave and numerous though they may be, don't appear to have any patience with the homeless. They seem to take joy in mentally bullying the homeless, easy targets as they are.

Twenty yards.

It appears to be a sport to break up the boredom of walking the beat. They don't have to interact with the homeless to do this. They just have to look at them. Their expression says it all.

I have seen you, scumbag ... That's it. Look away. Look away ... Don't make me come over there.

I don't think they even realise they are doing it.

Ten yards.

I am not yet conditioned to handle this. I instantly become incensed. I am not one generally for conflict, but there is something about badges that really rattles my pram.

Seven yards.

I don't have problems with authority, but ... Five yards.

I'm off.

I don't want to go. Well, I do I want to go but I want to take the pizza slice with me. But I have got myself all in a lather about the NYPD and the fact that they don't respect me and they should. They should respect me, shouldn't they? The truth is, I'm not sure. I can't think straight with this hunger. All I know is there's food everywhere but I can't take any because I don't want people to look down on me. But that enrages me further. I want to go back there and stop those two officers and say, 'Now you listen here! There's a pizza slice in that trashcan and I am going to eat it. You know why? Because I am hungry and I want it. I need it. There it is, look. Just so you know – a pizza slice. No! Don't touch it, I have had that once today and I won't stand for it again. That is my pizza slice. So I am going to take it now, from the trashcan and *you*, you'd better respect me.'

Of course, I don't go back. I don't even look back. Instead I am running across the road, over to Central Park and through the corner entrance and I'm in and …

Everywhere I look, people are sitting on benches, eating.

I feel dizzy and sick.

I sit down.

Breathe.

I listen to the conversation next to me between a very handsome and skinny gay guy and a fat woman. They work together in an office. There's a lot of 'N-o-o-o-o, he said that?' and 'I don't care …' and they just go back and forth, back and forth, with no breaks for air. But then the conversation takes a turn.

'Do you want to finish my noodles?' The skinny guy holds out a takeaway box to his friend. It looks as if it is from a deli and it looks as if he has eaten maybe 10 per cent of what is a NYC-sized portion of noodles, with vegetables and chicken. 'I just don't have an appetite today.'

I say, though not aloud, 'No, no, no, no, no, no, no …'

The woman says, 'Nah, I'm stuffed already,' and I feel like punching the air and gyrating my midriff in celebration.

Skinny slides his food back into a paper bag, gets up and starts to cross the path to a trashcan. This isn't simply about hunger any more and so before he reaches the trashcan I am already up and out of my seat, just a few steps behind him. He makes his deposit and we almost collide as he turns back. But I skip round, pick up the bag, which rests near the top of a fairly full trashcan, and remain just a few steps behind him as we both return to the bench.

I open the bag and there are a few napkins and a fork – the fork Skinny must have used. Now I am not about to tackle this with my hands, so I remove the water bottle from my backpack and pour a little water over the fork. I wipe the fork on my T-shirt, which is far dirtier than Skinny's mouth, and with little ado start shoveling the noodles into my mouth. I am once again overwhelmed with the desire to break into dance. Three mouthfuls in I notice a silence and turn to my left. Skinny and his friend sit with their mouths open. They look like cartoon fish. I say, and again only in my head, 'You will respect me.' And this sets me off giggling. I snort through my nose and start choking on noodles.

By the time I collect myself I am alone on the bench and I see that the woman forgot to put her chicken salad in the trashcan.

'Stuffed!' I think to myself and slide it over.

Fed now, I head back into midtown via 5th Avenue, intending to cut over to see JV. I haven't seen him in a long time. But first I come to the Presbyterian church on 5th Avenue. It is a gathering place for the homeless; large crowds have slept on the church steps for years. On these steps right now there sits a black homeless man in his sixties. He is not alone. In fact he is surrounded by at least fifty other homeless people who sleep on the steps of the church every night. It's 7pm and the sidewalk is still busy. People walking up and people walking down. But this one man, he stands out more than the others, simply because he is punching himself in the face as hard as he can. At times he hits himself so hard that he falls back on the steps.

Even then he doesn't stop, but continues to pound away at his face and body.

In a deep, mean voice he growls, 'Who you looking at, boy?' and he punches himself hard in the groin.

'I'm sorry, sir, I'm sorry, sir,' he says in a soft whiney voice.

Then in the mean voice he says, 'I'm gonna make sure you sorry, nigger ... stand him up, boys.'

'No, please sir, it was an accident, I didn't mean to look at you ...'

'Don't you try to walk away from me, boy!'

'No, please sir ...'

He punches himself five times in the eye.

'Put your face in that dirt, you stinking filthy nigger!'

'Please sir, let me go.'

'Don't be coming round here with your "I'm sorry" assed nigger shit!'

'Don't point your face at me, boy!'

He punches himself two more times in the groin.

For a moment he seems to calm down. Somebody nearby offers him a cigarette. He takes it and pushes it forward in his mouth while his companion lights it. They start to talk.

He says, 'Yeah, yeah, I saw he came around, I saw him the other day, he was looking good too, got himself all cleaned up.'

He punches himself in the face and falls flat on his back as the cigarette explodes into a cloud of sparks.

'Roll that motherfucker over!'

And with both hands he punches either side of his head.

'Oh yeah, you look pretty now, boy. Here, let me welcome you some more. You better remember who you are, monkey boy. What good are you to me? A snivelling fucking nigger!'

He says, 'I'm sorry, sir.'

Some of the other homeless people try to distract the man now and again with cigarettes and talk. It works for short periods, but for the most part there's nothing they can do.

I get up and make my way to Penn Station. I feel as if I need JV now. I could use some friendly positive energy. It is around two in the afternoon. The day is bright and humid as they often are in New York, so I walk slowly to reduce the outpour of sweat.

The police presence in and around Madison Square Garden is growing with every breath. On the steps are eight men, made menacing by their full body armour and mirrored sunglasses, and the large automatic rifles that sit across their chests. Their shiny helmets glisten in the sun. I recognise this scene from a hundred movies, but there is an added component: a crowd of tourists stands in front of this little Lego-man gaggle. Men and women alike click away, trying to capture the next screen saver on their digital cameras. I don't speak to any of them, but I am interested to note that without exception, the people taking pictures of this armed troupe are white Caucasian.

Further down stands JV and his cousin Remy. I haven't seen either of them for about seven days. I stopped by once to say hello but they were nowhere to be seen. They might have stepped off the block to smoke a joint, or they might have been in the multi-storey car park entertaining young ladies. Perhaps they were asleep.

Upon seeing me JV shouts, 'Hey, Alan! Where the fuck have you been, man?'

People turn, look JV up and down, look me up and down, and then assess that we are of little interest. The tables have turned on me somewhat. JV always keeps himself clean and presentable. It is I who stands in filthy dirty jeans, greasy-skinned and greasy-haired, with a greasy beard and dirt under my fingernails.

'You can't just disappear like that, Alan,' Remy says, and I look at him, surprised.

'Yeah, son. We been worrying about you.'

'First it was a day, and we're like, that's cool, he's hanging out somewhere …'

'Then two days …'

'And we're like, cool, maybe he getting some pussy …'

'Yeah, after three days we thought: he a white boy, he can't man the pussy for that long.'

Remy and JV crumple and twist in their own suppressed laughter.

'But damn, son! You can't just be stepping off the block for a whole week and not be letting us know that you is OK.'

'Yeah, we were worried about you.'

'You know I got your back, but damn, son, how I gonna take care a you if I don't know where your ass is at? It cool that you go off and do your thing, you know, but listen, you just gotta say: "Yo, JV, I'm stepping off the block for a couple a days. I gonna be up here with my boy. I'll be back in a few days to let you know I'm safe," you understand? Cool. 'Cause, I can't be having that shit.'

As soon as I agree to inform JV of my whereabouts at all times he calms down.

'Now,' he says. 'Tell us some stories, Alan, where you been at?'

# Day 20 – Getting with the Program

At night Time Square scares me. During the day I find it simply ridiculous, but at night, when I lie on the sidewalk trying to sleep, it is a different, daunting, place. Nothing could have prepared me for my first night-time arrival in Time Square. As you enter it from 43rd Street, you come upon a scene of madness. Thousands of people of all races and colours fly in all directions; yellow cabs honk and dive into the curbs to pick up tourists. Religious fanatics shout at the tops of their voices, proclaiming God to be black and the white man to be the devil. Steam erupts from manhole covers. There are people selling counterfeit sunglasses, police officers stuffing mustard hot dogs in their mouths. Homeless guys hold signs that read, 'Give me money ... for beer, drugs and pussy.' Four-piece bands blast music up into the neon adverts for Coca Cola, Virgin and the Gap. Smells invade your nostrils: car fumes, perfumes, sweat, puke, piss, shit, new, old, stolen. People are shouting everywhere, at nobody and everybody, but you can't hear much of what they're saying, words are lost in the hum of neon. As you stare skyward at million-dollar billboards you feel the buzz pulse through you.

I sit on the sidewalk, up against a construction awning. A

police car gives a burst of siren and pulls up right in front of where I am sitting on 7th Avenue, dispersing the crowd in all directions. Two officers jump out, grab a drunk who only has one arm. It's Joseph Lucas. I don't get to speak with him, though. He is quickly thrown in the back of the car and driven away. Nobody says a word, except for one guy who shouts, 'Watch where you're going, asshole!' at the police officer. Such is my exhaustion that I can fall asleep in almost any position these days. My plan was to make some new friends tonight, but I am too tired. Even here, alone with nobody looking after me, I am able to fall asleep. Such is Time Square that I wake up almost leaping to my feet as a yellow cab screeches to a halt by the curb in front of me, or when a fire engine screams through the cross-section with its horns blaring, passing by so close to me that I think I am about to become a twisted and bloodied corpse.

Somebody has just poured soda on my head. My eyes spring open to catch sight of a group of youths, but before I can stand up one of them has pushed another on top of me. I am tired and confused and thinking, 'Is this a fight?' Nobody on the street stops to help or even comment on the situation. It isn't a fight. The youths call me some names and move on. There are four of them, they must be thirteen years my junior, but even as they walk away, I am scared out of my mind.

It is impossible to sleep after this. I want to sit still and blend into my surroundings like a scorpion fish. Thirty minutes later I start to doze again and am woken by a McDonald's drink exploding next to me. When I look up there is nobody to pinpoint, only streams of tourists going back and forth.

I stand up and walk along 42nd Street to 5th Avenue. The sidewalk is completely empty, which gives me a whole other kind of fear. I look up and see the library. There are some concrete benches at the front, set way back from the road. It isn't ideal, in fact it is stupid, but I am not thinking straight, so I go over to one, place my bag under my head and drift almost instantly into a nervous sleep.

I wake up five minutes later, bathed in a sea of flashing red lights. A police car is parked right in front of me. The officers are just getting out of the car. They look at me and start to walk in my direction.

I have heard that the police are running a zero tolerance policy these days, what with the upcoming Republican Convention. If I think Time Square is scary, now I am wide-eyed with the realisation that I am going to jail. And what then, when they find out I'm not a US citizen?

The officers are in no rush, they are giving me plenty of opportunity to run. Stupidly, I even consider it.

Then a van pulls up. On the side is written 'The Bowery Outreach Program'. The doors open quickly and out jump two young men and a girl. They run, overtaking the officers, in my direction.

They say, 'You got two choices, you come with us or you go to jail.'

I go with them.

In the van they ask me a lot of questions and here is where my morality trip ends. I lie and I lie and I lie. Yes, I am homeless. Yes, I need shelter. Yes, I'll go into a state-run program. I say anything they want to hear, as long as it means they'll get me off the street.

They make some phone calls to the various shelters. They find one on 72nd and 2nd Avenue that has beds available. They take me there.

I sign in at the reception under a horrible green light. A woman takes my bag and gives me a ticket. I am told that I will go through enrollment in the morning, but for now I am to go to sleep.

The receptionist walks me down a dark corridor. At the end I sense that it has opened up into a big, dark room, but my eyes won't adjust and I can't see a thing.

She says, 'Here, give me your hand,' and she pulls me forward and places my hand on top of a metal bar. 'This is where you sleep.'

I still can't see. I do everything by feel and discover that what

I am holding onto is a chair back. There are four of them. I slide my hand down and find the little padded seats no more than a foot deep.

So this is my bed, four cheap dining-table chairs lined up in a row.

'This is impossible,' I whisper.

Someone, somewhere in the dark void, coughs. It is the mechanism that sends the entire room into a coughing and snoring fit.

I think, 'Christ, there must be a dozen people in here with me!'

I position myself on the chairs, thinking I daren't fall asleep, if I do I'm going to fall off. I lie there listening to the snoring and the breathing and the coughing.

When I open my eyes I am amazed to find myself still on the chairs. I look left and stare into the belly of a man so large of girth that I think he must be a Hollywood invention. My body feels stiffer than ever before in my life, but still I don't move for fear of falling on the floor and waking everybody up. I don't know how I have managed to stay on the chairs at all. What is really staggering is that the enormous man next to me is sound asleep on the same amount of chairs that I have. His trick is not to have the chairs facing the same way: he alternates them, so that he has two chair backs behind him and two in front. I try to peer over the top of him to see who else is in the room, but I can't see past his bulk. Struggling not to fall, I manoeuvre myself into a sitting position.

There are at least twenty-five other people in the room, all asleep on allotted rows of chairs.

Not all asleep.

Somebody looks at me and I lie back down as quickly as I can.

This must be some kind of holding station. Later today we will all be moved to a proper shelter, with proper beds.

An hour later people are up and about. For the man in front of me getting up is a full five-minute procedure. The chairs are put back in stacks around the edge of the room. Tables are pulled out. Coffee is made. Conversation is attempted, though these people have little to say.

Nobody speaks to me, the new guy, until a woman from the reception calls my name.

She says, 'OK, we can get you on the program. You'll be interviewed in one hour when the program manager gets here ...'

'But where is the program?' I ask.

'What do you mean, where?'

'I mean, is it near here? Is it downtown?'

'No, it's here. Right where you are now. All of those people in the room where you just slept are on the program. Some have been with us a couple of days, others several months.'

I stand there for a few seconds, taken aback, then ask, 'You mean that's where they sleep every night? They live like that?'

'Yes,' she says. 'That's where they sleep.'

'OK,' I say. 'I just need to get something from my bag,' and I hand over my ticket.

These people are actively trying to get off the street and this is what the authorities do with them? This is their chance? No wonder most refuse shelter. No wonder most prefer to stay on the street. Jerome's lifestyle is a hundred-fold what these people have in here.

Once I have my bag I walk out the door and head to Central Park. I don't look back as I walk away. I am mentally exhausted. I just can't believe that people are made to live like this, not here in the richest city in the world, not on 72nd Street, within spitting distance from Central Park, Zoo fucking York. I would have never believed it.

# Day 21 – The Mayor of Strawberry Fields

John Lennon was murdered on 8 December 1980 – shot in the stomach four times as he entered his apartment building on Central Park West. Four hours beforehand he had signed an autograph for the man who would shoot him. That man's name was Mark Chapman. He later told the police that he had heard voices in his head that told him to go and kill Lennon.

Yoko Ono and her son Sean still live in the Dakota building, on the steps of which John was shot. The building is opposite the 72nd Street entrance on Central Park West. In 1981 a section of Central Park, in line with the Dakota building, was renamed 'Strawberry Fields' in honour of John Lennon. A black and white mosaic was set in the pathway. In the middle of the mosaic is the word 'Imagine'.

Shortly after the memorial was placed, Yoko Ono donated one million dollars to Central Park. The money was to be used for the upkeep of Strawberry Fields. It is a place where fans still come to remember, where they come and place candles and flowers, even form circles and sing some of Lennon's songs.

Most days of the week, in the early afternoon until the early evening, Gary, a man the *New York Times* once called 'the Mayor of Strawberry Fields', takes over the Lennon memorial.

Gary and I sit cross-legged on the ground. Beside us is a bin-bag full of roses that have been thrown away by a local florist, no doubt having passed their prime. Gary and I pluck the petals from their buds and place them in a separate plastic bag.

'Yo, Lisa, come over here and help us with these petals. I don't wanna be doing this all day, I got work to do.'

In his previous life Gary was surely an elephant, not only because of his size, or because his legs are long and thick, but because he suffers the same lethargic disposition.

*Leth-ar-gy* n: a state of physical slowness and mental dullness as a result of tiredness, disease, or …

Drugs!

Gary likes to smoke weed.

His voice, although slow and lazy, is deep, and booms at one of those unnatural volumes that simply cannot be softened.

'Lisa! I said get over here.'

Gary's big chunky arms hang down like carcasses in an abattoir. His feet, huge on the end of tree-trunk legs, land amazingly softly. The movement is not graceful to look at. This mound of a man has no ballet about him. 'Lisa, I won't tell you again!'

His voice booms out and ricochets off the many tourists who stand around paying tribute to their favourite Beatle.

'Lisa, you're really pushing me today. If I have to deal with you …'

Lisa has her head way up in the clouds. She's tall too. Her pink flowery skirt, which would no doubt be long on the average woman, doesn't quite reach her knees.

Lisa shouts back from a bench about twenty feet away, her long blonde hair flicking round in exasperation, 'Gary, do you know what? Just shut up! I'm talking to Tony.'

Lisa's voice doesn't pack the same punch as Gary's. To make her words reach Gary she has to shout.

'Oh yeah, that's right. You think I'm gonna let you get away with that?'

'Gary, I don't even care.'

'Oh, you will. You think you can tell me to shut up? Go take a hike, Lisa! Get out of here. I'm sick of looking at you!'

Never before have I been so fascinated by rose petals. The tourists shrink back wondering whether this little confab is going to lead to violence. Or is it in fact performance art? Will Lisa and Gary soon be taking a bow and holding out a hat for donations? This is New York – it easily could be. But the tourists are unsure about what to do. They are not used to people airing their irritations in public the way Lisa and Gary do. All they want is to pay their respects to their favourite Beatle.

'OK, Gary. But when I go this time don't come after me, OK!' shouts Lisa. 'This time, when I leave, don't come after me. OK, asshole?'

People point their noses at the ground and sneak occasional glances, little glimpses of Gary and Lisa. They don't want to get caught looking. They don't want this bad energy to be turned on them. But still they can't help but take it all in. It's reality TV without the cable fee.

Gary pulls out another handful of roses. 'What are you talking about, Lisa? Come after you? You are so dumb I can't believe, I can't … I can't believe just how … You're so dumb!'

'You know what I'm talking about, Gary. Last week you came out with the same shit. Eight hours later you had the whole search team out for me. "Where's Lisa? Where's Lisa?" You're pathetic, Gary, you know that? Pathetic!'

'Oh, that's right, keep pushing me, baby. Keep pushing.'

'I'm not pushing anything, Gary. If you could just shut the fuck up and play with your stupid fucking flowers we wouldn't even be talking now.'

'Don't be calling my art stupid, bitch! It ain't so stupid when you run out of beer in the afternoon!'

'When did you ever buy me beer, Gary? Like once a fucking year!'

'What about last week, huh? You forget about last week already? That's how fucking dumb you are, Lisa. You can't even remember this morning, you dumb fucking crack head.' Gary looks up from his flowers and smiles at the two girls kneeling down by the memorial – two girls who have not been put off by the fracas. They came here to get a picture and aren't going to leave without it.

They beam up at the camera that a friend points at them.

Gary's voice, all of a sudden light and airy, calls out to the two girls. 'Hey, sisters! Peace sign! Peace sign! Don't forget the peace sign!'

They look at Gary uncomprehendingly and then speak to each other in French. What does this madman want, they wonder? Is he going to start on us now?

'Here, I'll show you.' Gary leaps up and kneels behind them. For a second they wonder if they are being robbed, in broad daylight, in front of all these onlookers. But quickly they become more concerned with Gary's dirty, grubby hands resting on the shoulders of their Louis Vuitton T-shirts.

Gary lifts one hand up and smiling proudly holds up a peace sign.

There's a *click!*

There's a *flash!*

Standing up, brushing his long dark hair back out of his face Gary says, 'I'm hungry, Lisa, what did you bring me?'

'I got you mash potato and meat sauce, from the All Angels.'

'Ah yeah, I had that before. That's real good.'

To me Gary says, 'You sit here and work away at those petals for me, I gotta get something to eat.' And he walks over to where Lisa sits. He takes a seat on the other side of the bemused Tony, who has remained silent for the last five minutes, and starts shoveling potato and meat sauce into his mouth.

# Day 22 – A Place on the Upper West Side

Lisa, while rummaging through a mountain of garbage bags, is engaged in an altercation with a gingery, red-faced maintenance worker at a residential building on 75th street.

He says, 'Listen, bitch …'

'Fuck you! I ain't listening to you, so fuck off …'

'Don't come back around here!'

'Fuck you, asshole. You can't tell me I can't come around here.'

'Why do you even have to act like this?'

'Act like what? You said, "Don't make a mess." I said I wouldn't make a mess. I'm out here every day collecting cans and I never make a mess. But you couldn't let it go, could you? You had to keep pushing. You had to keep playing the big man …'

'Fuck you, you fucking low-life whore, just get the fuck …'

'I'd rather be a low-life than a fucking rent boy cocksucker!'

'Fucking move, bitch, before I call the police on your fucking ugly ass …'

'Call them. I'll tell them you're just pissed 'cause I saw you sucking dick for two dollars, you fucking cunt! Why don't you just fuck off back to your own country, you piece a shit fag?

While others stop and stare, I continue to rummage in the trashcans for cans and bottles. I am trying not to laugh, shocked as I am about this torrent of foul abuse Lisa and the maintenance man bestow upon each other. The doorman from the building has come out to see what the fracas is about, but he doesn't join in. He just smiles in his neatly pressed uniform and lights a cigarette.

Lisa continues to go through the garbage cans while she argues. The maintenance man stands for a few seconds, dumbfounded by Lisa's last comment.

'"My own fucking country" – is that what you said?'

'You heard what I said. You want me to repeat it? Why don't you – cocksucker – fuck off back to your own country. You are not welcome here!'

'What, I look like an Arab to you? Look at me, I'm an American, you fucking pig-ignorant bitch.'

'Oh, you think so, with that attitude? Why don't you just mind your own business and fuck off.'

''Cause I don't like low-lifes like you coming around and rooting through the trash and dropping it all over the sidewalk.'

'Do you see anything on the sidewalk? I haven't dropped a fucking thing! Every bag I open I do back up, so what's your problem?'

'Like I said ...'

'Why are you still hanging around? I don't even have a cock and if I did I wouldn't let you suck it!'

'Oh yeah, you're really funny, bitch! Your husband needs to give you a beat.'

It occurs to me that he might be referring to me, that he thinks I'm Lisa's husband and I should give her a beat.

'He's man enough to do it if he wants to. Not like you, you fucking diseased cocksucker! Don't you have some fucking work to do instead of swallowing cock all day, you fucking immigrant?'

Throughout this little confab Lisa collects twenty-two Miller Lite bottles, seventeen Corona bottles, ten Diet Pepsi bottles, seven Heineken bottles, two 7-Up bottles and a peach Snapple bottle, twenty-two Coke cans, thirteen Sunkist cans, eight Bud Light cans and three Dr Pepper cans.

A trade-in value of $5.20.

The maintenance man walks around the corner.

Lisa shouts, 'That's it, cocksucker, go and service your customers!'

She moves on to the next building, to the next set of garbage cans.

She says, 'I wasn't going to work today.'

We walk along each street, from side to side, rummaging and collecting.

'But it's recycling day, it'd be stupid to miss it.'

It's early afternoon and the heat is at its peak.

'Was I a little harsh on that guy?'

She says, 'Cocksucker!'

Once both bags are full we lug them back to Columbus Avenue.

The Pioneer convenience store has a row of cash registers. Black girls serve customers and gossip among themselves. Near the cashiers, in a small walkway sectioned off by a large refrigerator are three recycling machines. One for plastics, one for glass and one for cans.

Lisa stands in front of the machines for cans and bottles, running both of them at the same time. She never lets the credit on each machine go over a dollar. She gathers her printed credit notes in her hand.

The glass machine gets full and can't take any more. Lisa presses the green button to get the receipt.

Seventy-five cents.

Lisa calls out, 'Sir, sir! Glass is full – thank you.'

A twenty-something man puts his soda down and ambles over as he sorts through a bunch of keys. Like the girls running the registers, he is a minority, minimum-wage worker.

He unlocks the machine and drags out two of the big plastic bins that are full with smashed glass of different colours. The third bin he shakes to make the glass settle down. He slides in two empty bins and locks the machine.

'Thank you,' Lisa says, sliding in a bottle.

The man nods and drags away the bins.

An old woman with hard reddened skin, warts and a sweat comes round the corner to a sighing halt. She puts her two bin-bags down on the floor. They clink and clank with the sound of tin and glass.

'What you got there, is that glass?' she asks Lisa.

'Yeah.'

'What about cans, you doing cans?'

'Yeah, I'm doing both right now. I won't be long though, I'm nearly done,' Lisa says.

''Cause I got cans and glass to do.'

'Oh, OK. Well, I'm nearly done.'

'Are you doing glass?'

'Yeah.'

'How did you make out today?'

'Not bad actually. It looked pretty grim at first, but then I got a bunch of glass.'

'Yeah? That's good. Where'd you go?'

'You know, 70th to 76th, between Amsterdam and Central Park West.'

'Oh – is it good there?'

'Sometimes.'

'I'm doing cans and glass when you're ready.'

'Won't be long now.'

Lisa finishes with receipts for $14.95. In the beer aisle she grabs two bottles of Polish beer at $1.29 each and takes them to the first cashier. She hands her three one-dollar credit slips and takes the beer in a bag.

She walks to the next cashier and hands over her three slips.

She receives three dollar bills and scrunches them up in her hand.

She goes to the next cashier. Three more slips. Three more dollars. Scrunches.

As we are walking out Lisa looks up and smiles.

She says, 'Hey, JR, how's it going?'

I freeze.

JR is V's boyfriend. I've invested many hours since being out here, waiting by the entrance to their tunnel, hoping to meet either V or JR. They were dull hours during which neither had materialised. But now here he is, standing before me, just as I remember him.

'Me, I'm having a great day,' he tells Lisa. 'I got me a six pack of Leila's in the fridge, just stuffed them in there and I'm gonna come back and get them when they're cold. As soon as I'm finished up today I'm gonna sit in the shade somewhere and drink them.'

'Sounds like a nice afternoon to me.'

'Right. What you up to today, you in the park?'

'Yeah, I'm gonna cash these in and go see what Marco is up to, probably drink some beers.'

'I might come over there later.'

'Why don't you? You know where we are.'

'OK, well maybe I see you later.'

'Bye, JR.'

Before we walk away I quickly ask, 'JR, do you remember me?'

He looks at me with a smirk. I can tell he does remember me, he is just trying to place me.

I help him. 'I'm the journalist. I met you and V, we came to your …'

'That's right,' he smiles. 'You and the photographer. So what you up to?'

I tell JR about my project. He says, signalling his own bag of cans, 'Well, I need to get these cashed in, but you know where I live, stop by.'

'Oh, cool,' Lisa says. 'You guys know each other. I'm just going to take him to meet Marco.'

'Well, when I am through maybe I'll see you both over there.'

We all say goodbye and go our separate ways.

I call out, 'Is V still around, JR?'

'Yeah,' he calls back. 'V's still around. We're not together any more, but she's still down in the tunnel. I bump into her now and again.'

Now we really do move on. But I think I am the only one with goose bumps.

When Lisa reaches Central Park she does not go immediately to Strawberry Fields, where Gary is no doubt flinging himself into tourists' snapshots. Instead she turns left at the first available path. She says hello to an old Cuban man named Sabatino who sits on a bench in the shade, his shopping trolley parked nearby. She carries on up the path to a wood-chipped recreation area that has three bark-covered benches.

The benches are taken up by three men, Marco, Tim and Jonathan. Marco is from Cuba. His long greying hair is bunched up in a red bandanna, and behind his drooping moustache is a very happy, easygoing, clever and articulate man. He sits on the furthest bench, feet up facing the others, drinking beer from a McDonald's cup complete with a lid and straw.

Tim is from the Bronx. His expression says, 'Be careful where you tread' – because he knows he vomited somewhere around here, he just can't remember where. His face is red from drinking and his hands shake, also from drinking.

Jonathan is a man who many moons ago spent a full morning sneaking into a Patty Smith concert. After relaying in much detail his fence-climbing escapades Jonathan says, 'I was walking in Time Square the other day. This woman says, "You wanna help beat Bush?" I said, "Yeah, I'll beat your bush. Pull your panties down, you fucking bitch." *Ha Ha Ha Ha.*'

Lisa shares one of her beers between the three men. Marco tops the beers off with the tequila that he keeps stashed in his sports bag. Also in the sports bag is a gallon of water and the remnants of what used to be ice – odd little forms that bob hither and thither in their last moments of being frozen.

An Iranian arrives on a mountain bike.

'Give me a beer, Marco!'

'This was from Lisa ...'

'Lisa, give me a beer, please. I buy more soon.'

'You missed it. That was it. But someone will go to the store again soon.'

'Here, I have tequila,' says Marco, passing the bottle. 'How did you make out today?'

'Seven hundred dollar,' the Iranian answers with a tequila-strained face. 'Not bad, eh?'

'Seven hundred!'

'Yes, seven hundred. It was just in time. I have to give five hundred in rent tomorrow, otherwise I am thrown out, so I have rent, and the electric and some food. Now I have sixty dollars left.'

The Iranian pulls out a crack pipe, loads it and hits it.

My curiosity overcomes me. Without thinking how stupid a question this is, and how stupid a time to ask it, I say, 'How did you make seven hundred dollars in one day?'

The Iranian's face twists and I know instantly that this isn't only the crack taking hold. My back stiffens.

The Iranian's back straightens.

The Iranian walks over to me. Staring deep down into my soul the Iranian, barely an inch away, says with menacing lucidity, 'Like I'm going to fucking tell you when I just met you!' He is almost nose-to-nose with me, ready to attack. After a few seconds he sits back down and gives his attention once again to his crack pipe.

I decide that the Iranian's choice of career is best left to the imagination.

Silence reigns for a short time after this altercation. But very soon everybody digs in their pockets for a whip-round. Tim is sent on a beer run. Lisa and the Iranian go to a payphone on the corner of 72nd Street to call their dealer.

I slip away quietly to see how Gary is getting along.

Tourists flock in and out of Strawberry Fields, mostly in twos or threes, but now and again a walking tour stops by with a crowd of thirty-odd sightseers. The guides are known to the Mayor Of Strawberry Fields, as he is known to them, but they rarely acknowledge Gary's presence. The guides tell the story of John Lennon. Gary acknowledges their presence by calling out to correct them whenever they get the story wrong.

'She still lives there, you idiot! Yoko Ono still lives there! So does Sean! How are you still getting it wrong?'

'Yo, brothers!' Gary suddenly booms out, making several people jump. 'Don't forget the peace sign!'

'Dude, what are you talking about?' asks a teenage boy, with complete bewilderment all over his face. His reply comes a little aggressively; he doesn't appear to want random conversation.

'What am I talking about? What am I talking about? Oh, brother! You don't know what I'm talking about? Brother, you're kneeling down on John Lennon's memorial and you don't know what a peace sign is? Shame on you, brother. Here, shift over. I'll show you.'

Gary flings himself clumsily into the picture. The college kids from Middle America don't know quite what to make of this bulk of a man who has just infiltrated their vacation pictures. Gary loops an arm around one of the youths and pops the peace sign above the head of the other.

'There you go. The peace sign. Hands up, brothers, with the peace signs. This is Strawberry Fields – you need to show some respect to the legend. Where are the peace signs? Brothers, come on, arms up! Peace sign!'

The two boys realise that it's easier to give the peace sign.

'There you go!'

There's a *click!*

There's a *flash!*

As the tourists leave, Gary grabs a handful of petals in each hand. He places them in the centre of the memorial. He grabs some more and lays them just below the first batch. He is starting what will grow to become the vertical line of a peace sign.

He doesn't rush the job, his *art* as he calls it. He takes time to think about the colours of the petals. Using purple to contrast the pink, and yellow to contrast the red, he starts a diagonal arm that branches off from the top of the vertical line.

Gently, from a bottle, he pours water on the petals to keep them in place. Then he remembers Mary-Jane, his black Labrador, and he goes over and rummages through his shopping trolley until he finds her bowl. Mary-Jane sits up and licks her lips as Gary pours water for her. Looking over his shoulder he curses a cluster of petals that blow free from his incomplete peace sign.

Visitors continue to squat. Some hold up their two fingers and wave their own peace sign. Others need to be told.

'Brother! Sister!'

Slowly but surely Gary's art starts to take shape. He has a border of peach and red working its way around the circular memorial, possibly six feet in circumference. But he doesn't rush. The memorial is never finished. Gary will be there, weighing the petals down with water, repairing patches made by errant gusts of wind, until the sun goes down.

Three girls from Spain squat behind the once black and white memorial, careful not to disturb the rose petals. They smile up at the camera, waving a peace sign on each hand and singing:

> Imagine there's no heaven,
> It's easy if you try

In no time at all there is a crowd of over thirty people singing:

> No hell below us,
> Above us only sky
> Imagine all the people
> Living for today … aha-o-a-wow …

Gary is up on his tiptoes, waving his arms around like a conductor – an unlikely instigator. But it doesn't stop the new arrivals thinking he *is* the instigator – he does, after all, carry it off rather well – and they drop dollar bills into his hat.

As the shadows take over Strawberry Fields, Gary gathers his things and together we walk over to join Lisa, Marco and the others. I am instantly aware that I am more welcome than Gary. This is essentially Marco's crew and space. Marco and Gary don't like each other very much and this quickly becomes apparent.

'Where's Lisa?' Gary demands of Marco.

'I don't know where she went. She said she'd be back though.'

'Marco, just tell me where she is. I don't want to deal with your bullshit.'

'Maybe if you didn't beat her all the time, Gary, you'd know where she is. She'd be with you.'

'Watch your fucking mouth, Marco. I don't beat Lisa.'

'Yeah, why is she always covered in bruises then? She should have left you a fucking long time ago, asshole.'

'Leave me? What, for you? You'd like that, I know, but she ain't about to leave me for a fuck-up drunk like you, Marco.'

'You're right, Gary, I might be a drunk, but your woman is addicted to crack, 'cause it's the only way she can escape you.'

The argument, in a circling teenage fashion, doesn't let up. In fact it gets louder. The others standing around seem to be used to this; they don't join in or look over. They just raise their own voices so they can be heard within their own conversations.

The argument is so intense that nobody notices when the police arrive. It is dark at this point and it is only when the two officers start shining their flashlights in faces that Marco and Gary quieten down.

Crack pipes, liquor and beer bottles are quickly kicked under benches or stuffed into pockets and bags. The now ten-strong crowd all try their hardest to look sober. The result is comical and cartoonish.

'What's the problem here?' a lean-looking policeman asks.

'It's no big deal, officer,' Marco begins. 'This guy here beats his wife and I don't like it, so I'm telling ...'

'You better watch your mouth, Marco, or ...'

'Hey you!' The officer cuts Gary off. 'You beat your wife?'

'I don't beat my wife, officer. He's just trying to cause trouble. She'll be here in a minute, you can ask her yourself.'

'She's too scared ...'

The officer shouts, 'Both of you shut up.'

'Yeah, shut up, Marco. You drunk.'

'*Hey!*'

The officer shines his flashlight onto Marco's McDonald's cup and then up into Marco's face.

'What's in the cup?' he asks.

'Just soda, officer.'

'So if I open that up I'm not going to find liquor in there, am I?'

Gary is jumping as if he wants to say something. But he has a tin full of weed in his pocket and knows that if the officers do decide to search, he is in more trouble than Marco.

Quickly, my own eyes are filled with a flood of light from the police officer's flashlight.

'What are you all doing here?' he asks.

'Just hanging out and talking,' I tell him.

'Why here?' he asks.

'It's Central Park, it's a great place to sit and hang out with friends.'

It turns out I am a good choice to continue a dialogue with. I am stone cold sober and this is obvious.

The officers leave, and although they know exactly what is in Marco's cup, they don't search.

'Keep the noise down,' The second officer says as they walk away.

As soon as they are out of sight Marco reaches into his bag and removes a beer. He nods at me and throws it in my direction. The drinking and the drug-taking continue. An hour later Gary has left and although Lisa has come back, she is without doubt chemically challenged. As I continue to refuse the crack pipe, and try hard not to make eye contact with needle sharers, I realise that this isn't a safe place for me to fall asleep. The recreation area is starting to look more like an apocalyptic wasteland. Quietly, and without anybody noticing, I take my leave.

At around 2am, as I sit alone dozing on one of the benches next to Central Park on Central Park West, the big booming voice of the Mayor wakes me up. 'Alan, what are you doing?'

He sits down next to me and hands me a very cold forty-ounce bottle of Budweiser. 'Keep it out of sight.'

He pulls a newspaper from his trolley and starts reading.

After a few minutes Lisa trundles up to the bench with her trolley, 'Hi, Alan,' she says, but quickly breaks into a screaming rage that is aimed at Gary, who spits rage back at her. In among the 'cocksuckers' and 'whores' they wave their arms and look to the sky in disbelief.

Eventually they walk off, but quickly stop and turn to look at me.

'Where are you sleeping tonight, Alan?' Gary asks.

'I don't know.'

'You don't know what you're doing, do you? Come with me, I can't leave you out here.'

I get up and follow them. We walk several blocks, the Mayor and Lisa continuing to defy the meaning of the word *obscenity* all the while. Eventually we climb a grass bank down by the West Side Park. The Mayor and Lisa bed down right at the top, out of sight but right next to the highway. Then, remembering me, the Mayor gets up and searches the bushes for a suitable spot where I will be comfortable and out of sight. He crashes into the bushes, huffing and puffing and stamping until he has flattened a sizable patch of shrubbery.

'They're kinda springy. You'll be real comfortable there!' and then he bounces off. The yelling picks up – although a less intense version – then it stops abruptly. Lisa appears at the exit to my bush cave.

'Oh yeah, this is nice,' she tells me. And then, holding out her hand, she says, 'Here, I got a blanket for you. If you need anything, you know where we are.'

I spend a minute or two arranging the blanket. Then I lay myself down on what is the most comfortable surface in … how long? The springy shrubbery really is just like a mattress, better than the mattress I sleep on at home, in fact.

I can't help but listen to the now hushed voices of the Mayor and Lisa as they continue to fight.

'Fuck you, Gary. I'm going to sleep!'

'Fuck me? Fuck you, *I'm* going to sleep!'

'Then shut the fuck up and go to sleep.'

'Why don't you shut the fuck up and go to sleep?'

'I'm trying to shut the fuck up and go to sleep but you keep talking, don't you, Gary?'

'Who was talking then? Was that me? *No!*'

'Oh God, you're so dumb, Gary. I can't even believe it sometimes.'

'Yeah? That's because I can never get any freaking sleep 'cause you always yapping!'

'Oh yeah, right. I make you dumb.'

'Lisa, fuck you. I'm trying to sleep.'

'No, fuck you, Gary …'

I am the first to fall asleep.

When I awake it is around 7am. The noise from the traffic is loud and continuous. I know I'm not going to sleep any more and decide to head down into the park where there are toilets. I put my trainers on, sling my bag over my shoulder and walk up the hill to where Gary and Lisa are sleeping. They are lying arm in arm in a peaceful, loving embrace. I leave the blanket by their feet and walk away.

# Day 23 – $2 on the Nose of Whichever Horse Wins the Next Race!

I sit by the fence that blocks public entry to the Freedom Tunnel. I am more patient now, knowing that JR and V are both still living in there; if I sit here long enough it's just a matter of time before one of them comes out.

Caught up as I am watching joggers, it is JR who sees me first. 'Hey, you wanna come play the horses?' he asks as a way of greeting.

I slip my trainers on and together we leave Westside Park.

The OTB is loud and smoky. The OTB is depression. The OTB is joy.

There are no young people in the off-track betting shop on 72nd Street. Middle-aged men with beer guts and old women with few teeth rule this domain. The elderly segment, prominent features being gums and hearing aids, sit in couples, man and wife. Form sheets shake in their spotted dry hands. Eyes swell behind bifocal bullet-proof spectacles. Transparent skin stretches as they squint up at the screen, rarely knowing where their horse finishes.

'First?'

'Fourth?'

'Fifth?'

'Second?'

The middle-aged men – vests, shorts, baseball caps and cheap gold attire being the official garb – strut up and down in front of a bank of screens. They are the noisemakers. They shout at anything and everything.

At the screen one man shouts, 'You son of a …'

At a horse another man shouts, 'You lazy good for nothing …'

At each other two men shout, 'Fuck you!' And then, 'No! Fuck you!'

Into cellphones they say, 'I'll be home when I'm home!'

To the cashiers they say, 'To win, *all of it*!' Then they hand over two crumpled-up, dirty dollar bills.

They are peacocks with too many feathers and no women to impress. They are the atmosphere and soul of the OTB.

One man is doubled over, riding an imaginary horse. 'This is what you do …' He gallops on the spot, building up a good speed. In his right hand there's a handful of betting slips. He uses them to whip himself into a faster gallop. He has a 150-pound gut that dangles beneath him in the space where a real jockey would expect to find his horse. In total you could chalk him up at around 260 pounds. '… In the final bend, that's when you start to go forward.' He's an expert.'… You don't pull on the reins …' He increases speed, giving everything he has down the final straight. 'You lean way forward.' Beads appear on his forehead. 'You cross the line …' Damp patches appear under his arm. 'And I take my 8-1 and 100 down and I'm laughing, baby!' He stops, contorts his face and begins to rip his betting slips into as many pieces as possible, fury dribbling from his mouth in droplets of spit as he showers the floor with the torn pieces of paper. 'You son of a bitch!'

Onlookers laugh those silent, shoulder-hunching laughs like dogs in a cartoon. The jockey turns and walks back to the cashier to place another bet.

JR selects form sheets from the horizontal rack that stands

beneath the screens lining the wall as you enter. His greasy ponytail hangs limply from his baseball cap, moving only with the whim of selection. There are many races to choose from. JR walks away with the form sheets for Belmont Park, Bay Meadows and Meadowlands. He leans on the railing by the entrance and studies the forms.

The form sheets list the day's races for each track. They tell you who's running, who's riding, who's training, what the odds are, and how the recent form has been.

JR looks from the sheets to the screens as he chews lightly on his bottom lip, releasing it now and again to whisper to himself. He walks towards the cashier, changing his mind with every step. He slides his dollar bills through the glass partition.

He watches the screens.

Three minutes until the off.

Outside the OTB, JR stands four dollars lighter than when he entered. The loss has no effect on his smile.

We walk up 80th Street, stopping to search every trashcan outside every house. Jauntily JR takes the steps that lead down to the half basement level where the trashcans are kept. His hands form pincers, twisting and pulling at the plastic to undo the knots. In no time at all he finds himself up to his elbows in yesterday's life, oblivious to the twitching blinds and staring passers-by – or maybe not oblivious, simply indifferent.

He rummages …

He finds a bottle of hot sauce.

'I could use that,' he tells me.

At the third house JR runs his hand over an as yet unopened black plastic bag. His eyes brighten. The bag is cold. It means that somebody has *just* emptied out their refrigerator. He pulls at the knot. Sitting on the top is a half-frozen pack of eight chicken thighs. He removes them. Studies them. Sniffs them. He searches for a date: June 28, 2004 … that's today.

'Hmmmm … Well, I guess I'll just have to eat you tonight!'

He places the chicken thighs on the lid of an adjacent trashcan and reaches back into the cold black bag. He removes a packet of unopened chorizo.

'Mmmmmm.'

A bottle of Jägermeister.

Half a bottle of white wine.

Italian vinaigrette.

A large unopened packet of salmon.

JR goes through the same ritual with the salmon that he went through with the chicken, twisting it and turning it and smelling it. Is there a date? June 28, 2004.

'Now there's a dilemma!' he says to himself, 'Do I eat the chicken or the salmon tonight?'

He picks the chicken back up and stands there, weighing his options.

A young man walks past with fifteen dogs, all on leashes, that scurry along ahead of him.

'Chicken or salmon? Well, if I eat you then you're no good to me … but I could … eat you and salt you and save you till tomorrow! Yeah, that's what I'll do, chicken tonight, salmon tomorrow.'

JR continues to search the contents of the bag. Items that appeal to him are placed on the trashcan lid to his left, the items that don't go in the open binbag in a trashcan to his right.

'French mustard,' he says to himself. 'Now I got me some of that, but what … What about an onion? Can I get an onion here?'

The front door to the neighbouring house opens and closes with a bang. A large woman appears, wearing an expensive sports outfit. She is possibly on her way to the sports centre that she joined more for social reasons than for health. An hour drifting on the rowing machine should be good for gossip. Her hair is blow-dried into a storm of waves. Her Chrysler car keys dangle in her left hand.

At the bottom of the steps she stops abruptly. What's that noise? Is it a rat?

No.

She studies JR. A little man who looks like he never found his way home from a Led Zeppelin concert. She tries to make out the items as he piles them up.

'Watcha got there, honey?' she asks as she sidles around the front of the house. She reaches the gate and hops down to JR, who continues to rummage.

'Oh, a bunch of stuff.'

'What's that? Salmon?'

'Yeah, today's date though. I think if I salt it, it might keep another day.'

'Why not just eat it today?'

'Well, this chicken here also has to be eaten today …'

'Oh I see, salt the salmon then. Plenty of salt, mind.'

The woman walks past JR and stops at a trashcan two down from him. She pops a bag open and starts to rummage. JR hears the clank of glassware but doesn't turn to look. The woman holds a couple of glasses in the air, one in each hand. They are thick glass, fogged from twenty-five years of hard service, the kind old aunties still serve their lemonade in, worthless to some but purchasable at twenty dollars apiece if you take a liking to them in a trendy second-hand store. They would be the ones labelled as 'retro tumblers'.

'Oh, these are nice,' the woman says, holding them up for JR's approval.

'Pretty,' he assures her. She leans over, places them on the wall in front of her and digs back into the bag, coming up with two more of the same.

'Oh, what a shame. This one's cracked,' she says before coming out with a set of brown on brown sixties-style plates. She turns them over, studying them from different angles before deciding on the lot. Six plates and three tumblers slowly climb the stairs to her house before disappearing behind the big glass, paneled door. A dishwasher starts its cycle while JR tops up his vodka bottle with Jägermeister.

JR takes his time packing the food into his trolley. He stands

as if playing Tetris, trying to figure out the best order for packing, the system that will take up the least space. He packs and
unpacks, spreading his bounty over the sidewalk to study the
shapes. Eventually he covers the food with a large empty binbag
and moves on.

Three houses down, JR breaks into a smile. In a plastic bag he
has found twenty-five porn magazines, mostly seventies retro
chic – *Big Titties, Bum Shanks, Tender Steaks* – along with ten porn
DVDs. He wastes no time in collecting the treasure and, as is his
style, packs them carefully into his trolley.

He continues on his way.


On 75th Street, between Amsterdam and Columbus he finds
two *still* ice-cold Miller Lites and a Budweiser. On 73rd he finds
an almost new hardback biography of F. Scott Fitzgerald. On
72nd he finds a copy of *The Complete Idiot's Guide To Camping*.
On 71st he finds five tins of soup, two breaded chicken breasts
and a bag of carrots. He also collects bottles and cans for recycling. After two and a half hours of touring the neighbourhood, JR's trolley is three-quarters full. He digs out the pornog-
raphy and separates the magazines from the DVDs. The DVDs
go back in the trolley under a bag of carrots. The magazines, in
a bag of their own, are placed on the top of the trolley. He
drags the trolley behind him as we head back to 72nd Street.
We stop at the lights at Amsterdam and 72nd. We stand, like the
other pedestrians, and wait for the crossing light to change.
Unlike the other pedestrians, however, JR picks a cigarette butt
up off the floor, lights it, finishes it with two puffs and throws it
back again.

The lights change.

The trolley can just about be heard as it crosses the road, rat-
tling over ridges and holes. It clanks as it catches the rise in the
curb on the other side but comes to a silent halt next to a man
fifteen yards on who sits next to a table, on top of which are
three milk crates.

The man's expression and body language suggest that he doesn't want to interact with the white man. But business is business.

JR hands over the magazines and walks away. Standing by the window of the Gap he removes his vodka bottle and takes a swig. He tries to pay no attention to the man looking over his magazines. The man looks at the titles, inspects the magazine's condition and flicks through the content. He puts them back in the bag, stuffs the bag behind a milk crate and walks over to JR, removing singles from his pocket. He counts out five and holds them out to JR.

'I'll have some more stuff for you later,' JR says, smiling. The man nods his head to acknowledge that he heard what JR said, and walks back to his crates. JR grabs his trolley and together we begin to work the streets that we hadn't visited earlier.

The trolley trundles along. It stops at every other house and waits to see if it will bear more load. JR rummages and rummages, collecting more food than he can possibly eat.

More chicken cutlets, some drumsticks and a lettuce.

Everything is stacked precariously in the trolley.

Flicking through a pile of unread computer magazines he says to himself, 'I'm not too sure what to do with this stuff,' and he turns them over and over as if the answer will reveal itself in the handling. He looks at the CD-ROM taped to the front of a magazine, reads the writing, and puts it down. Next he picks up a book, a big thick volume of dull text.

*Mac Made Easy.*

He looks at a book cabinet that's standing on the sidewalk, says 'Hmmmm,' and rubs the side of the tanned wood. 'This could be nice for the house.' He tilts it on its side, and rubs a scratch, feeling its depth with his thumb. The cabinet's shelves are loose in the bottom. He picks one up and examines it, turning it over and over. He looks at the trolley, loaded up. 'Ahhh.' He's still turning a shelf over in his hands. 'Too much hassle.'

He puts the shelf down, straightens the cabinet to leave it as he found it and moves along to the next house.

Aha!

JR ran out of olive oil three weeks ago and here's a half full bottle of Eliki. He unscrews the lid and pours a little onto the sidewalk to be sure that it is olive oil.

Aha!

He loads it into the trolley.

What else do we have here?

Half a jar of pickles.

A bag of peas.

A jar of sweetcorn.

A roll of tinfoil.

He finds a book.

He reads the cover: '*The Gates Of Fire* … Steven Pressfield.' He turns the book over and starts to read the synopsis. He asks me if I know the book, but I don't.

'Well,' he says, 'I'll let you know if it's any good.' And he puts the book in his trolley and, as if this constitutes some kind of signal, he calls it a day.

On the way home we stop once more by the man with the milk crates and a large market share of seventies porn magazines. He removes the DVDs. The man raises his eyebrows and places the pile on the table. He goes through them one by one, reading the covers, checking that the disks inside match the covers. He removes the disks from each box and checks the play side for scratches. He blows on them and sets them back in their casings.

JR puts the thirteen singles in his pocket.

He turns to me as we walk away and asks, 'You want to sleep on my couch?'

I laugh. 'Oh yes.'

'Good,' he says. 'You can help me eat this chicken.'

It's dark outside when we reach the Freedom Tunnel. JR walks along the fence to an area where the dirt beneath it has been dug out. Taking the bags from the trolley he slides them through one by one, being careful to keep the bags upright so that the contents don't spill into the dirt. There are seven bags in all.

He makes his way over the metal fence by his usual route, hooking his fingers into its sharp little holes. He squeezes through a gap to an old plank of wood that flexes as it leads him down to the ground. I follow suit and by the time I am on the other side JR has unhooked his trolley and is over gathering the bags that he slowly and meticulously reloads into the trolley.

It's pitch black in the tunnel. The humming and bumping of cars as they race over the uneven surface of the highway above obliterate any sound below. JR walks in. Unafraid he walks an unmarked path with his heavy trolley, and I follow obediently behind him.

'That's where V lives,' he says, pointing to a mezzanine up in the roof.

JR stands for a few minutes calling out to her, but there is no reply.

'Ahh,' he says. 'Maybe we'll catch her for breakfast.' And we start walking again.

As we walk I look out for her dance floor. Even though it's dark, I'd love to see it. But I can't find it.

Then, seeing a plywood hut that wasn't there before, I am prompted to ask, 'Is she still dancing?'

'No,' JR says. And, with a nod, he adds, 'That's her dance floor. The workmen ripped it up to use as storage for their paint.'

We walk on in silence.

After about five hundred yards there's a flicker of white ahead. Minimal light makes its way in through small grilles above, but there's enough, just for a split second, to pick up the movement of a white shirt.

'Who's there?' JR asks, not so much in enquiry but in greeting.

An Indian man in black trousers and an untucked white dress shirt steps into view.

'Hey, how you doing, fella? I ain't seen you in a while.'

'Hello. I have seen you.'

'Yeah, how you keeping? How's that cough?'

'It is much better now, thank you.'

The two men continue their exchange for a few minutes. Talking about the weather, the Yankees, and the police who came into the tunnel a few days ago.

'Yeah, I couldn't believe it,' JR says, with a big smile just about visible in the dark. 'They even came up to my house, climbed up the ladder and everything. That's brave. Anyways, they call out so I poke my head out, you know, as you do. And they're like, "Hey, we thought you were still here. We brought you some coffee." And they gave me two cups of coffee. I was like, "It's 3 o'clock in the freaking morning. I gotta whole tin of coffee in here!" They were just laughing. It was nice of them anyway.'

The Indian man tells JR he is going for a walk.

JR replies, 'Yeah, you take care of yourself. You know where to find me if you need anything!' And off the two men go, one on his way out, one on his way in.

The trolley is stowed in a dark corner, out of view from train drivers and passengers. JR picks up a ladder that is lying on the ground and leans it against the wall with a swift, practiced motion.

'Wait there,' he tells me as he gathers some of his shopping bags and mounts the ladder. It creaks under the strain. As JR climbs, the bags bounce off his legs and hips. JR keeps climbing. Every rung of the ladder needs to be used. At the top he swings the bags up and into the darkness of a small entrance before he descends and hands me two more.

'When you get up there, just stand still and away from the edge, then when I get up I'll let us in.'

At the top there's a thick metal handrail made of tubing. JR grabs it and pulls himself up onto the ledge, pushing me a little further into the darkness. He doesn't poke his head back out to see if anybody is there, or if anybody was watching us as we climbed. He simply turns and with another of his practiced actions lowers the ladder back to the ground with a cord he has attached for that very purpose. Now we stand in the dark entryway. His reception area.

A heavy blanket hangs on the left wall. Beneath the blanket there's a rug. JR pulls both back to reveal a large square hole. He reaches in and gropes the inside wall until his fingertips touch a cable. He tickles his way along the cable to the switch and turns it on.

And then there is light.

'OK, in you go, just hop on the wall and then walk down the ladder.'

I do as he says, though I don't make it look as easy as JR makes it sound. The wall is quite high and I have an embarrassing moment where I try to scramble over it, eventually only managing with some assistance from a laughing JR.

JR, considerably shorter even than me, swings his left leg up into the hole in the wall with ease.

On the other side is another smaller ladder. It is positioned like a ramp, leading up to the square portal. The ladder is partly covered with fabric, more blankets and rugs.

I hold my breath for a second.

JR doesn't notice the smell any more. But to me the smell is strong, a mixture of food, sweat, smoke, feet, dirt and excrement.

On the immediate left, tucked into the corner, I see a white plastic garden chair. There's a hole cut into the seat. Beneath the hole is a bucket. Next to the bucket are four extra-large water bottles. They are filled with a foggy, yellowy liquid that appears to have random brown shapes floating about inside.

JR puts his shopping down.

The room is about ten feet wide and twenty-five feet in length with a ceiling that must be fifteen feet high. There is stuff everywhere.

STUFF!

Unidentifiable stuff.

Plastic shopping bags that bulge in different shapes and sizes are spread all over the floor. All of the bags are tied at the top, with a simple little bow. Most of the bags are adorned with the red and blue Duane Read logo stretched out of shape. It is not possible to know what is in each bag. Even JR doesn't know.

'I mean, my guess would be food and clothes – mostly – and you know – *stuff*.'

For June the room is surprisingly cool.

'I got the place insulated about three months ago. I passed a site where they were in the process of renewing the insulation, so I got the old stuff for free. It works great too. I got it going all around. You can see it on the ceiling. Keeps the heat out in the summer and keeps the cold out in the winter.'

Fabric hangs on most wall surfaces. A huge maroon-coloured duvet cover is draped over the exit. It is splattered with sunflowers of many different sizes and hangs crooked to where it rests on the ramp. The back of the room is split into two levels. A wooden ladder leads to the upper level, which is JR's sleeping area. The lower level serves as a kind of living room. There's a two-seater sofa pushed up against the left wall, mostly covered with dirty clothes and porn magazines. In this living area, two different fabrics have been chosen to add homeliness to the dwelling. On the left wall, behind the sofa, is a seascape fabric. Blue and turquoise waves are littered with fish: yellow fish turn back on themselves; pink fish with blue zigzags swim from left to right. The back wall is covered in a big square of deep-red velvet. It hangs from ceiling to floor like a stage curtain, the row of multi-coloured Christmas lights that run along its top only adding to this impression.

Two pictures – watercolours on card – are pinned to the top of the red velvet wall. The first is of a faceless woman tending a vineyard, the second is a landscape of a pretty European village. Other homely touches include a circular mirror framed in gilded metalwork, a Monopoly board game and a copy of last month's *Playboy*.

Along the right-hand wall are cabinets and shelves. There's a stereo, a stack system with a turntable, two tape decks and a radio. In the middle of the wall there's a plastic shelving unit holding condiments: salt, black pepper, ketchup, mustard, honey, vinegar, oil, peanut butter, hot sauce.

Next to the shelving unit is a large oblong table, stained dark brown. Stacked up on the table are pots and pans, enough to man a small restaurant: six frying pans, four small saucepans, three medium saucepans, two large saucepans and five chopping boards.

There is no free space in the room. All flat surfaces have items stacked on them. The small table next to the sofa holds a lamp, an empty vodka bottle, an ashtray, five light bulbs and a medium-sized indeterminate sculpture. All surfaces hold empty liquor bottles, mostly vodka, but also beer bottles.

'Make yourself at home,' JR tells me after spotting me standing there a little unsurely. He attempts to move some cloths from the sofa, but only clears a small space. 'Sit there,' he says and hands me the *Playboy* magazine.

As a ritual, JR always gathers a few bottles of fresh water from the water fountain in the basketball courts that are en route to the tunnel. Inside his room he has an oversized bucket that catches the dirty water as he washes a pan. He places a bottle of washing-up liquid on the third shelf of the plastic unit.

He swishes the water around with his hand as he sits on his knees. He doesn't move the detritus around or beneath him, and doesn't notice any discomfort as an overloaded plastic shopping bag causes him to sit crookedly at an odd angle. Twisting over his right shoulder, he looks around, then he looks over his left.

'Er ... Er ...'

Finally he sets the pan down on a plastic bag in front of him.

JR's electricity is stolen from a power box that sends electri-city up to the highway. The two-hundred yards of cord needed to feed the power into his lodging was found in skips around building sites.

JR leans over and switches on the stereo.

'What we need now,' he tells me, 'is some rock and roll.'

He presses play on the tape deck and the room is filled with an unimaginable sound. I don't know the band, but I know after the first bar that they are heavy rockers, punching the living daylights out of their guitars and, by the sounds of it, their producer too. The volume is high and the sound bounces off the walls, but this doesn't stop JR from turning the music up even louder. Now it's so loud it's painful to listen to. But JR, who nods his head and plays air guitar, is having so much fun that I don't have the heart to ask him to turn it down.

Instead I scoot down on the sofa and rest my head on the back. Within a minute my eyes start to flutter. My last thought, before I slip into a deep abyss, is, 'Surely I can't fall asleep in this noise?'

But I do exactly that.

# Day 24 – Fear and Loathing in the Eyes of People I Know … and Those I Don't

New Yorkers collectively devote serious time and effort to not looking at homeless people. Pedestrians go to such pains to not look at … no, to not *see* the homeless, that it must be measurable in terms of units of energy. It's incredible to watch. People burn calories under the strain. If you could scoop up all that energy you could run the subway from it.

Why don't people look at the homeless? After all, it's a spectacle, and people are drawn to spectacle. Yet the instinct is to look away. Is it because the homeless are unpredictable, because they might fly into a rage? Partly. But it's more than that: behind this raging, mad person might be someone just like you, someone who once had a job and family. Among the homeless I have met so far, there have been schoolteachers, police officers, a fireman and two bank managers. If homelessness can happen to a bank manager it can pretty much happen to anybody.

New Yorkers know how fragile their existence is and they are constantly reminded of it in the most dramatic ways. They can't look at the homeless because they daren't tempt fate.

Best not to look.

Best to avoid eye contact at all costs.

Many of the articles I have written over the years have been set in New York and in that time I have worked with various newspapers and magazines. I have made friends and acquaintances among photographers, editors, writers, people that I have interviewed and written about, people I have met at parties and in bars and parks – a network of New Yorkers. Some have become good friends, others are people that I hook up with now and again. Some of these people know what I am doing in NYC right now. Some don't.

Take Donald for example. To avoid embarrassing him I will call him Donald. It's as good a name as any.

Finding myself in his neighbourhood I decide to pop over and see if he is around, just to say hello.

Donald stares back at me in trepidation.

What's really interesting about Donald, somebody that I have hung out with on many occasions, is that having explained to him that I am living homeless to research a book, he doesn't know whether to believe me. He knows that I am a writer. He has read my articles. Is what I am doing really implausible?

It isn't from where I am standing, of course. But Donald, judging by the speed with which he leads me away from his apartment (announcing what a lovely day it is), may not entirely believe me.

Now I am agog.

Does he think I am lying? That really I am homeless and have made up this elaborate cover story? I can't quite believe this, but still, it's quite funny.

That is, until the penny drops.

Believing that I am homeless, my friend, Donald, is not going to offer any help: not so much as a shoulder to cry on, a sandwich or some spare change, and certainly not his sofa while I sort myself out. In fact what he is doing is getting me as far away from his neighbourhood as possible. What he'd really like to do is walk me to another state and leave me there. Christ, now I know what John Rambo felt like.

All of a sudden 'agog' is not the right word. But what is? I don't think I have one that conveys what I am feeling right now.

I know that Donald and I aren't great friends. I catch up with him when I am in town – anything from one to five times a year. Of course he owes me nothing. I know this, but it is still rather shocking.

I met Donald through my wife. He is, given his fear and behaviour, stupid enough to ask after her.

What I want to say is: 'She's at home … under platform 8 in Grand Central Station. You should drop by one day. She'd love to see you.' Upset as I now am, I feel that this is what he deserves: 'Hey, bring a six-pack and stay over.'

But I don't say this.

Donald tells me he has been ill. He tells me that because he has been ill he has been out of work. He tells me that because he has been out of work he has no money. He tells me that because he has no money he is on government support. He tells me his apartment is a mess. He tells me that it's full of boxes. He tells me that there are so many boxes, there's barely room for him.

I believe everything Donald is telling me. I just wish he would breathe between sentences, because I am worried that I am going to have to give him CPR.

I can't help but feel hurt and upset. Although, in fairness to Donald, maybe it was dumb of me to turn up. If he has been ill the last thing he needs is an acquaintance turning up and throwing a curve ball into his life. He doesn't know me well enough to understand that I wouldn't turn up on his doorstep asking for help.

Maybe he does believe me. It *is* a beautiful day for a walk. Maybe I am being paranoid.

When I was planning this project I didn't think for one second I would ever have the first clue as to what it is really like to be homeless: just knowing that I could give up this project and walk off the streets any time makes this impossible.

But now and again I feel get a glimpse. It may only last a few seconds, minutes at the most, but when it comes it really hurts.

The Salvation Army mission on 3rd Avenue and 14th Street has turned into one of my regular haunts. The sermon is always entertaining and the food bag generous. It was Jerome that first took me there. He describes it as 'my church', by which he means his church of choice. He sings in the choir, when the choir sings.

Most of the people who attend the church are homeless.

Today, when I enter, there is music playing: piano and drums. But the two instruments don't play together, or, at least, they don't appear to. At the piano sits an elderly lady who looks fragile but still holds her back perfectly straight. She sits high on the stool, looking almost regal, with her bright white hair capturing all the light. The piano sounds hollow. The timing seems to come and go like waves of sanity.

On the drums is a man who is probably in his late forties. His clothing is tinted like an old Charlie Chaplin film – all tones of brown. The rest of the world is in colour, but he has been left behind. His swept-back receding hair is brown and grey, as is his moustache. His drum kit consists of one tom, a snare, a bass drum and a cymbal. Now and again he drops into a funky jazz beat. His face brightens as his shoulders start to feel the rhythm. But as soon as the rhythm joins him for a few seconds it dumps him and goes back to the old lady on the piano. The drums fall off into the sloppy snare while the old lady gets all jaunty and sparkle-eyed. They sound like a wind-up bandstand toy where the instruments are played by pink teddy bears.

Most of the people that enter the church pick up one of the red-bound songbooks from the book cabinet to the right of the doors. Joey and Savage are here tonight. They don't take a songbook though. Joey sits, having long fallen out with God, and blasphemes under his breath. He still can't believe that

God could have done what he did. Savage sits with a notebook and sketches pictures of demons fulfilling demonic tasks.

They don't sing and they don't stand for any of the hymns until eventually I ask them to. I don't believe that God could have done what he did to Joey because I don't believe in God. But the people of this mission, who come in early every day and put food bags together for us, for the hungry to eat, they believe in God, they *really* believe in God. It is for them that I stand.

I don't normally sing, but tonight I join in, the tunes having become familiar by now:

> On Calv'ry's brow my Saviour died,
> 'Twas there my Lord was crucified;
> 'Twas on the cross he bled for me,
> And purchased there my pardon free.
>
> O Calvary! Dark Calvary!
> Where Jesus shed his blood for me;
> O Calvary! Blest Calvary!
> 'Twas there my Saviour died for me.

Once I start to sing I can't stop. I join in with all the hymns and find myself happy and uplifted to take part. I don't bellow out into the room like some people do. I doubt anybody can even hear me. I can hear me though, and that's what is interesting.

> Dark is the night, and cold the wind is blowing,
> Nearer and nearer comes the breakers' roar;
> Where shall I go, or whither fly for refuge?
> Hide me, my Father, till the storm is o'er.
>
> With his loving hand to guide, let the clouds above me
>     roll,
> And the billows in their fury dash around me.
> I can brave the wildest storm, with his glory in my soul,
> I can sing amidst the tempest – Praise the Lord!

Tonight, for the first time, I see the church in a different light. I don't fall deep into a religious stupor. I am still an atheist. But within this church I see a group of people who need God, not so much as a deity to worship or to be judged by, but as a reason to turn up. The church provides them with a place where they can come and be joined with others. Where, by their hopes and beliefs, they can become one voice. When they sing their hymns it isn't so much to God but to each other. It doesn't matter what the belief is, just that they all share and feel it.

The chapel is not big. It is lined with wood paneling, like a courtroom. Sitting up front, facing the congregation, are two bitter-faced women. One, tall and thin with light-grey curly hair and glasses, looks as if she could produce fire. One flare of the nostrils could turn the entire congregation into sun-dried raisins. Her companion looks less dangerous, only because she is shorter and a little fuller in the face. But you can still read her message loud and clear in her eyes. Never before have I seen so much anger and disappointment on a human face. It doesn't sit well with the whole *servant of God* thing. The pair of them look as if they snitch straight back to the highest office. (The one in the fifth row, Lord, who was snorting and giggling, he wasn't listening to your prayer, Lord, he was sketching, in your house, the cousins of the devil himself – may you strike down that little blond head, Lord, and peel back those boyish looks to reveal his rotten and putrid skull!)

This impression is confirmed when the two ladies take the stand and start ranting into the microphone.

'If you continue down your path, if you continue to take in vain the Lord who loves you, the Lord who created you, the Lord who watches over you, that Lord will send you to hell. And in the hell is the almighty fire. But the fearful, and unbelieving, and the abominable, and murderers, and whoremongers, and sorcerers, and idolaters, and all liars, shall have their part in the lake which burneth with fire and brimstone, which is the second death. Revelations 21, Chapter 8.

'And that's the truth. And while that stirs around you, and you call out to the Lord, he will not hear you. It will be too late then. And you will burn for eternity. Now let me tell you a little something about that flame, about that heat, about the sensation of burning in hell ...'

Tonight people give testimonies. They stand one by one and talk of the drink and the drugs and the gutter and the whoring and how one day God had looked down on them and smiled.

'And if you just look up he can save you too, brother!'

Joey says, 'This has got to stop. I can take this shit any more!'

Savage draws another one of the devil's cousins, a bony wretch of a character relaxing in an armchair.

After the men (I have only ever seen one woman in the congregation) have worked themselves up, one of the Salvation harridans stands and says, 'Thank you, Charlie, for sharing,' or, 'Thank you, Edward, for sharing,' or 'Thank you, Stephen, for sharing.' And then, just when I think it is all over, after the women have stared down everybody who hasn't testified, trying to will them through telepathy to stand, a little skeletal man rises and says, 'Let me tell you a thing or two about Jesus' and he starts shaking his tired fists until his body shakes from exhaustion.

'If you can find anything wrong with Jesus, after the service you come over, ask for me, and you show me where he did one sin even ... You couldn't find it. Because he was perfect. He never did a sin ...'

Joey says, 'He's gotta be fucking kidding me.'

Savage says, 'Snort giggle snort giggle.'

The little old man, short and in his late seventies, wearing a suit of matching years, rasps on. 'I believe in the Lord Jesus Christ. I'm not ashamed! I'll stand in front of ... of ... fifty thousand rabbis – the ones with the beards like this ...' Here he raises his right hand and grasps his chin before quickly bringing it down to the middle of his belly to signify beard length. 'I'm not afraid!'

Even the stern-looking lady preachers are giggling now.

This little fist-throwing fart is the only thing between us and our food bags, but nobody minds. And if anybody does, he isn't about to say so.

Because we can see that he isn't afraid.

I had expected to see Jerome in the mission, but he wasn't there. I say goodbye to Joey and Savage, who go off to eat their food bags, and make for Broadway and 20th, Jerome's corner. When I get there he is sitting on the ledge, reading a newspaper.

'Hi, Jerome.'

He looks up at me and mumbles an unhappy hello.

'How have you been?' I ask.

'Good,' he says, without looking up, as I sit down on the ledge.

He seems irritable. He seems irritable with me and I can't fathom why. When I told him about the book project he seemed to think it was a great idea. We talked about it excitedly for an hour.

Maybe I am just being paranoid. Maybe it isn't me. Maybe he just had a bad day.

I ask, 'Is it cool if I crash down here tonight?'

'No, no, no, no, no!' comes his fast and firm answer.

I sit for a few minutes, shocked. I hadn't been expecting this. I had been expecting, 'Sure, crash. So tell me where you've been. What have you been up to?'

After a few minutes, feeling hurt and deeply embarrassed and unable to understand Jerome's change towards me, I get up and walk up Broadway.

'Goodbye, Jerome.' I say.

He doesn't look up. I hear him say, 'Yep.'

I come to a shop. It's one I have known for years from earlier holidays and from the time I lived here: a lighting shop, with a window full to capacity with lamps of different styles.

The shop is closed, permanently.

The doorway isn't wide enough for me to spread out, but still I find some card and lie curled up like a foetus. I look in the window of the closed-down lamp shop and see a sad face look back. What happened between Jerome and me? I visualise him saying, as an add-on to what he actually said, 'No, no, no, no. You can't treat this place like a hotel and come and go as you please.'

Whatever the reason for Jerome's change of heart, I feel hurt and saddened by it. I close my eyes and wish for sleep, hoping that my own light can be switched off, just like the glowing light of Jerome, and the lamps in the shop window that I used to love to stop and stare at.

# Day 25 – Just a Naked Cowboy

It's just about a perfect moment. I am sitting in Central Park, cross-legged on the Great Lawn. I have taken my trainers off. My feet are enjoying what to them feels like a cool breeze. It is the first time they have been free in forty-two hours. To my left, nestling in the grass, is a hot cup of coffee bought from a pretzel stand. In my right hand I hold a book, Paul Auster's *New York Trilogy*, bought for four dollars from a street vendor opposite Washington Park. Wrapped in cling film, though open, is a peanut butter and jelly sandwich that was handed out by Midnight Run the day before. I go back and forth, from coffee to sandwich, at whim.

I am in no rush, as I sit here with my small luxuries, the proceeds of a morning collecting bottles and cans for recycling. A lesson Lisa and JR taught me well.

If I want a sip of coffee I take one. If I want to nibble my sandwich I do so. I could also just gulp the peanut butter and jelly sandwich down if I wanted to. I have another in my bag.

I am in no rush.

It's just about a perfect moment. I miss my wife, but just over there is a girl with the most tremendous legs. I will content myself with those for the moment. I miss my daughter, of course, but here there are kids everywhere and though I can't grab them and throw them up in the air, I superimpose her face onto theirs. I spoke to my wife this morning – called her up and ran down the last of my twenty-dollar phone card.

We spoke about sandals. seven-hundred-and-fifty-kroner sandals, to be exact. U.S. that's $123. For sandals. For my daughter who is one and a half.

I am in no rush.

Here in Central Park I can have it all, as many kids as I like, as many wives, $100 sandals for her, $1,000 sandals for her, why not? The best thing about it, though, is that here in Central Park somebody else pays. I just watch and take the pleasure. I sip my coffee and eat my sandwich. I peer out from behind the *New York Trilogy*, free from burden, free from debating the necessity of $123 sandals for a one-and-a-half-year-old. Those conversations belong to that guy over there, with his wife and three kids and what has to be $1,000 a month in health insurance.

My wife told me that I forgot to pay for my web-hosting before I left. (Something I had been planning to put on standing order for over a year, but somehow never found the two minutes needed to stuff a bill in a pre-paid envelope supplied by my bank.) It's only a six-dollar-a-month bill. I just paid a $50 late fee. My wife told me that my office has been broken into. I am not to worry, the police caught the guy before he made it out into the street. My $3,000 Mac is safe.

Who cares? I don't need it. It's not as if I can plug it into that oak over there.

There's a man to my left practicing Tai Chi. He has passed his sell-by date and is therefore, and quite rightly so, being attacked by a wasp. His movements are slow and whimsical and prove of little use as the wasp continues to dive-bomb his face. He grunts and farts and generally spirals around in a losing battle. It's as good entertainment as I have ever seen on any cable-fed, more than flat, plasma doodah TV. I am in no rush. Why would I be? I can stay here, where my only concerns are warm coffee, peanut butter and jelly sandwiches and reading matter.

This right here feels like a perfect moment.

But then I go and meet up with Nancy and Kim, whose moments are generally less than perfect.

Standing in the central reservation, opposite the Virgin Megastore in Time Square, there's a man wearing nothing but underpants, a cowboy hat, a pair of cowboy boots and an acoustic guitar. His straight blond hair hangs all the way down to his underpants.

He calls himself the Naked Cowboy.

Twenty yards over, on the opposite central reservation, stand Nancy and Kim.

The Naked Cowboy plays his guitar and sings. He sings mainly about being naked and being a cowboy.

Nancy and Kim also have a song that they sing. They sing about disposable cameras, a bargain at five dollars a piece.

Occasionally the Naked Cowboy stops his playing and singing and takes hold of a child that is being offered to him. The parents stand back and take pictures. They slide a dollar bill into the Naked Cowboy's underpants and move away.

Nobody offers Kim or Nancy a child to hold. But that doesn't stop people from trying to slide dollar bills into their underwear.

IIIIIIIIIIII'm a naked cooooowbooooooooooy
*Five dollars, five dollars!*
Just a naked cooooowbooooooooooy
*Disposable cameras*
I'm a
*Five dollar*
Cooooowbooooooooooy
*Get your cameras*
Sure, what's his name?
*Disposable*
Where are you guys from?
*Take your fucking*
Cooooowbooooooooooy

*Hands off me*
Just a
*Asshole*
Cooooowboooooooooy
*Leave us alone*
IIIIIIIIIIIIII'm a naked
*I don't care*
Sure you can take another one
*I don't want a drink*
One two three
*Just leave us alone*
IIIIIIIIIIIII'm a naked cooooowboooooooooy
*Where'd you get*
Naked
*Those cameras?*
Just a
*Oh, fuck me*
Sure, where you from?
Oh, she's cute
Cooooowboooooooooy
*You have two choices*
What's her name?
*You either come and party*
Naked
*With me and my friends*
*Stop pulling at me*
*Or I'm gonna get the cops*
Enjoy your stay
*Pow!*

I am standing to one side, thinking that any second now I will have to step in. If it turns into a fight it will be the first since a silly drunken brawl when I was eighteen. But Kim quickly pops the harasser in the face and runs through the dense pack of tourists with Nancy hot on her heels. I am tempted to run after them, but dither for too long. Instead I watch as the plastic bag containing the cameras gets caught on a passer-by and splits.

Disposable cameras fall to the floor. Nancy tries to grab some, but over her shoulder Kim sees the man she just punched in the face coming after them. He is a middle-aged white man with a sweaty brow and a swelling eye. He is just a little bit angry.

Kim shouts to Nancy, 'Leave them. Come on. Let's get out of here!'

They run into the road and almost double back on themselves as they head in the direction of the Naked Cowboy, banging into his guitar as they pass.

'Easy, ladies … I'm just a naked cooowbooooooy …'

They jump into a yellow cab and yell at the driver.

'Drive!'

Their assailant stands panting among the tourists as he watches the yellow cab drive away. Kim's arm is extended out the window, offering him the finger.

I know that Kim and Nancy have left their bags with a street vendor on the corner of 43rd and so I go there to wait for them. I am expecting a wait of at least an hour, but they turn up only ten minutes later, shouting at each other.

'Hey, Kimmy,' the vendor says when he sees the girls approaching. 'How you doing, baby?'

'Don't ask, OK! It's been a fucked-up day and now we have to head up to the park where we'll be sleeping on a fucking rock tonight.'

He says, 'You know I'll get us a room for the night.'

'Look, Jimmy, I'm not in the mood, OK?'

Jimmy sidles up to Kim. His black wavy slicked hair and gold accessories sparkle in the sun. 'Look, fuck her,' he says, nodding a dark chin at Nancy, speaking quietly so that she can't catch his words. 'Me and you, we'll get a room, some nice food, some wine …'

'Jimmy, fuck you. You're supposed to be a friend.' Kim tries to walk away.

Jimmy says, 'Yo. Wait, come here!' and grabs her by the arm, but Kim yanks herself free.

'No, I won't come here! Fuck you! What kind of friend are

you? Why don't you shut up and go home to your wife and kids, huh?'

'Fuck you, Kim,' says Jimmy, re-tucking his white T-shirt into his black jeans. 'Don't ever come back here!'

'Oh, that's great. A real friend you turn out to be. I'm OK to come round as long as you think there's a chance I might fuck you, but outside of that ...'

'Kim get your shit and get outta here! And don't come back here asking to leave your stuff with me, you ain't welcome here any more.'

'Oh, I'm going!'

Kim drags the holdalls out from under the vendor's table and passes one to Nancy.

'What was all that about?' Nancy asks.

'That?' Kim says, still angry. 'That was just the asshole trying to get me to send you away and for me to go and fuck him in a hotel room all night.'

Flushing red, Nancy drops the bag on the floor and turns, saying, 'That's fucking *it* ...'

'Nancy!' shouts Kim, grabbing her arm.

'No, Kim, fuck him! I'm not gonna let him get away with that shit!'

'Nancy, come on, baby. The day has been hard enough as it is. I just want to go and sit in the park. I can't take any more bullshit today.'

Nancy picks her bag up. 'Yeah, well, the next time he pulls that shit, I'm gonna be there.'

'There won't be a next time.'

'Oh, of course there'll be a next time, Kim ...'

'He won't let us leave our stuff there any more.'

'Oh, that's great! So we have to carry these bags everywhere we go now?'

'Nancy, what do you want me to do?'

Nancy doesn't say anything. She just adjusts the heavy bag on her shoulder and walks along in silence, trying to get through the throng of oncoming people, through the banging elbows and barging shoulders. She seems to be wishing that for once she could be part of the crowd walking the other way. But she is not and this is spelled out only too clearly when she and Kim arrive in Central Park, at their rock, where they bed down, tired from the day's stress, for an early evening nap.

It's still quite early, so I decide to come back to Nancy and Kim in the morning. There's a chance that I'll miss them, but I want to go and see JV. After all, I haven't seen him for five or six days and am in danger of another rebuking.

When I find him he is standing outside Penn Station as the crowds hustle up the steps for an Eric Clapton concert. He is a tad upset. 'Alan, son,' he says. 'Can you give this cracker his miracle and get him to shut up? I can't work with his shouting, people can't hear what I am saying.' I look over. 'This cracker' is a huge white man with a drooping moustache who is shouting continuously: 'Miracle? Miracle? Who's got my miracle?'

I recognise his bulk immediately. It's Gary.

'Miracle? Miracle? Who's got my miracle?'

JV shouts back, 'Yo, if you don't shut the fuck up you gonna get *my miracle*!'

To JV Gary says, 'Take it easy, brother.'

To the world he says, 'Who's got my miracle? Come on, baby. I know you out there! Bring me my miracle.'

# Day 26 – Another Day, Another Dollar

When Nancy awakes it's to the sound of rustling paper. She turns over to find Kim sitting up, in her lap a pile of paperwork from Family Services.

'Morning,' Nancy says, slowly sitting up.

'Hey, babe. I got the whole day worked out. Today is going to be different.'

'Yeah?'

'Listen, it's six now, we'll head down to Penn Station and get a UHO table and do that until one, OK? Then we'll go to my program and I can get fixed. Then, we'll see how much money we've got and we'll make up the rest with cameras. We'll go downtown to get them. Then we need to go down to Family Services to get a certificate stating that we are a couple, that we're recognised as a couple. Remember, the woman said that we need to get that ...'

'Yeah, then what?'

'Then we go back to the EAU and they'll have to take us in together 'cause we'll have the paper.'

'That's gonna take days to sort out.'

'Not necessarily, we could be in a room tonight, you heard what the woman said last time. Plus we'll make our money on the collection bottle and the cameras and tonight we'll be free from all this shit.'

'Do you know where we have to go to get the certificate?'

'Yeah, baby, look, I got all the paperwork right here, you see. I got the paperwork.'

'OK, so let's go. Can we get a coffee on the way?'

'How much do we have left after the cab and the cigarettes?'

'Five dollars.'

'Yeah, we'll share one …' Kim starts to put the paperwork back into the envelope, 'No, bullshit, we're not sharing a coffee. We'll get one each. Today's gonna be different, trust me.'

'I love you, baby.'

'Hey, I love you too, and tonight we'll be in our own room.'

'Come on. Let's go before all the good tables are gone.'

'I'll take that bag.'

'No, I'll take the heavy one.'

'No, come on, baby. Let me do it.'

'No, you'll start feeling sick soon. I've got it. I don't mind anyway.'

'Nancy, I've got it.'

'No, I've got it.'

The girls start giggling at each other.

'Come here, baby!'

Nancy and Kim make thirty-two dollars with the bottle at the UHO table down on 7th Avenue. Kim steals six cameras and sells them in Time Square without incident for five dollars each.

At 4pm they pick up their bags and head down to Family Services.

The subway at this time is packed. Nancy and Kim force their way on with their holdalls. People huff and puff at the inconvenience of luggage. Nancy and Kim do the same.

To a man in dirty overalls holding a toolbox, Kim says, 'If you touch my ass one more time I'm gonna punch you so hard in the face!'

The man smiles.

'You think I'm kidding, you piece of shit? You're wearing a wedding ring, why don't you go and grab your wife's ass?'

A woman standing two feet away, wearing smart clothes and carrying a Louis Vuitton handbag looks Kim up and down with disgust.

At Chambers Street, Nancy and Kim force their way off the subway car with their bags and follow the signs for City Hall.

They have only taken four steps into the building when a man wearing a green blazer and a badge says, 'Hold on! Back up! Where are you going?'

The two girls seem to lose all strength. They stand like beaten boxers who can't find their own corners. They drop their bags. Their arms hang limp. Frustration seeps out of every movement.

'Take a deep breath,' Nancy whispers to Kim.

'We're going to Family Services …'

'They're closed!'

'What? But we called and we were told to come down between three and five and …'

'Closed on Wednesdays!'

'Oh man, why …'

The security guard suddenly senses the depth of their despair. 'I can see you're frustrated. I'm sorry. They really should have told you this when you called them.'

'Are they really closed?' Nancy asks.

'No, really they are. I mean, they're here, but they're closed to the public today. I really can't let you in. But let me get a pen and write the hours down for you so that you have them.'

The security guard walks back to the reception desk and starts writing on a piece of paper.

Returning, he says, 'I know it's a pain, but here, these are the opening hours. They're open tomorrow. Can you come back tomorrow?'

'I guess we'll have to.'

'Do you smoke?'

'What?'

'You want a cigarette?'

'Oh yeah, please.'

The security guard once again walks back to the reception desk where he retrieves a packet of Camels. 'Here, keep the packet.'

'Are you sure? That's really nice of you.'

'Thank you, sir. You're really kind.'

'Sure, don't mention it.'

The security guard walks away.

Outside Nancy and Kim light cigarettes.

'He was a nice guy.'

'Yeah, he was.'

They sit on the floor, leaning up against the building.

'What now?' Nancy asks.

'It's the same old shit. We have sixty-odd bucks and nowhere to stay. I wanted to be able to save this money, make another sixty tomorrow, then that would be a week's rent at the other place. If we could just get in the EAU for a week we could make the rent and the deposit.'

'Yeah, but we didn't get a place, Kim, so what now?'

'We got money and I can't face the rock tonight. I don't want to *see* that rock tonight.'

'Me neither ... Fuck it! Come on then, let's do it!'

The steps are dirty and lit by a fluorescent strip light that makes everything look green. Nancy and Kim climb the steps with their bags hoisted over their shoulders. At the top is a glass partition. Behind it a man sits in a cloud of cigarette smoke. He is dirty and sweaty and doesn't appear to be willing to turn away from the portable TV that sits on the desk in front of him.

'Sir?'

Nothing.

'Sir?'

Nothing.

'SIR?'

'Yeah, gimme a second.' He doesn't look up. He can't look up. Judge Judy is about to pass verdict.

GUILTY!

'Yeah, what can I do for you?' the man asks.

'Basically we got fifty-five dollars and we were told you could take care of us for that.'

'Who sent you here?'

'I can't … do you remember his name?' asks Nancy, turning to Kim.

'No, he was a tall guy with dark hair.'

Nancy turns giggling back to the guy behind the glass. 'A tall guy with dark hair.'

'But you can't remember who it was?'

'No.'

'Please help us. We really need this. We've had such a bad day.'

'I gotchya, I gotchya, let me see …'

Nancy grabs Kim's hand and gives it a gentle but apprehensive squeeze.

Kim squeezes back.

'You got your cash?'

'Yeah, here you go.' Nancy pushes fifty-five dollars through the gap in the glass.

A telephone starts to ring

'Now take this. You know where you're going?'

'No,' both Nancy and Kim say.

'Go up to the third floor, turn right when you come out the elevator, third door on the right.'

'Thank you, sir.'

'Yeah, thank you.'

'You got it. Go knock yourselves out.'

The door is a faded green. Nancy inserts the key that the guy downstairs gave them. Together they tiptoe in, anxious about what they might find inside.

'This isn't so bad,' Nancy says.

'For fifty-five bucks it ain't bad.'

'Does the air conditioner work?'

'Try it.'

The room is filled with the humming of the air conditioning unit. Nancy and Kim jump on the bed and start bouncing up and down, shouting with joy.

When they finally stop Kim says, 'A room with air con and a TV for fifty-five bucks in New York is pretty good. They don't come much cheaper than that.'

'They come prettier,' Nancy laughs. 'But they don't come much cheaper. Let's not leave this room until we have to.'

Kim, looking at the two towels on the bed, says, 'Shower!' and both of them go back to bouncing and screaming.

Forty-five minutes later the girls pad back into the room wearing PJs and with towels wrapped round their heads. I quickly get off the bed where I have been watching MTV on the television.

I would like to shower myself, but I am paranoid – given that every man on the street seems to try and get Nancy and Kim to perform sexual acts – that my request to take a shower will be misconstrued. I know how stupid this is, but the feeling is still there. That, and the fact that, unlike Nancy and Kim, I don't have other clothes to change into. I would still have to put these dirty, horrid jeans back on.

Nancy and Kim cuddle up on the bed while I sit in the only chair. We are watching *Fear Factor*. A woman is having cockroaches poured onto her head.

Turning Nancy's face towards her with her hand Kim asks, 'Why would you even bother?'

Nancy says, 'I don't know, why would you?' Then they kiss for a few minutes, stopping only when the telephone rings.

'Hello?' Nancy holds her hand over the receiver and whispers, 'It's him again.' 'Thank you so much,' she tells the telephone. 'You're so kind. I'll be there in a second.'

Nancy leaves the room.

The guy from reception has been calling Nancy and Kim for the last few hours. He's staying in a room down the hall and has been giving them cigarettes all day. He calls every thirty to forty-five minutes. He would like both of them to go and join him in his room. But Nancy always goes on her own and brings the cigarettes back to their room.

Kim says, 'Hold on, I can't hear her ...' goes to the door and steps out into the grubby hallway. 'Did she go in? The stupid ... Oh, here she comes.'

Nancy gallops into the room.

'Why did you go in there? I told you not to.'

'I just stepped in there quickly ...'

'But don't. You can tell what this guy is like ...'

'But listen, he said, "Hey come in a second." And so I step in and, like, on the table there's, like, loads of crack, and then I look back at him and he's just grinning ...'

'Really? Did he have a lot?'

'He invited us to go get high with him ...'

'Of course he did!' Both the girls start laughing.

'Shall we go?' Nancy asks.

'Nah, not tonight, babe.'

'Why not?'

'Because Alan is here. We're hanging out with Alan.'

'Alan won't mind.' And then realising that I am sitting there Nancy turns to me. 'You don't care, do you? You should just come with us, but don't tell him you're a journalist 'cause he'll piss his pants!'

More laughter.

'Nah. Come on, babe. Let's not.'

'Why?'

''Cause I don't want to expose Alan to that. We don't know this guy. I'm not gonna just take Alan into this crack head's room, you know. If it was just us then we'd only have ourselves to worry about, but I'm not gonna put Alan at risk. Just ... just no, babe.'

'Oh ... you're right.' Turning to me Nancy says, 'Sorry, Alan, that was rude of me.'

I say nothing. I just sit there flabbergasted.

# Day 27 – A Yankee Supper

'Yo, dude, stop playing, stop playing, I got to tell you a story, brother …' says Gary to a man sitting on a bench in Strawberry Fields who is playing 'Miracle Man' on his acoustic guitar.

'Well, you interrupted me mid-song, it better be good, this story of yours.'

'Brother, listen, it's like this. You see that woman over there, tall, blonde, drinking from a McDonald's cup … yeah, that's my girl. We've been together four years … no, that ain't right, it's seven years, six months, no, six years then some months and a week and a few days and some hours. She'll tell you exactly if you ask her. You know where we met?'

'I have no idea where you met.'

'Eric Clapton – 1998 – in The Garden, Pilgrim Tour. I was sitting two seats away, on my own, and she was there with this other couple and I knew she liked me 'cause every time she got up to go on a beer run, when she was passing, she faced towards me, you know what I'm saying, brother …'

'I hear ya, I hear ya.'

'So I knew she was into me right from the get go, OK? After

a while I starts talking to her and we rearrange the seating so we're next to each other and it's going great and she buys me some beer and we get drunk and then we smoke some weed and we get high and it's … we're having fun, you hear me, brother?'

'Oh, I hear ya, I hear ya. You know he played here last week, in The Garden, right?'

'Now what do you have to go and do that for? I'm out here telling my beautiful story and you … Oh, man …'

'Carry on, carry on!'

'*Damn!* So anyway, after the concert she takes me back to her place and we, you know … we been together ever since, excluding when I was in jail and this other time she had a restraining order on me for a while, but even when we're apart we're together, you know what I'm saying?'

'I hear ya …'

'So, as you know, Eric Clapton just played three nights at The Garden and I wanted to take her, you know. It's where we met and so … but I don't have that kind of money. I'm out here every day and I make a bit from my art but, you know, we're homeless. Homeless don't have two to three hundred bucks for Clapton tickets.'

'I hear ya, I hear ya.'

'So I says to her, get dressed, we're going to the Clapton concert, and I just had this feeling, you know, brother? I knew it was meant to be. I didn't doubt it for one second. But Lisa was like, "Oh, come on, Gary, we ain't getting in," and I said, "Trust me, baby, trust in … *the miracle.*"'

'The miracle?'

'*The miracle!* So we goes down to The Garden and I says to Lisa, "You just wait here," and I stand out front shouting, "Miracle, who's got my miracle? I know you're out there, baby. Bring my miracle …" and I'm doing this for like two hours and I start to get frustrated, you know? Nobody's giving me my miracle. But deep down I know, so I don't give up. But then it's like, Clapton is due on stage any time now, and I'm getting annoyed, when this guy steps up and says, "Here you go, buddy, I got your miracle right here."'

'Oh, wow! And he just handed you two tickets?'

'Yep, two tickets. We were sitting next to each other and everything. It was perfect, dude. You know what I'm saying?'

'Oh, I hear ya, man. Beautiful. Was it a good show?'

'Oh, brother, was it good? Was it good?'

'I hear ya, I hear ya.'

'Anyway, I just wanted to tell you that story. You were playing the Miracle Man and, well, that's me, or it was me for one night. Anyway, have yourself a good night, brother, and don't ever be too proud to ask for a miracle.'

'I hear ya.'

I am back at JR's place, sitting on his sofa, reading *Playboy*. JR sits with his head resting on his right knee. His left leg curves out and around the hotplate. On the hotplate there's a frying pan in which several chicken breasts sizzle away. JR sits with a chopping board on his lap. He chops an onion with heavy-handed irregularity, ignoring the little pieces that occasionally dart off at obscure angles. He scrapes the onion into the pan. The sizzling is loud, just like the Yankee game:

> *Swinging a high fly ball into White, jumped on it, Sheffield back to the wall – She's GONE! A two run-homer for Kaz Matsui.*

JR appears to nurture the food as he cooks it. When he turns the chicken pieces he does it gently and calmly. When he adds more oil, it's with a slow fluid motion.

He opens a carton containing a half-eaten mixed salad. He takes a sniff.

'That ain't bad,' he says to himself. 'Hmmmm.'

He looks at the salad for a while, trying to make up his mind. He starts picking out pieces of red pepper and lays them gently in the frying pan.

He says, 'Yeah, there you go.'

He reaches up to one of the shelves on the plastic racking unit and removes a salt shaker.

'… a little salt … now what else do we got up here …'

His eyes flit over the shelves, from label to label, from jar to packet.

His eyes light up.

'Oh, there you are,' he says, picking up a salsa jar. 'Yeah, that should do nicely.'

He twists the lid off the salsa and, out of habit, inserts his nose into the opening.

'Wow, smells good, you got plenty left in you, but still, your days are numbered, buddy. Sorry, but I gotta eat ya!'

He places the open jar to one side and goes back to tending the chicken. Saying, 'Do you know what…?' he reaches up and takes down one of many half-empty bags of pasta. He turns the temperature on the frying pan down low and turns the other hotplate up high. From under a table he takes a pan, gives it a wipe with a T-shirt he finds on the floor, and then starts to fill it with water from a water bottle. He puts it on the hotplate. He has no lid for the pan, so he covers it with another frying pan. It's smaller than the one he cooks with and fits just right when it is upturned.

He freezes.

> Mike Mussiner faced eight hitters in the first inning, he got three runs. Ah, they'll never get him … will they get him with that speed? What a play! Wow, wow, wow!

He picks up a DVD case: *Fresh Jugs*.

He doesn't have a DVD player.

Flipping it over he starts reading the back cover out loud. His shoulders start to rise and fall with quiet, husky laughter: 'Jugs a-plenty!' Join us for a celebration of the biggest, bounciest, most squeezable all-natural fun bags ever to bust out of a bra. Perfect pairs of splendid sweater puppies, saline-free sacks of nature's joy, and swollen mounds of fleshy-soft mammaries stack and pack this collection of melon-loving mayhem. Fresh

jugs is jiggling with juicy jizz-dripping cones, perky nipple licking, tasty tit-tugging, and hardcore fucking and sucking. No
matter what you call those big round soft hangers, we call them
the greatest gift ever to man: 100% ZT Approved Fresh Jugs!
ENJOY!'

He throws it back and selects another.

He laughs louder this time.

Then another, although this one is not so funny.

The moment has passed. He throws the case back and lifts
the frying pan off the water pot.

'You're just about ready for some salt,' he says.

Before pouring any salt in, he twists the shaker around in his
hands, acknowledging that he needs to find some more. Then
he pours the remainder into the pot and replaces the frying
pan.

The slow rattle of a train can be heard approaching in the distance. JR reaches out and turns the radio up.

> *Up the middle ... Matsui gets to it, spins, throws off balance –*
> *a beautiful play to get it ...*

That will be in the highlights reel somewhere! Posada does not
run very well ...

'Ah, come on, Posada!' he says.

There's a hissing sound and JR quickly flips the frying pan off
the water pot before the water boils over.

'Goddamned Yankees, getting their ass kicked and making
the water boil over.'

He pours pasta into the pot and then looks at what's left in
the bag.

'Ah what the heck!' he says and pours in the rest.

From a plastic bag that he has to stand up to reach, JR removes a can of Budweiser and passes it to me. He tends his
chicken, turning the heat back up a little. He flips the peppers
so they don't burn and stirs the onions.

'Damn. Those Mets are really kicking some Yankee butt. Ha ha ha.'

JR starts to cut up the chicken breasts while they still sizzle in the frying pan. He cuts each breast into about four pieces. He mixes everything together: onions, peppers and chicken all sizzle in a group. Then he adds the salsa. The noise is loud. A little smoke cloud wafts up into the air. He stirs the salsa and leans in for a sniff, then removes a pepper pot from the racking unit and unscrews the lid.

'Just a pinch!' he says to himself as he dips his fingers in.

Taking a knife and fork he prepares a mouthful of food as a taster. He makes noises of approval, adds a little more pepper, makes another noise and then prepares another taster for me.

'Mmmmm,' I affirm. We really do make quite the domestic couple.

JR turns his attention to the pasta. He pokes at it with a fork until he manages to harpoon a shell. He tests the consistency with his teeth.

'Ow!'

'A couple more minutes and you'll be done,' he says, and then, turning to the frying pan, 'but *you're* done now,' and he turns the heat off. From under the table he takes a colander and a large pan. He sets the colander inside and sits impatiently waiting for the pasta. He pours the pasta into the colander, transfers it back into its cooking pot and puts the contents of the sizzling frying pan on top of the pasta. With a wooden spoon he stirs it all in.

Sniffs.

JR tips the contents onto two plates and repositions himself with his back up against the sofa, facing the stereo. We sit blowing on our food and listening to the Yankees.

# Day 28 – A Song for Jessie

Joey and I sit alone in Union Square. I have the feeling that he wants to confide something.

'I haven't quite told you the truth about my daughter's death,' he says.

That's fair enough. It's a distressing topic and we haven't really known each other much more than five minutes. But perhaps that's exactly why Joey wants to talk to me.

'I come from Belfast, as you know. My father was … *is* in the IRA. He's doing time over here. All of my brothers too – I mean, they're not doing time, but they're all in the IRA. It's why the grandparents brought me over here. My dad always called me a pussy and a coward because I wouldn't join.'

Joey takes a breath and looks around.

'My dad did some fucked-up things in his life and he's serving time for some of them. When my daughter was killed … it wasn't a robbery, it was a revenge killing. They didn't mean to kill her. They were only supposed to kill me. They fucked that one up. I wish they'd got it right.'

'Who was it?' I demand, more out of shock than anything.

'It was the UFF, you know who they are? The Ulster Freedom

Fighters. My dad had killed the son of one of theirs and so they came after me … And Jessie's dead.'

'Do you ever speak to your dad, or hear from him?'

'I'd like to punch him in the throat, so, no. We don't speak much. I really miss my mum though, I'd like to bring her over, someday I will. When I'm straight. She can't see me like this. I have to get straight first.'

'Your wife obviously knew what … I mean why.'

'Oh, fuck yeah, she knew. That's why she blamed me. She knew it was directly about my family.'

I suddenly feel thoughtless and tactless having talked so much about my own daughter to Joey.

'What? No! Are you kidding me? I kept asking about her. I wanted to hear about her and I could see what she meant to you and I liked hearing about her. It made me remember the good things about Jessie when she was alive instead of just, you know, what happened. Don't be sorry, be glad.'

We sit quietly for a while.

'You know, like, the other day I was remembering how she used to laugh. Her little eyes would sparkle and … She was such a daddy's girl, man. I took her everywhere. That's the stuff I want to remember, you know? Will you come with me somewhere if I want to show you something?'

Immediately I jump to the wrong, morbid, conclusion. I don't want to see this little girl's tombstone. I am scared of how I will react, that I won't be strong and do the right thing for Joey. But the right thing is to try, I guess.

I say, 'Sure, Joey.'

Standing, he says, 'Oh, and my name's not Joey. It's Colm.'

We walk in the tremendous heat along 14th Street. We don't talk. Enough has been said, I guess. We stop abruptly at a large music store and enter. We head straight downstairs, leaving all the glittery rock guitars up on ground level. Joey sits down at a keyboard. He switches the keyboard on, turns it up and starts to play.

'I come down here a lot on my own and play for Jessie,' Joey shouts over the sound of other people playing other instruments. 'I've written several pieces for her. I write them in my head and then I come down here and play them.'

Joey sits there playing, his black ponytail wobbling every now and again with the subtle movement of his head. His sandalled feet work away gently at imaginary pedals.

I'll never know whether this new version of how Jessie died is the true one. Perhaps there are even other versions. Nonetheless, although I am standing to the other side of Joey, I can still picture the scar where the bullet entered his mouth, shattering bone and teeth before leaving him to kill his daughter. I want to cry and hug him. I want to go home to my own daughter. Yet I do none of these things. I just stand there, listening.

Between the drumbeats and squealing of the other electronic sound machines, I hear a beautiful ballad. It's always startling when somebody sits at an instrument they have completely mastered, having never before spoken of music. But every few bars the noise around us invades the moment. I can't believe this is where Joey comes to honour his daughter, a music shop in the middle of New York City. So much noise and interference, and buried beneath it all, a ballad.

A kid over to our right is making an awful racket with a box of switches and dials. I want to say it myself, but of course Joey beats me to it.

'Yo, dude, can you shut the fuck up with that noise? I'm trying to hear this keyboard!'

The kid groans something unintelligible and leaves the store.

Joey turns back to the keyboard.

He plays songs for Jessie.

# Day 29 – Don't Forget Behind the Ears

Washing would be a much pleasanter experience if I'd had the brains to pack a hand towel. I like washing. I don't like dirt. I don't like touching dirty things. I always knew this would be a problem with this project.

My wife finds it funny that I soap behind my ears. But I know I can't be alone. In fact, until she brought it up and started mentioning it at dinner parties, I thought everybody soaped behind their ears.

She recently told me that she has never seen anybody soap and scrub their genitals the way I do.

To which I thought, I should hope not, you're *my* bloody wife.

I haven't soaped behind my ears or my balls in … it tickles and shames me to say, over a week. I came to this realisation with a start. It's easy to forget when you live in exhaustion and fear.

I am relatively clean. I have been rinsing my face and body every day and brushing my teeth like a good boy. Still, there are three main areas of concern. Behind the ears, my groin and my feet. The ears of course aren't so much of a problem. It's just a bit greasy back there is all. The ears can be easily tended to.

The feet, well, I have avoided dealing with them because at the end of the day, once I clean them I have to put a very soiled pair of socks back on, plus they hurt like hell. Then of course there's the groin, an area I have tried my damnedest not to think about.

I just don't have what it takes to walk into an open public toilet, stand in front of a sink, strip down and start washing myself. One day maybe, but it certainly won't happen in thirty-one days. I am just too private about such things. I need a closed door.

I *am* in a public toilet, but not an open, multi-stalled one. It's a single room with toilet and sink. I want to tell you exactly where I am, but, for fear of putting New Yorkers off their coffee for life, I shall keep it to myself. Also, I risk devaluing a brand, several lawsuits and a life where every cent I earn belongs to somebody else. At best I am breaking a dozen health codes.

I scrape paper towels round the backs of my ears, removing all the surface grease before slathering them with soap from the dispenser.

It feels goooooood.

I do my feet next. They are black, but mostly this is cotton embedded in my skin from my rotting socks. The other socks in my bag, though soiled, are in a much better state than these, so I deposit the rotting socks in the bin provided.

I block up the sink with wet paper towels and run some warm water. My feet are continually sore from not getting enough time out of my trainers, so when I do manage to get my right foot up and in the sink, the warm water stings sharply. I am surprised by how much it hurts, and ooh and ahh as I soap my foot.

I need to be quick in case somebody tries to come in. It's 7am, but still.

I go through the same procedure with my left foot.

There's a hideous smell in the air now – it's not just sour but somehow putrid – and I feel bad for the person who will follow me. But now comes the part I have been dreading.

After rinsing the sink I fill it again with fresh warm water. I sense that I am resigning myself to a big task.

Up to this point I have had my jeans on, just in case I have needed to leave quickly. I take them off and they are so dirty I can stand them in the corner. I take my boxer shorts off.

I am not tall, very average in height actually – short, if the truth be known – so to get my balls and penis into the sink, I have to rise up on tiptoe.

Instant pleasure.

I was once told a story by a gay friend – a New Yorker. He told me that English gay people are weird, or, at least, into fetish. He told me about a night when he picked somebody up in London. He went back to this guy's apartment and when they got there his new-found friend ran a bath, sat in it and demanded to have water splashed over him until he came.

Rather odd, I agreed at the time.

But as I stand here now, balls and cock immersed in this lovely warm water, the first warm water they have experienced in a while, I understand what that guy had been driving at. I don't start splashing myself, but I do acknowledge the desire to do so.

I set about the ghastly task of pulling back my foreskin. I don't look at what I am doing. I look at the ceiling because just imagining the deprivation of my penis sends shivers of repulsion down my spine. Disgusted, I quickly empty the sink, soap my hands and refill it. This time I soap my balls and penis and quickly find myself getting an erection, which I don't mind as it makes the task of washing that much easier.

For a second I think about masturbating.

I am masturbating. Celebrating as much as anything the fact that in all this time nobody else has tried to use the bathroom.

I come into the toilet, flush, wash my penis again, clean the sink with soap and get dressed as quickly as I can. I put on boxer shorts and socks taken from my rucksack; they are dirty but feel cleaner by having not been worn for a while. It's my jeans that surprise me most. Of all the clothes I have to put on it's my jeans I am most repulsed by.

I do a round of the bathroom, mopping up the floor with paper towels and wiping the sink again. Then I hobble out, my feet hurting a lot more for having been washed. But I don't care, I feel somewhat clean. This isn't the worst start I have had to a day.

The girl behind the counter gives a moody, unimpressed look.

I smile back and head out into the street.

I sit myself down on a fire hydrant and lean against the wall. I am spent now, and I find myself drifting in and out of sleep.

I wake up. A man in a really awful condition stands there, his denim shirt covered in vomit, wavering as he struggles with balance. He says his name is Dean.

### Dean's Rap

Where's the subway?
Over there?
Where am I?
I'm in Brooklyn, right?
Manhattan?
That can't be
When I went to sleep I was in Brooklyn
How'd I get here?
It don't matter
You English?
The Beatles were English
Liverpool
You from Liverpool?
Where?
The 'Bottom' of England
HUH!

Lovely Rita Meter Maid
She look like a military man
With that thing on her back
Lovely Rita
I had a friend who loved the Beatles
In the jungle
He used to play the Beatles
In the jungle
No, no, no, not tape
Records!
Records!
On the turn thing
Yeah, in the jungle
I was a medic
196 Light Infantry
You got a cigarette?
You believe in God?
That don't matter
You a nice fella
Better than me
They tell me I'm like a dog
I ain't no better than a dog
If you don't believe in God
Where do you think all this fucking
STUFF
Came from?
Look at it
Stuff fucking everywhere
I like the baseball
You like the ball game?
I like DiMaggio
He was good
And he could pitch like a motherfucker too
And he play good outfield
I never see England
The White Album

Out there in the jungle
They all dead now
Where the toilets?
I need to change my clothes
I … I … I can't go around like this
You like Frank Sinatra?
I had an Irish friend once
He hated him
We went to a place up on 57th
There was this poster
FRANK SINATRA
And he rip it up
And punch it
I says
Eh, whassamatta wi ya
He says
*ITALIAN!*
*ITALIAN!*
Wassat gotta do with anything?
I asks him
He says
Italy is near to Africa
So what, I says
Some of the best people in the world
Come from Africa
Maybe I go to Rockaway today
See my friend James
James Martin
He a rapist
A rapist
Used to be anyhow
Used to rape old ladies
He younger than me
But he always liked the old ones
I like the young'ns myself
I don't need this

What do I need this for?
What a thing to be drinking, eh?
Fucking Listerine
But I ain't gonna kill myself
That's the only thing I don't believe in
I ain't doing that
I didn't even attend my mother's funeral
Or the wake
That's the kind of bastard I am
Too drunk!
Ah, Denver?
I don't like basketball
Bim
Bim
Bim
Bim
Bim
Bim
Fruff
We got an atheist over here
Don't matter none
I a believer
But he's a better person than me
Get that, he don't have a God
But he still better than me
I didn't play baseball
My father left me
Thanks, *Pop*!
He said to me
There ain't no good
You ain't no good
When you're dead
'Cause when you're dead
You're dead!
Wonder where he is now?
I know he's dead

Maybe in paradise
Or maybe what?
Fucking …
Fucking …
Purgatory
I hope he's dead
But I don't believe they're dead
No sir
They live for ever
The sister hit me
Smacked me right across the face
I says to her
You think Jesus woulda hit me?
So she hit me again
Sometimes they hit me with sticks
But the sister
What she gonna do, she only five one?
And she's wearing all that
Shit
What can she do?
She can't hurt me
Not no more
I don't need this
Fucking Listerine
Don't need it

Dean disappears down the street, but just as one madman leaves another one turns up on the scene. Suddenly a big bear of a black man is standing in front of me.

'Yo, son. You OK?'

'Yeah, I'm OK,' I tell him.

'When was the last time you ate?' he asks.

'Yesterday,' I say.

'How much money you got?'

'About eight cents, but I'm OK. I'm going to head up to the Holy Apostles in a while.'

'Fuck the Holy Apostles. Here. Here's twenty bucks.'

The man opens his left hand. Compressed in there is a wedge of twenty-dollar bills. He peels one off and hands it to me.

'Take a walk with me,' he says. 'I just gotta get me some liquor from the corner here.'

In the store he orders half a pint of vodka and then tells me to pay for it. I hand over the twenty that he gave me. The cashier holds out the change to me, but he steps in and takes it. Then as we walk away he says, 'Oh here, my man, that was very kind of you to buy my drink for me. Here, take this!' And waving it around in the air for everybody to see he hands me another twenty.

We walk back around the corner to the Toys 'R' Us.

'I need to get bubbles for my gun!'

From his shorts he removes a battery-operated bubble gun with a Disney character at the front. When you pull the trigger bubbles fire out of Goofy's mouth.

Back out on the street, the man, whose name is Steve, stands in the middle of the crossing shooting passers-by with bubbles.

He warns them, 'I am a Green motherfucking Beret. Do not fuck with me, people, 'cause I blow you away with my bubbles. Yeah, you can run, son. I'm a fucking Marine. I get you when you're sleeping, motherfucker!'

I don't have the energy for this and as soon as a moment presents itself, I slip away.

I find Joey and Savage and tell them about the strange guy who woke me up and gave me twenty dollars.

'Probably robbed somebody down the block, snort giggle,' says Savage.

This makes me freeze, and Savage notices.

'Hey, don't worry about it. It ain't like you're gonna find them and give them their money back.'

'If you got a problem with it, I'll take it!' laughs Joey.

We save the twenty dollars until later that evening, for our own little 4 July celebration. We don't go to the 3rd Avenue mission for food, instead we go to Pronto, a cheap pizza parlour that also has a cheap Chinese takeaway in the back. I order special fried rice while Joey and Savage order vegetarian dishes with tofu and broccoli. Then we pop round to a deli on University Place and buy a bottle of cheap Chardonnay and three paper cups.

'Where shall we go now?' I ask.

'We should get up on one of those buildings and watch the fireworks,' says Joey.

'That sounds cool. What about this one here?' asks Savage.

'How are we going to get up there? The guard is right there.' I ask.

'Just follow me,' says Savage as he goes in.

To the guard, he says, 'Hey, how's it going? We're going up to a party on twenty-one.'

'OK, just sign in here.'

We all sign in under various names. Joey and I are too quiet so Savage fills in the dead sound by asking the security guard if many people have turned up.

'Nah, you're the first.'

'Coooool,' says Savage. 'We'll get the best seats.'

We jump in the elevator and select the twenty-first floor.'

'Oh man, 'says Joey,' that was too easy.'

I say, 'I can't believe we got away with that.' knowing in fact that *we* didn't. Savage did. It's the kind of thing I would never do on my own.

'We didn't get away with anything,' Savage responds. 'He knows what we're doing. He just don't give a fuck.'

Still, we do get off on the twenty-first floor and walk the last four floors. When we reach the exit to the roof Savage takes out a pencil from his jacket and wedges it in the door jamb so that we won't get locked out.

'Probably doesn't lock, but I don't want to find out the hard way!'

The view from the roof is fantastic. From the north side we can look down directly over Union Square and up into the city.

The fireworks are over on the East River and start up almost as soon as we get there. It's the usual fanfare of exploding balls of red, white and blue – the things that we have all been disappointed with before, yet somehow always look forward to every year.

Joey takes the wine and smashes the top of the bottle against a wall, which seems somehow more symbolic of our 4 July. He pours wine into all three cups.

'Remember to check for glass before you drink it down.'

The three of us stand there eating our barely warm Chinese food and drinking wine, grateful to the Green Beret madman with his fistful of dollars, regardless of how he came by them.

We can look down on other rooftops where people are also out watching the fireworks. We can see into apartments where large groups are crammed into small windows. We are higher and have a better view than all of them. A small triumph, but with a belly full with Chinese food and wine, it feels much bigger.

'Are we gonna go back down to the park?' Joey asks once the fireworks have ceased.

'Nah, I don't think so, at least I'm not. Why spoil a nice evening? I'm thinking of just going to sleep.'

'Where?'

'Right here, in fact.'

'You serious?' Joey asks.

'Yeah, why not, it's safe. I was gonna see if that hut was open 'cause it looks like it might rain.' He nods in the direction of a white Portakabin.

Savage walks over and tries the door ... it's open.

He looks back at Joey and me. 'I'm sleeping here, there's plenty of space if you don't want to sleep at Cooper tonight.'

Joey and I go over.

The hut is empty, for the most part. Metal shelving units line the walls, but the shelves themselves are empty, apart from one single roll of packing tape.

We each select a patch on the floor, all doing our best to keep our heads away from each other's feet. We lay our blankets down on the hard floor. We lay our bodies down on the hard blankets.

I say, 'Good night.'

Joey says, 'Don't let the bed bugs bite.'

Savage snorts and giggles.

# Day 30 – Man and Trolley

It's market day in Union Square. People sit at tables selling paintings, photographs and crafts, and there, at last, is the trolley with the flags. Once again it is loaded with black bin-bags. I ask some people if they know who the trolley belongs to.

'That guy is a total asshole,' comes the first reply. 'Stay away from him!'

'You don't want to meet that guy,' comes the second reply. 'Trust me!'

Before I ask anybody else, I see him for myself. He is a black man in his mid to late fifties with a grey curly beard and glasses. His wears jeans and a Day-Glo orange workman's bib that are dark with grime and dirt. He looks livid and moves angrily. Whenever he finds a can or bottle he drops in into a big black bag. When I say the bag is big, if he is 5 foot7, the bag itself is 5 foot. He fills the bag to the very top, leaving just enough space to tie a knot. He appears oblivious to all those around him. He is like a machine, unrelenting. His expression is irate, tight. He looks ready to trample anybody that gets in his way.

Is this a man to speak to about canning? I have already canned with JR and Lisa. Is there any more to know?

The thing with this man here is that he just doesn't seem approachable. Which is exactly why I must approach him. Also he is canning in a different way. He is not canning until he has enough for some beers, he is canning until he can't carry any more.

But should I just present myself now or wait until he has finished collecting cans?

Still I wait.

He takes his beaten baseball cap off and finishes his drink. Taking a little look around the park, he walks over to the trolley, which contains three more gigantic bags, all bulging to capacity. He removes the bags from the trolley one by one.

He attaches one bag to another by tying rope to each of the bag's knots, and then does the same to the other two bags. Once they are secure he takes two bags, placing the rope over his right shoulder, and walks them to the entrance of the Union Square subway. He comes back to the trolley and picks up the other two bags, then walks them to the entrance of the subway. But this time he doesn't stop, he takes them down the steps and walks them over to the service gate that is twenty yards in. He climbs back up, collects the other two bags and signals for the attendant in the booth to open the gate.

Click.

He slides all four bags inside the gate so that it can be closed. Then he throws two bags on his shoulder and walks them fifty yards, through rush hour commuter traffic, to the top of the stairs that lead down to the 5 train.

He goes back.

Comes back.

Down.

Up.

He walks the bags, two at a time, to the far end of the platform and stands waiting for the train.

This seems like as good a time as any to introduce myself.

After the usual explanations – homeless, England, book, etc. –
'Alan.'

'Preston.'

Preston speaks to me.

He says, 'I been doing this fifteen years, you know why?'

'No.'

'America is the land of the poor. Home of the idiot. This is
what I have to do to put food in my belly 'cause the *white* man
has had his foot on the neck of the black man for ever. But not
me, *you* try to tread me down and I'll put you on your back! If
*you* try to talk down to me I'm gonna put *you* on *your* back! If
*you're* gonna come to me you better come as you. White people
treat the black man like shit.'

He says, 'I do this 'cause I ain't gonna play *your* white man
game no more!'

And, 'I ain't gonna be treated as second class and fight my
brothers for the little tidbits of life the white man throws our
way every now and again.'

And, 'I ain't gonna fight my brothers and sisters the way the
white man wants me to.'

And, 'I got my own way of surviving.'

And, 'I don't need *you!*'

Preston speaks like this while we ride the 5 train all the way
from Union Square to 149th Street. It is hard to take everything
in. I get the impression that he hasn't spoken to anybody in a
while. When the train doors open at 149th Street he jumps off
with two of the bags. I follow with the other two.

'Well, what are you doing now?' he asks when he sees me with
the bags over my shoulder.

'Well, I'm here now,' I say. 'Why don't I just help you with
these?'

He says, 'You wanna try it? Well, OK, let's go.'

Off we go, Preston leading the way, me five paces behind.
There's an elevator at this station that takes us straight up to
street level. Outside we turn left and walk back on ourselves
along a road overflowing with people who stop at vending stalls

for batteries, belts and socks. People march up and down with thin transparent plastic bags that look as if they will split and break. There are mothers with litters of children hanging off them and fathers selling knick-knacks from foldaway tables. Dollar stores. Drug stores. Five-T-shirts-for-ten-dollars stores. We cross, turn right, cut between a police car and a postal van and start walking away from the throng and up a hill via a side street.

We keep walking. Now and again Preston turns around and asks if I am OK.

The bags are heavy – really heavy. Manageable, but heavy. I'm thirty and in reasonable health. This is the first thing I've lifted in weeks, maybe even months.

It is manageable, but for how long? What does this weight feel like to Preston, who does this 'job' four days a week, every week of the year? What do these bags feel like to a 63 year-old man?

'OK, let's rest up a minute,' says Preston halfway up the incline. 'It ain't far now.'

We walk for maybe another five minutes.

We turn a corner.

Along the outside wall of a supermarket there are ten recycling machines. Some take bottles of one size, some take bottles of another, and the rest take cans.

In front of these machines stand a collection of human beings that you might expect to see on an envelope for the Red Cross, a collection of people so thin and drawn it is deplorable. There are men, magically held up by thin wiry frames and then thrown off balance by swollen bellies, and women dressed in rags, in T-shirts that are too small and full of holes. They stand in shoes that are falling apart.

Not only is every machine in use, with two supermarket employees manning the machines and fixing jams, but every machine has a queue of people waiting to use it. Carts and bags full of collected cans and bottles sit in rows, their owners sitting on top of them.

'Sir?' asks a woman desperately to a man at the front of a

queue. 'Please can I go in front of you? I've only got a small bag and I need to get diapers for my baby.'

The man, although shaking his head, tells her to 'Go ahead.'

What is he shaking his head at? The inconvenience or the desperation? Best not to ask, I wouldn't understand. But could it really be that this woman left her house with the sole purpose of collecting enough cans so she could buy diapers for her child?

No, it's easier to think that she lied, that really she's going to buy half a pint of tequila.

I follow her into the store.

She buys diapers.

She takes them to the checkout, hands over her printed credit note and receives no change. She leaves and I make no attempt to talk to her, to find out about her life. What could I tell her? That I am writing a book about it?

Bully for me.

This is the most desperate gathering of people I've ever laid eyes on.

They are in New York, struggling and fighting for food.

Preston says, 'This is America's slave labour force. This country is run on slave labour, even right down to this here, canning. We get five cents a can. What do you think the supermarket gets per can? Who else is gonna do this for five cents a can? The fucking hungry, that's who.'

He says, 'Yeah, I saw your face on the train, you thought I was full of shit. You thought racism was a part of history. But tell me, who's the only white person standing here?'

I look around.

'I am,' I say.

It is hard for Preston, who comes here daily, to grasp my shock. He leaves his bags in the queue and takes me over to the deli where he buys me an iced tea.

'In your weeks living on the street, how many Vietnam vets did you meet that were homeless?' he asks.

I confess the number is high.

'They take the lives of these young boys and when they can no longer function, when the atrocities that they had to witness and commit in war for their country breaks them down mentally, this country turns its back on them. Their own country leaves them hungry on the street, calls them names, "filthy", "animal", "nigger", "boy", "bum!" The black man is good enough to die face down in the mud for his country. But he ain't good enough that he can get a decent job, a yellow cab, a safe place to sleep after he gave his youth to this here USA!'

Back in the supermarket I stand next to Preston while he slot cans and bottles into the machines. Almost fatherly he says, 'You wanna try?'

I find myself thinking: there's a hole with a spinning belt, what is there to try? But I take the bottles anyway and feed them in. The machine just keeps sucking. Whether there is a bottle there or not. It just keeps sucking.

After five bottles Preston steps back in and takes over.

'I don't expect you to do them. I just wanted to see if you got it.'

I don't think he is referring to recycling.

## Day 31 – So Long and Thanks for all the Filth

Itry to say goodbye to as many people as I can on my last day, even though part of me worries that it might be wrong for me to wave goodbye as I head back to my own comfortable and privileged life. But I think it would be worse still to have made all these friends and to then just slip off as if it has all been a one night stand that I regret the following morning.

The last people I manage to track down are Kim and Nancy.

Kim goes into a store to steal cameras. I sit outside with Nancy. She starts to tell me about her life back home, before prison, before Kim. She tells me about how much she loves Kim.

'But I'm still *in* love with my fiancé,' she says.

'Fiancé?' I splutter.

'Yeah, fiancé. He's at home in Miami. Oh God, Alan, it's just such a mess. He and I both got prison sentences together and he served his sentence back home and I got sent up here where I met Kim.'

'Does he know about Kim?'

'Oh yeah, I've never lied to him or her. Even when we both

got sentenced he said to me, you know, "Have some fun, baby, while you're in there." So he's totally cool about it.'

'Except?'

'Except he got out two days ago and I want to go home to be with him. I'm in love with him. I need to be with him. I'm not meaning to string Kim along. Really I'm not. I really do love her so much. But the last time I told her I was going home she tried to jump out the sixth-floor hotel window. It was all I could do to hold her back. She made me promise never to leave her because she'd kill herself if I did.'

'Oh shit, Kim, that's … that's …'

'I never intended to stay. But she got out a week before me and when I got out she came and picked me up and she had like 1,700 bucks and she just kept spending it. She bought me a necklace and a bracelet and we stayed in hotels and ate in restaurants and got high. We just kept partying.'

'Then the money ran out?'

'Yeah, and then I couldn't leave 'cause like, we'd spent all her money and now she was on the street … Well, that's not true. She's allowed to stay at her mom's place, but I'm not. That's why we're on the street. So we can be together.'

'But … *you* don't want to be together!'

'What can I do? What if she kills herself? But I can't go on like this, sleeping on a rock! I want to go home, to my family, to my fiancé.'

We sit in silence.

I want to look at Nancy but I am scared that she might be crying, scared because I don't understand any of this and, if she is crying, I don't know how to comfort her.

'What am I gonna do? I was supposed to take a flight two days ago. I still have a ticket waiting for me at JFK.'

'I have no idea, Nancy, really I don't. I guess … I guess …'

'She could just come with me if she … No, that wouldn't work, if I go back I'm going back to him.'

There's a pause.

'I'm going to be gone by the end of next week.'

'Shit, Nancy, you really need to pick your moment well, and the place. Don't go telling her in any sixth-floor hotel rooms or when she's high or about to get high or … Are there no friends you can call so that they can be there?'

'No.'

'Do you think she knows?'

'Maybe. I mean, she knew I wanted to leave because I told her I was going back home to my fiancé. That's when she went mad and tried to kill herself. I could just go right now, I mean like, *right now*. But I love her and I can't do that to her.'

Then Nancy says, 'Shhh! Here she comes. Promise you won't tell?'

# Epilogue

I was in New York for another two months after I came off the streets and I stayed in touch with many of my friends from the homeless project. A lot of them didn't recognise me at first sight, what with my clean-shaven face and shortly trimmed hair. JV and Remy were the easiest to find. Whenever I was wondering what they were up to I just went to Penn Station. It was a moving sight to watch their faces brighten when I approached them one day with my daughter in her buggy. You could see the joy they got from telling my wife stories of what a vulnerable little fellow I had been and how they had to take me under their wings and protect me. They told her of a homeless black woman in her fifties who had all but fallen in love with me. She followed me up and down and wanted to find places where we could cuddle up for the night. JV and Remy were clinging to each other with laughter as they recounted the story.

I bumped into Lisa while she was canning in Central Park, again with my wife and daughter. We spoke for a few minutes, then Lisa burst into tears.

She said, 'I'm not sad. I'm just so happy to see you with your family, you're all so beautiful.'

Savage, I heard, went back to South Carolina and moved back into the apartment that had been sitting paid for and vacant the entire time he had lived on the streets of New York. I saw Joey again in Union Square. I was with my wife and daughter and felt a pang of guilt for being back in my normal life, surrounded by love. Joey of course brushed it to one side. Then I saw him again a month later, long after my wife and daughter had gone back home. He was drinking a five-dollar concoction from Starbucks and had an SLR camera slung over his shoulder. He had met a girl, Erin. They were living in a short-term lease studio flat just off Central Park, the Upper bloody West Side! When Joey asked me where I was staying and I told him that I was heading out of town as I had outstayed my welcome on a friend's sofa, he offered in a flash to let me stay. At this point I had just ten days left until my flight back to Copenhagen, and I slept on Joey and Erin's sofa until two days before my flight. I was so overjoyed by the turn of events, to be staying as Joey and Erin's guest, I never once considered checking into a hotel. I rarely saw Joey again without either a Guinness or one of those five-dollar concoctions he had grown so fond of.

I don't know what the financial situation was with Joey and Erin. Even though Joey hadn't found a job they signed a new lease together for a two-bed apartment in Brooklyn. We all went to the storage house in downtown Manhattan to collect Erin's furniture and possessions. We spent the afternoon cleaning and scrubbing and mopping up the new apartment that looked as if it had been squatted in. At least, Erin and I did the cleaning. Joey sat on the futon, rolling joints.

Preston, my beautiful angry black man who blew away my naivety in a single hour, took me to where he lived. Since an accident with one of his bungee cords had left him needing eye surgery, he had been living in what is called an 'SRO', single room occupancy. We sat on his bed while looking at pictures of each other's children. Whenever I think of Preston now I don't see the angry black man, I see the grandfather who giggled while he told me about one of his granddaughters, who had called him asking for pocket money.

I did bump into JR again, as he was coming out of the OTB. We shook hands and laughed and joked on the street. He asked how the family were and told me I knew where to find him if I ever needed a place to stay.

I had one more thing I wanted to do before I left New York. I wanted to go to Westside Park, to the Freedom Tunnel, and just sit and wait and watch. Knowing that V was still living in the tunnel meant I couldn't just leave. Again and again I had looked for her, but I never had any luck. I had to give myself one last chance. Otherwise I knew that I would always be wondering what had happened to her. So the day before my flight home I did exactly that; I sat and waited and watched for hours and hours.

Three young girls, aged maybe six, eight and eleven, stand with bare feet, digging their toes into the wet sand. They have already enjoyed the giggles that come with flicking sand at each other as well as at their mother, who stands off to the side, watching. Now the three girls stand in a row. The eldest, wearing a white and blue polka dot dress, with long dark hair, takes the lead. Her two younger sisters, one in denim dungarees, the other in black leggings and a pink vest, step to their sister's command and on the count of three they all flick sand over the fence and into the junior baseball pen in front of them.

In the pen a young boy aged six stands poised. His baseball bat is held at forty-five degrees to the horizon. His mind no doubt dreams of the almighty cracking sound that will come from his bat striking the baseball, which is about to be thrown by his father. His enthusiasm doesn't appear thwarted when he hears the clank of the ball hitting the caged fence behind him. Instead he remains coiled, ready for the next pitch. His orange Mets T-shirt shines brightly in the afternoon sun. He wears the number 25, probably hoping to emulate Matsui, his Mets hero, and, the boy takes another swing. Once again the ball falls to a clanking halt behind him. Another pitch and this time the baseball whizzes past the wayward bat and skims the nose of a Mexican who is passing his time walking laps of the baseball pen. His name is Raul. He is homeless and he has just completed his thirteenth lap.

Raul marches on, unfazed by the baseball. He looks at the ground as if searching for pennies that will bring him luck. Although the sun is high in the sky and beating down a tremendous heat, Raul walks with the hood of his green sweat top pulled over his head and tied tight beneath his chin. His hands are buried deep into the sweatshirt's pockets.

'No, no, no,' begins the father emphatically. 'You need to coil. Don't hit the ball with your arms. Unwind the body as you swing, that's where the power comes from. Now try again.' The irritation the father suffers at his son's inability to hit home runs with a bat twice his size floats across the pen. But it doesn't seem to affect Raul. Maybe the words don't even make it into his head. He is indifferent to the world around him.

The father for his part also pays little heed to Raul. He does not think to hold his pitch back as Raul, now on lap fourteen, walks once again behind the batting plate. He does not think to lower his voice or soften his rebukes when it is clear that Raul, if he were interested, could hear every word.

'Why don't you listen to me? Hold the bat higher, watch the ball and when you want to strike, uncoil!' The father offers an empty-handed demonstration. 'Like this!' he says, swinging his belly as he demonstrates.

Raul removes his own baseball from the pocket of his sweatshirt. He kicks it along the ground in front of him as he walks round. The father and the boy don't appear to notice this, or at least they don't acknowledge it. Likewise, Raul does not acknowledge the loud crack as he passes once again by the batting plate.

'Whoa!' the boy cries as the baseball that he just struck soars high into the air, over his father's head and on to clear the fence lining the pen. The ball disappears into the long grass. The boy's eyes are wide and sparkling, his body still numbed by the sensation of the ball striking the bat. So that's what it feels like to hit a home run? For a split second the boy is Matsui; in this moment he is not wearing another man's jersey, the jersey is his and he has just hit a winner for the Mets. The imaginary cheering and clapping from the fans registers on the boy's expression, but only for a split second.

'That was better. Go and find the ball.' The father lights a cigarette and Raul begins another lap.

The boy follows the path of his ball. He can't help a glance at the Mexican as their paths near. The peak on his baseball cap, made in size for the same person as the baseball bat, obscures his view and so he tips his head back so that he can see the Mexican in his entirety.

'Hurry up!' cries the father and the boy drops his head and scurries on.

It takes a few minutes for the boy to find his ball. By the time he rounds the fence and enters back into the baseball pen he and the Mexican are once again on a collision path. The Mexican does not acknowledge the presence of the young baseball player and the young baseball player, no doubt having learnt the lesson, does not acknowledge the Mexican. They pass each other like a pair of lepers, neither one wanting to see the markings of the other.

Imagine my surprise, at this moment in time, as I turn my head and I see V.

She must have actually walked past me.

She strides along in her stripy blue cotton combat pants, dark grey and blue sweatshirt, gold lamé headscarf, NY baseball cap and a pair of enormous sunglasses.

She is moving from trashcan to trashcan. Even her black bag is worn and frayed.

I run after her.

'Yes, I remember you. Of course. How are you?'

'I'm good, how are you keeping?'

'Yes, well. Did you see what they do with my dance floor? They have … how do you say? Smash it and so I don't dance any more.'

'I saw. Who smashed it up?'

'Some assholes! They take the wood and make a hut with it!'

'Can you not make another one?'

'What, so they can do it again? Why are you here anyway? Are you no longer in Denmark with your wife?'

I tell her about the book. I am ready to cancel my flight.

'But you must not live on the street. It is no good for your morale. You must get off.'

'But it was only research for a book …'

'What book?'

'The one I just told you about. The one about homelessness.'

'What about your friend, Michael? Can you not sleep on his sofa for a while until you get a place? You know the pictures he give me, they are gone now! Somebody stole all my things and those pictures were there and now they are not.'

'I'm sure Michael will just print some more for you. I'll ask him.'

'No, don't ask him about the pictures! Ask him if he can help you. If he is a true friend he will help.'

'But V, I'm not homeless. I stayed with a friend in his apartment last night. I fly home tomorrow. I was living homeless but only while I was working on the book.'

'What book is this?'

'The homeless book. The homeless portraits. The one I told you about.'

'You cannot come and live with me. I cannot have you there. I have enough problems. I cannot take care of you.'

'V, I'm not trying to live with you.'

'Well, good, because I am not having it.'

I forget all about doing a portrait of V. I want to see if there is anything I can do but she just gets angrier and angrier. Not with me. She is shouting about being harassed by the police. About people being assholes. Sometimes I turn and she is staring intently at me, scowling almost.

'V, are you hungry? Can I get you something to eat?'

'If you want to do this you can do this.'

At the next trashcan she finds a pizza box with a slice inside.

'Now I have my dinner. Now I don't need anything.'

I walk away, trying to work out how I am going to tell my wife that I want to take money from our already overdrawn bank account to buy V a plane ticket home. But when I track down JR, to ask his advice, he tells me that at the beginning of the year she wrote to her father and asked for money so that she could fly home. He tells me that her father had sent her a check for fifteen hundred dollars to a nearby church that allows her to have mail sent there. He tells me that V spent that money within a couple of months, surprisingly on clothes.

On my final morning in New York I take a train, with my luggage, to Penn Station, where I have arranged to say goodbye to JV. We hug and laugh until eventually JV says, 'Don't forget me now, Alan.'

I promise him, truthfully, that I never will. He takes my suitcase and wheels it over to the taxi rank, lifting it into the trunk when my turn comes.

During the cab ride to JFK I receive two phone calls on my cellphone. The first is from Kim, who tells me that Nancy has gone back to Miami to visit her family and that she will be back on Friday.

'But actually I don't think she's coming back,' she says. We'll see. 'Anyway, Alan, I just wanted to say goodbye and it was great meeting you and give your beautiful daughter a big hug and kiss from me when you see her. I hope one day we'll see each other again.'

The second phone call is from Joey.

He says, 'I'm out here again, man.'

'Out where?' I ask.

'Back out on the street. I'm sitting in Union Square right now.'

'Shit, Joey, why? What happened?'

'Ah, you know. She was just bugging me, man. I can't even explain it. I woke up at six this morning and just thought, "Fuck this." And I threw some clothes in my backpack and just headed back out here.'

'But Joey, there must be more to it than … *Fuck this?*'

'Alan, don't worry about it, man, just, you know …' Joey sighs into the phone and for a couple of seconds I stare out of the window, watching the buildings slide by.

'Just …' says Joey, as New York recedes into past tense '… goodbye.'

Alan Emmins is a freelance journalist who was born in England in 1974. Alan's texts and images have sold worldwide and cover a wide range of topics, from point-of-interest features to investigative journalism. Accompanied by his images, his stories have appeared in *Playboy*, the *New York Post*, the *New York Daily News*, *Politiken*, *Berlingske Tidende* and others. After living in New York he relocated to Copenhagen, Denmark, where he now lives with his wife and daughter. Alan is also one of the founding editors of *Spoiled Ink Magazine* (www.spoiledink.com).

Also by Alan Emmins

'Salty, sassy, running-off-at-the-mouth commentary.'
*The Times*